IMAGES
of America

WOOLAROC

On the Cover: For Frank and Jane Phillips, entertaining at Woolaroc was an art form. From business associates to family and friends, the Phillips family ensured that their guests to Woolaroc were treated like royalty. Here, on the occasion of the Cow Thieves and Outlaws Reunion, Frank Phillips holds the grandchild of Osage Chief Fred Lookout on a cradle board. Some important figures in Western history are seated with him. From left to right are George Miller (101 Ranch and Wild West Show), G.W. Lillie (Pawnee Bill's Wild West Show), Frank Phillips (with large hat and glasses), and Osage Chief Fred Lookout.

IMAGES
of America

WOOLAROC

Michelle M. Martin

ARCADIA
PUBLISHING

ISBN 978-0-7385-1047-1

Published by Arcadia Publishing
Charleston, South Carolina

Printed in the United States of America

Library of Congress Control Number: 2013933996

For all general information, please contact Arcadia Publishing:
Telephone 843-853-2070
Fax 843-853-0044
E-mail sales@arcadiapublishing.com
For customer service and orders:
Toll-Free 1-888-313-2665

Visit us on the Internet at www.arcadiapublishing.com

Dedicated to the memory of Carolyn Jean Cooper, who uncovered, shared, and preserved history for others. History and gardening were her greatest passions, and we all benefited from her friendship and humor. She left us far too soon.

Dedicated to the memory of John Hughes, a true gentleman rancher and great friend of Woolaroc

Contents

Foreword

Every time I go through the gate, it seems like I'm entering a time capsule, a journey through another world. It starts with rocks laid bare by time. Blackjack oaks twist around prairie streams. In the distance, like apparitions dodging shadows, beasts emerge. From another place, exotic animals plod forward, as Isak Dinesen described in *Out of Africa*, "as if they had an appointment with the end of the world."

This is Woolaroc, where time stops for a few precious moments while we are there, long enough for the ancestral peoples to provide a proper "welcome."

I can see an Osage hunting party down by the lake, some oil prospectors in the distance, skins staked out at Mountain Man Encampment, and there, on horseback, is a 10-gallon hat moving through low branches. Frank Phillips is enjoying an afternoon ride among his "tribe."

And it doesn't end. The real illusion is how the living gallery outside melts into a permanent home inside. It is a perfect place where art meets reality. On brightly lit walls are scenes frozen in time in one of the world's great collections of Western Art. It is hard to know where to look. This documentation tells a story of Native American culture, of dancing and hunting, and of costumes and faces. It is priceless and adds its own "magic" to Woolaroc.

All of this comes together in one small place—on the bluff overlooking the woods, lakes, and rocks sit awhile and let the wind talk to you. You will hear the whispers of children laughing and the chatter of parties inside the lodge not far away. This was Woolaroc through the years past. It will be Woolaroc for years to come. Such is the magic of Woolaroc.

—Bill Kurtis
Broadcast journalist and former member of the Woolaroc Board of Trustees

ACKNOWLEDGMENTS

For any author, the Herculean task of finding, sorting, and making sense of information obtained while researching a book is daunting. My greatest thanks must first go to the staff at Woolaroc. Without the assistance of Ken Meek and Linda Stone at the Woolaroc Museum, this book simply would not be possible. Ken and Linda are not only amazing museum professionals but also good friends. Their guidance and humor were invaluable and made this project enjoyable. A great debt of thanks is owed to Bob Fraser, the CEO of the Frank Phillips Foundation, Inc. Bob's vision and passion for all things Woolaroc makes working on any project connected to the site a joy.

I was not familiar with Woolaroc until broadcast journalist Bill Kurtis suggested that I spend an afternoon there. Upon my first visit in 2005, I came to realize that Woolaroc is not an afternoon experience; it is a lifetime experience. To Bill, I owe a debt of thanks for introducing me to an amazing treasure in the heart of the Osage Hills.

My family, friends, and colleagues always play an important role in my work. They oftentimes put up with my incessant chatter about the research, writing, and editing process, and for that, I am grateful. A thank-you goes to my family, Dale, Susan, Michael, Amelia, and Nicholas Martin. I was pleased to be able to share the magic of Woolaroc with my Michael, Amelia, and Nicholas when they spent a family vacation with me in Bartlesville. Seeing Nicholas's eyes light up when he held a baby rabbit in the Petting Barn or hearing the joy in his laughter while playing on the playground and feeding Buffo, the garbage-eating buffalo, are precious memories that we will always cherish. Special thanks go to my Bartlesville friends Jim and Kim Goss, Lawana Leach, Kay Little, Molly McCown, and Scott Perkins, and my Kansas, Missouri, and Nebraska friends Deb Goodrich Bisel, Jenna Blum, Alan Chilton, Carolyn Cooper, Stephanie Dodson, Rosie Frey, Sandra Haimerl, Jim Reed, Arnold Schofield, and Kari West. They always support and encourage me to follow my historical dreams.

Lastly, many thanks go to Dr. Donald Fixico for his encouragement and guidance. Don listened to me chatter endlessly about the photograph collection at Woolaroc. Thank you so much for listening patiently and being so supportive and for spending an afternoon with me at Woolaroc that was magical.

Unless otherwise noted, all photographs are courtesy of the Woolaroc Museum of the Frank Phillips Foundation, Inc.

INTRODUCTION

Nestled in the rough-and-tumble Osage Hills of northeast Oklahoma, Woolaroc is a place of magic. You can hear it in the wind whistling through the blackjack oaks or the water lapping against the shores of Clyde Lake. You can experience it as the thundering hooves of a herd of American bison cross the prairie. This symphony of nature plays daily on the 3,700 acres of woods, lakes, and rocks called Woolaroc. Once the retreat home of oil magnate Frank Phillips, the founder of Phillips Petroleum, Woolaroc was a place of inspiration for his family. Here, he was able to escape the more refined atmosphere of his grand home in Bartlesville, Oklahoma. Phillips could unwind and relax in his rough-hewn lodge. Woolaroc quickly became a destination for more than family. Business associates and dignitaries from the world stage came to Woolaroc for a taste of Oklahoma hospitality in the heart of an exciting new venture that would help reshape and build America—oil. This was oil country, and Frank Phillips and his brother L.E. built their fortunes from the black gold that bubbled up from the Oklahoma soil.

Built in 1925, the lodge at Woolaroc is a log cabin–style structure on a grand scale. Boasting eight bedrooms, many bathrooms, a great room, and large dining area, the lodge at Woolaroc was the perfect setting for Frank Phillips to close business deals. Many of the furnishings and artwork in the lodge were gifts from family and friends. They create a portrait in time—the heyday of the great Oklahoma oil boom. Exotic animal heads and skins adorn the walls and floors of the lodge and came from Phillips's collection that roamed the grounds of the ranch. Paintings, pottery, woven rugs, and other artifacts of the American West found a home in the lodge. This would become the genesis of a major museum collection that visitors can still see today. The lodge at Woolaroc is a showplace that fills visitors with awe and preserves the history of a pivotal period in Oklahoma's history.

Phillips added an airplane hangar in 1928 that would evolve into the museum to hold his extensive collection of Western and American Indian art and artifacts. Additional buildings, a herd of exotic animals, and the Osage Hills rounded out his amazing complex that is known today as Woolaroc.

These days, Woolaroc is administered by the Frank Phillips Foundation, Inc., and is a tourist attraction like no other. With the rugged beauty of the wilderness, animal life, the weekend home of an Oklahoma oil baron, and a world-class art museum, Woolaroc is truly a place where magic lives every day. Perhaps Frank Phillips himself summed up the importance of Woolaroc:

> During my lifetime, I derived a great deal of pleasure in building Woolaroc Ranch and Museum. Through this medium I tried to preserve and perpetuate a part of the country I knew as a young man . . . I hope the Ranch and Museum can be preserved and maintained as a monument to the West as I knew it in the days before Phillips Petroleum was organized.

The pages that follow are a photographic journey into the world of one of America's most successful businessmen and the passion that inspired him to leave something of value for future generations. Saddle up, hang on, and enjoy the ride!

One

A Lodge in the Osage Hills

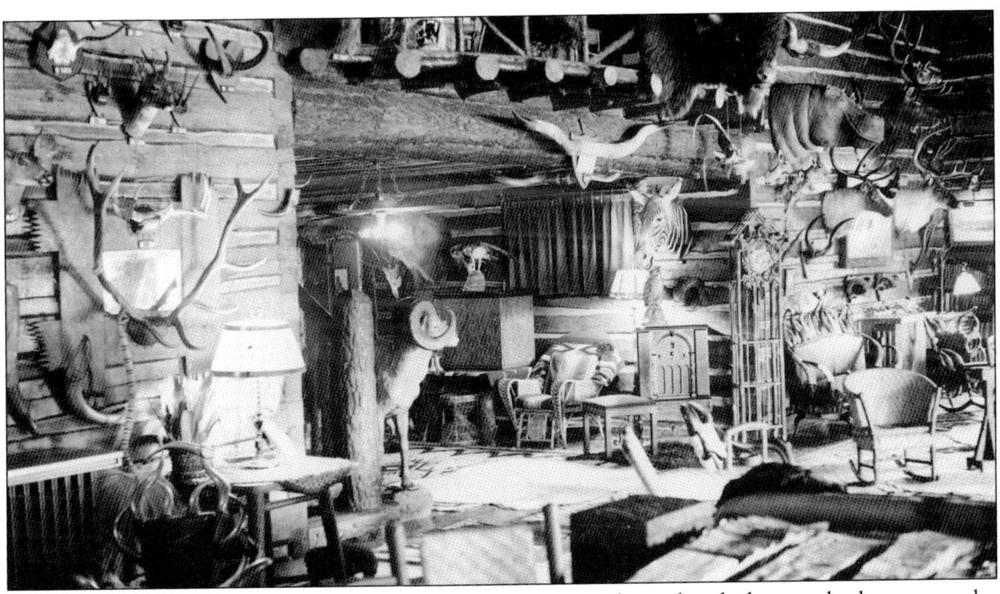

In 1925, Frank and Jane Phillips began construction on a log cabin lodge perched atop a rocky hill overlooking woods, lakes, and rocks in the Osage Hills of northeast Oklahoma. Intended to be a family retreat, the lodge at Woolaroc would become one of the most important tools in Phillips's business arsenal. The rustic, rough-and-tumble lodge would become a place where Phillips would entertain family, friends, politicians, business associates, Hollywood starlets, and world-famous aviators and humorists. This interior photograph of the lodge shows the rough-hewn logs and backwoods decor that made it a place of wonder and curiosity for visitors that passed happy hours within its walls.

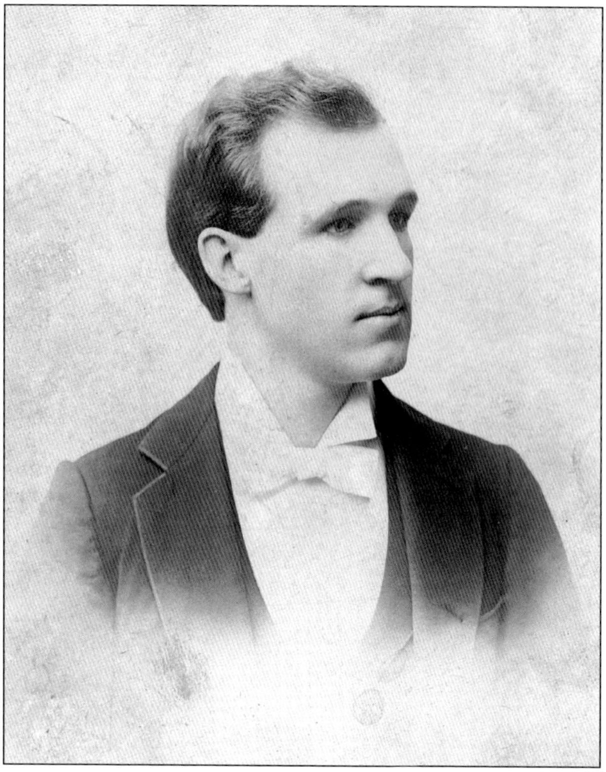

Born in Scotia, Nebraska, on November 28, 1873, Frank Phillips was 1 of 10 children. Life for his family was at times difficult. Grasshopper plagues in the 1870s and 1880s decimated crops and forced the family to move to Iowa. By the age of 14, Frank had become a barber's apprentice in Creston, Iowa. Local banker John Gibson was a loyal customer of young Frank and was the father of a rather attractive young lady—Jane Gibson.

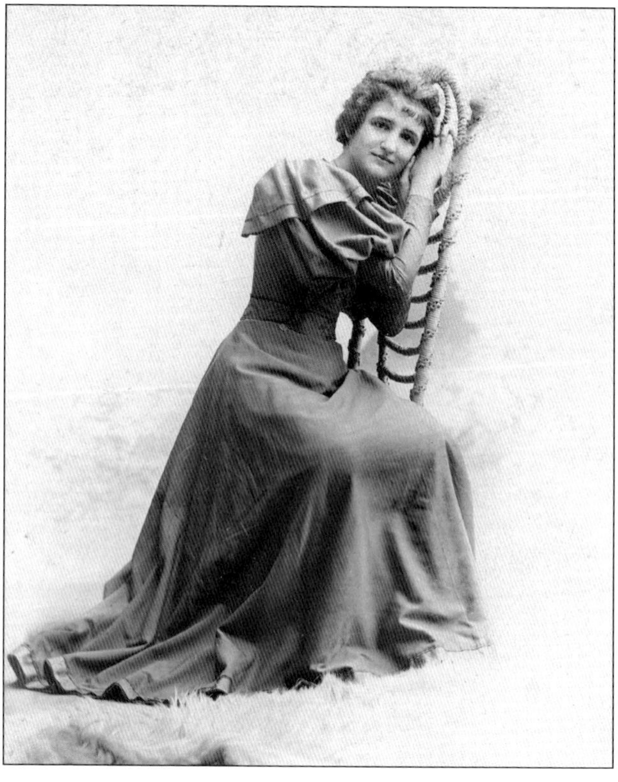

Jane Gibson was born in Creston, Iowa, on August 8, 1877, to John Ebbert Gibson and Matilda Jane Martin. Called Jennie or Jenn by her friends, she was called Betsie by her close family. Her beauty and poise attracted the attention of Frank Phillips. For him, winning Jane was easy; her father, however, was not sure of young Frank's ability to provide for his daughter on a barber's salary.

John Gibson decided to test Frank Phillips and gave him the onerous task of selling bonds. Unknown to Frank, the bonds were not of great value and none of Gibson's other employees had been able to peddle them successfully. Frank worked hard and sold the bonds. On February 18, 1897, Frank Phillips and Jane Gibson were married in a double ceremony with Jane's brother Josiah Gibson and Marcelene Miller in Creston. The young couple's only son, John Gibson Phillips, was born on December 9, 1898, in Creston.

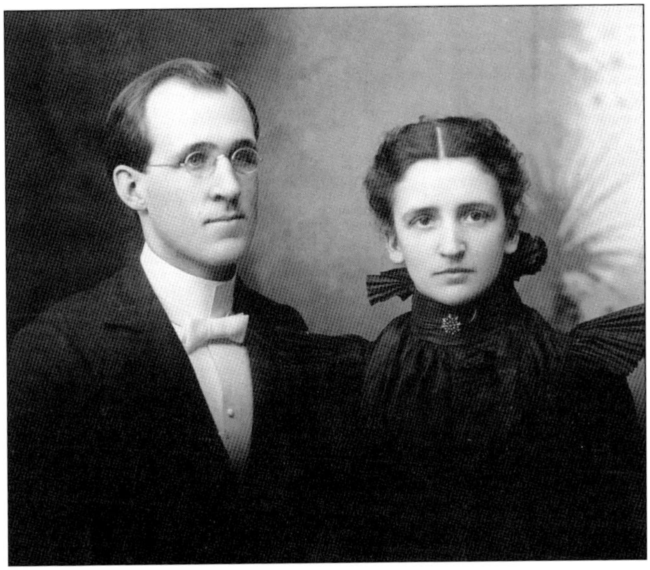

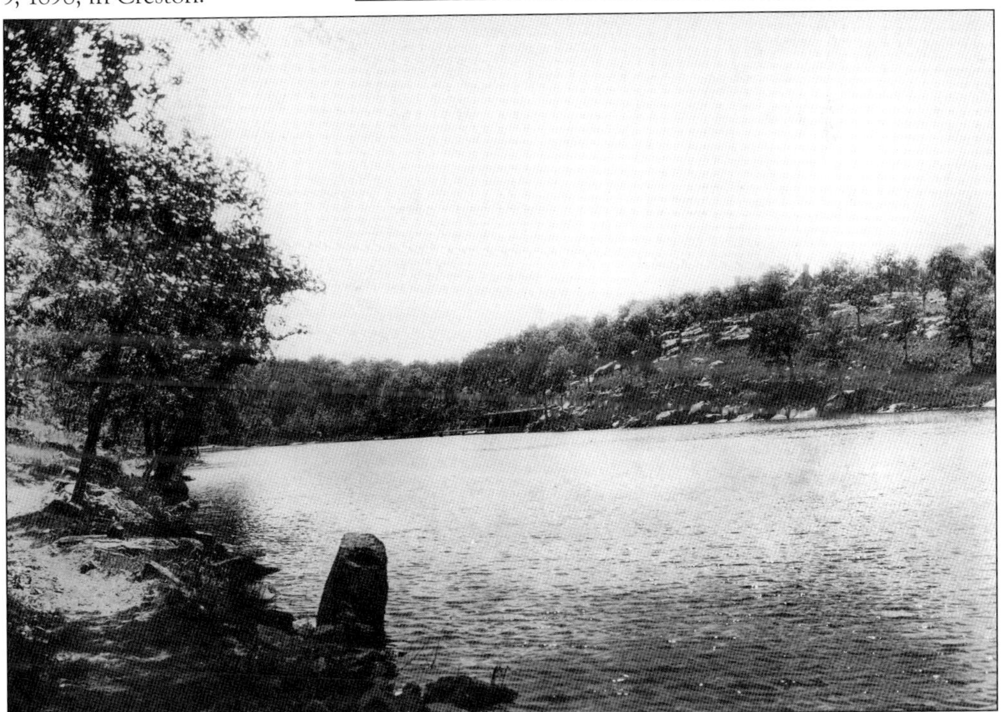

After leaving the barber's trade, Frank Phillips went to work for his father-in-law in the banking industry. In 1903, the oil boom in Oklahoma Territory was underway. With the first commercial oil well drilled in Bartlesville, northeast Oklahoma, was attracting wildcatters, speculators, and would-be oilmen. In 1904, Frank and his brother L.E. Phillips arrived. On September 6, 1905, they struck oil. After their well the Anna Anderson came in a gusher, the brothers drilled 81 consecutive wells that spewed black gold. The landscape of northeastern Oklahoma was important to the brothers and their business ventures. The woods, lakes, and rocks made up the name Woolaroc. Clyde Lake, seen here, is one of the features that attracted Phillips to purchase his 3,700-acre ranch.

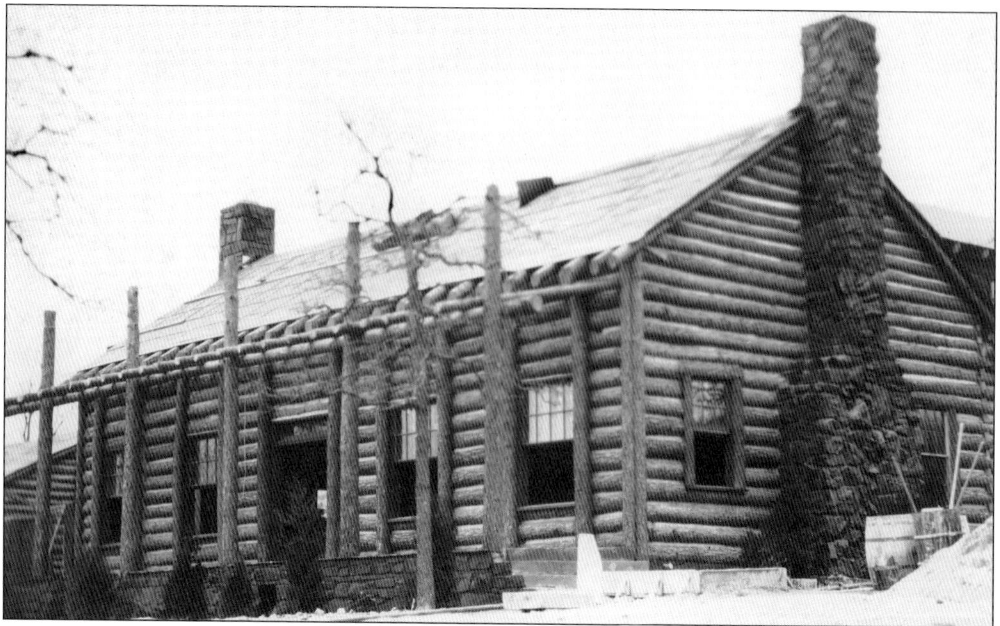

Pine logs from Arkansas were hauled in to build Frank and Jane Phillips's lodge at Woolaroc. In March 1926, the lodge was still unfinished. With no chinking between the logs, it became a haven for small animals that could shimmy their way in the open spaces. For Jane Phillips, who preferred the creature comforts of their 26-room mansion in Bartlesville, the lodge was rustic and wild. Numerous incidents involving flying squirrels forced Frank to have workmen put chinking in between the logs to keep the vermin at bay.

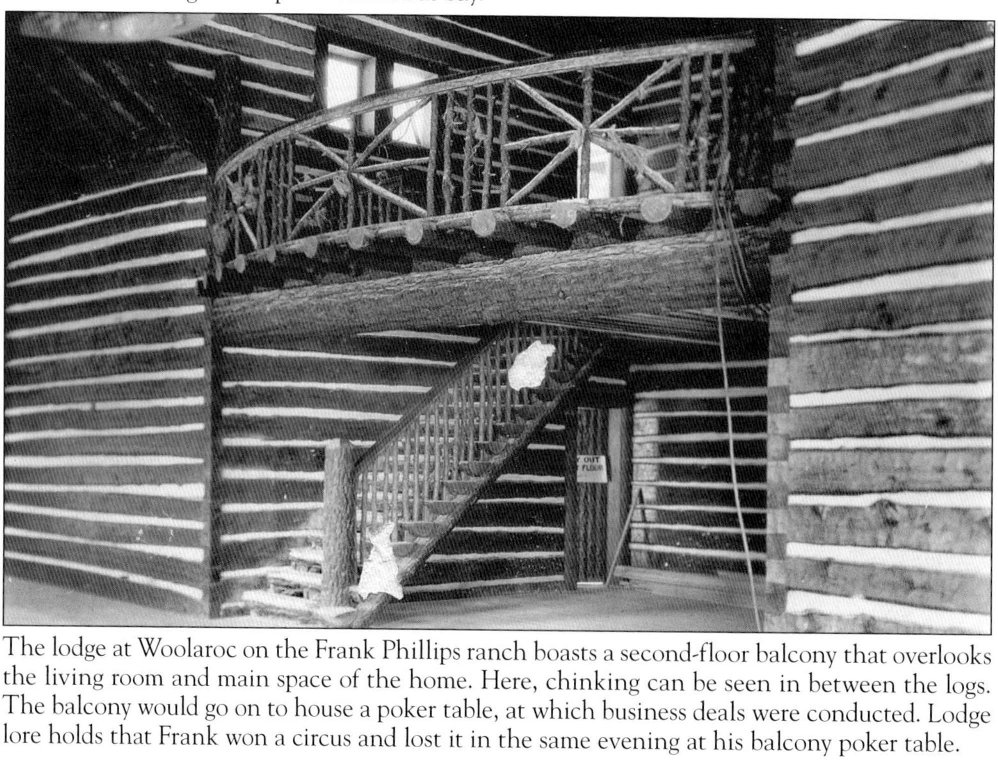

The lodge at Woolaroc on the Frank Phillips ranch boasts a second-floor balcony that overlooks the living room and main space of the home. Here, chinking can be seen in between the logs. The balcony would go on to house a poker table, at which business deals were conducted. Lodge lore holds that Frank won a circus and lost it in the same evening at his balcony poker table.

The rustic exterior of the lodge, seen here around 1926, was accented with animal horns collected from the grounds of the ranch. With herds of native deer, sheds were commonplace. The porch was a favorite place for the family to sit, relax, and enjoy the evening Oklahoma breezes. The lodge porch looks out over Clyde Lake.

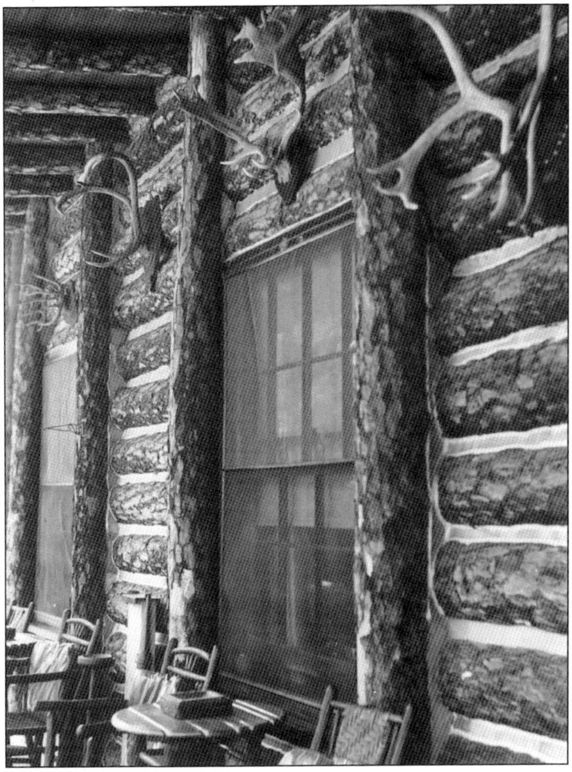

Once completed atop the high ground, the lodge at Woolaroc was an impressive sight from below. As seen from one of the spillway dams, the lodge and adjacent dining area take up the hillside. From here, Frank and his family, which would grow to include foster daughters Sarah Jane, and Mary Frances, enjoyed the best of nature and civilization.

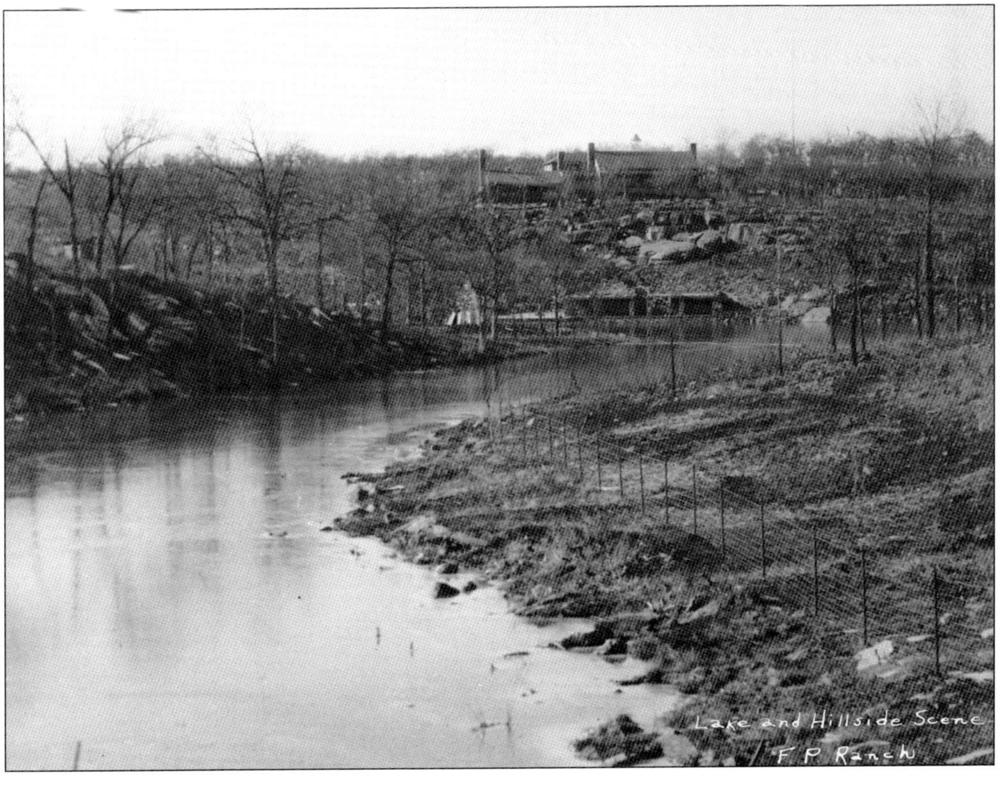

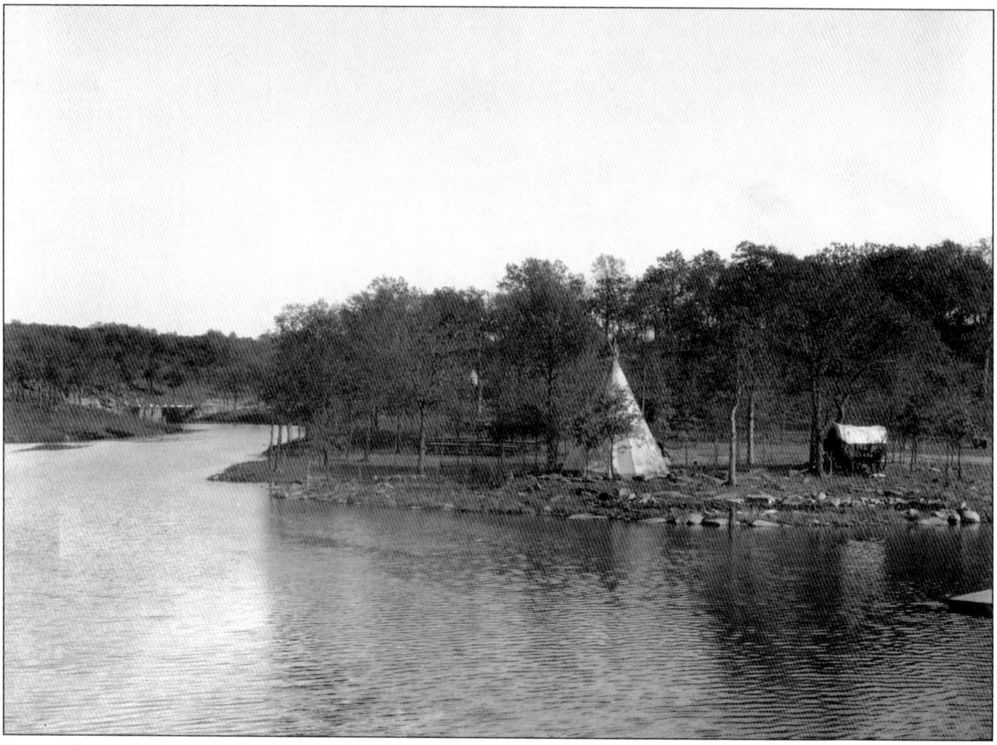

From the rocky outcroppings in front of the lodge, Frank and his family could sit and take in the majesty of the Oklahoma landscape. This view looking toward Clyde Lake is one of the most picturesque from the lodge. Clyde Lake would become a gathering place for the Phillips family, friends, and business associates. From 1926 to 1930, the famed Cow Thieves and Outlaws Reunion would be held at Clyde Lake.

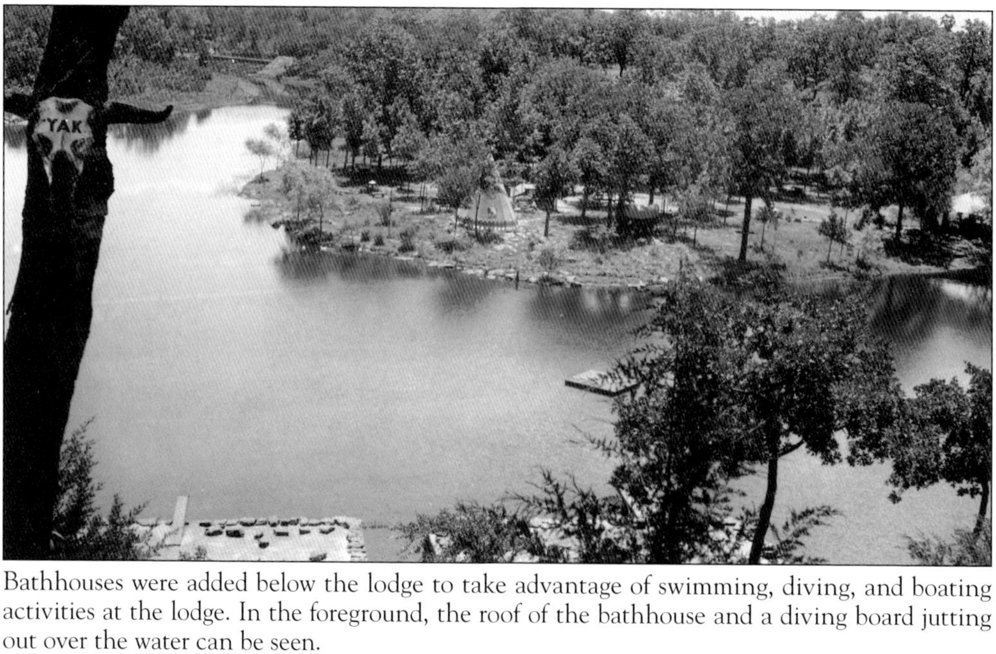

Bathhouses were added below the lodge to take advantage of swimming, diving, and boating activities at the lodge. In the foreground, the roof of the bathhouse and a diving board jutting out over the water can be seen.

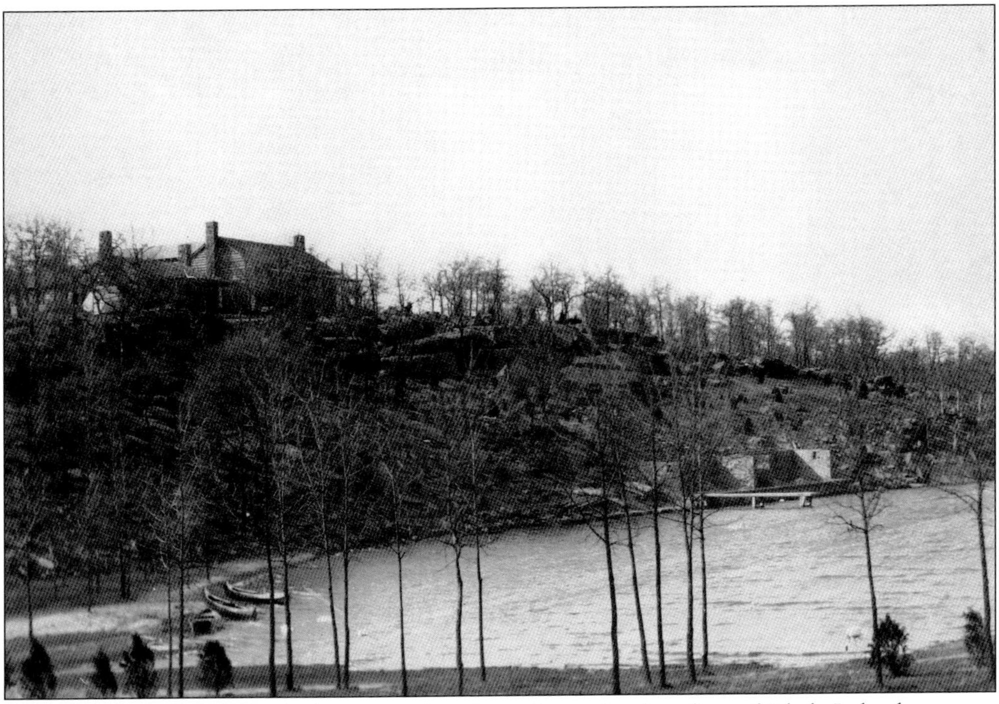

By the spring of 1926, the lodge was in fine form. From the shoreline of Clyde Lake, boats can be seen along the lakeshore as well as the dock and diving board in front of the bathhouses. For many Oklahomans this was the first view of the lodge they saw when it was published in the *Tulsa Daily World* later that spring. Perched atop the rocky hilltop, the lodge sits like a sentinel overseeing life at Woolaroc.

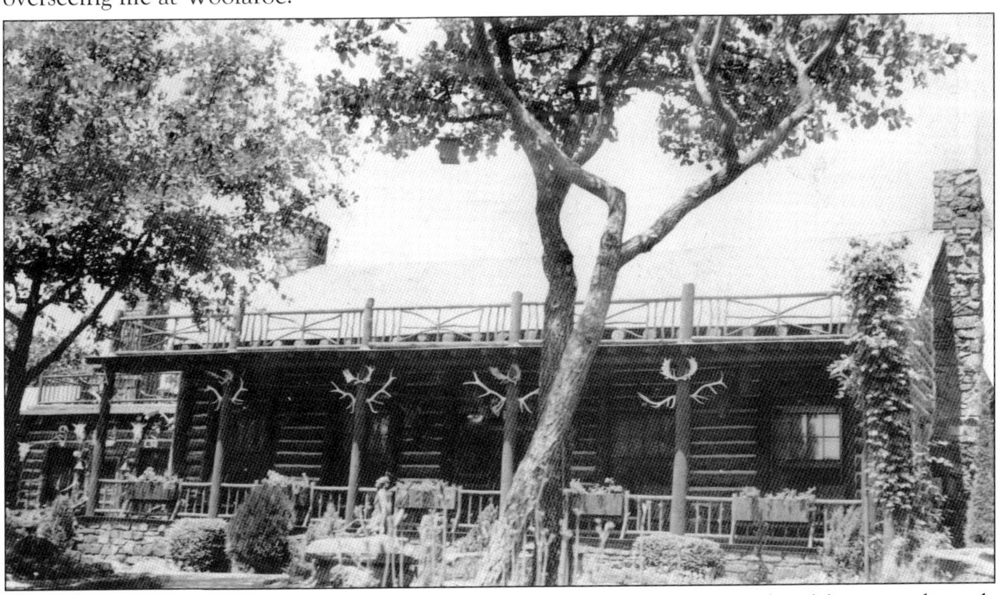

The lodge quickly became a retreat for the Phillips family. Here, the completed front porch, with animal horns adorning the posts, is fully viewed. Planters on the railings and furniture made from wood on the ranch complete the space. For Frank, the task of furnishing the lodge would entail numerous trips to purchase rugs, art, and other items that can still be seen at Woolaroc today.

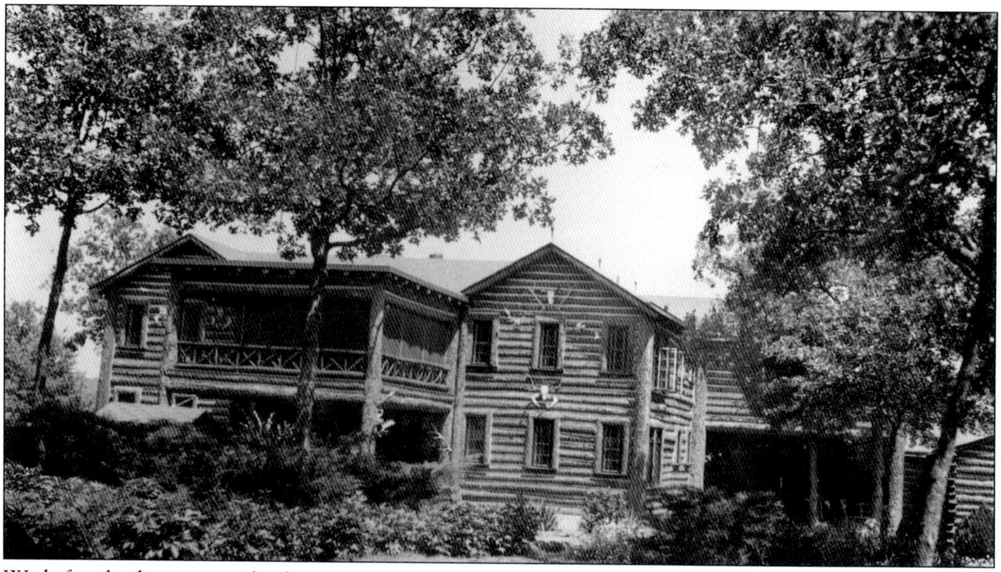

With five bedrooms, six bathrooms, a large dining area, a grand hall, screened private porch, and a front porch with a commanding view of Clyde Lake, Phillips found that Woolaroc was the ideal place to bring his Eastern business associates for meetings.

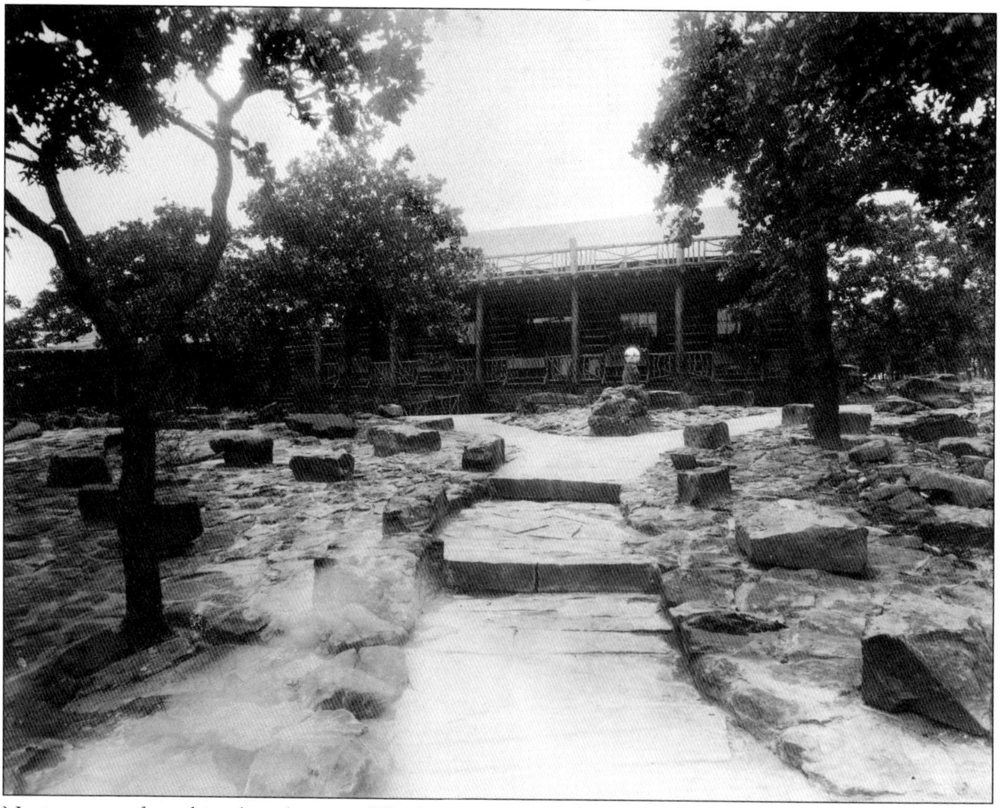

Native stone found in abundance at Woolaroc comprised one of the main building materials used for walkways and other buildings that Phillips needed on his ranch. Here, the native stone has been used as part of the sidewalk and garden material.

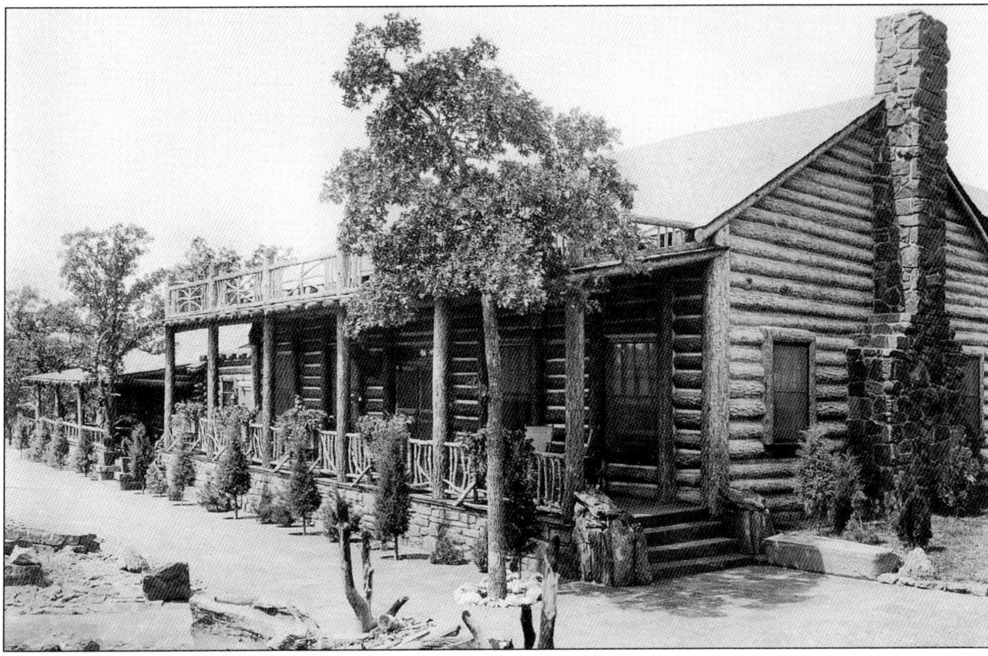

With the completion of the lodge, Frank Phillips realized his dream of a country retreat in the Osage Hills. Arthur J. Gorman, Frank's handpicked architect and contractor, must have been pleased with the end result. Gorman would go on to build the airplane hangar, the museum additions, and many of the additional outbuildings that would later comprise Woolaroc.

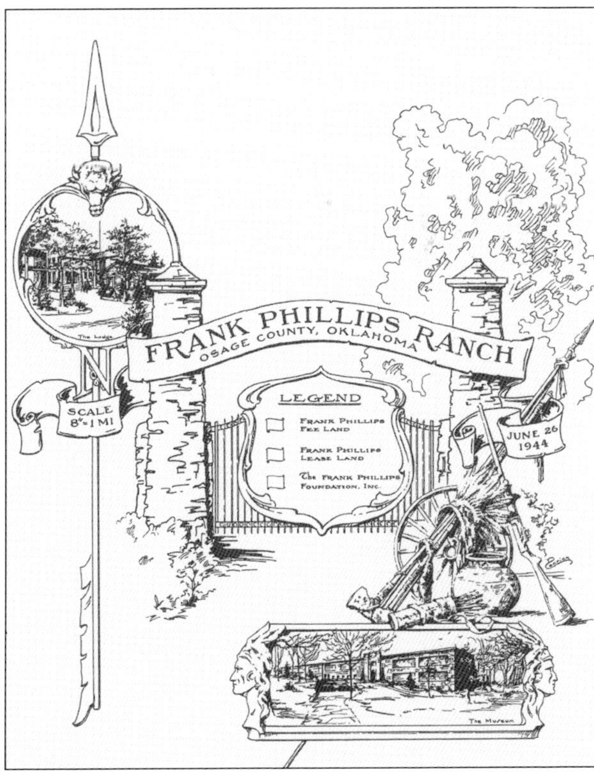

This map created in 1944 highlights many of Woolaroc's most popular attractions. Within the arrow to the left is the lodge. To the bottom right is a depiction of the museum building flanked by two Indian chief heads. Of course, the most prominent feature of the map is the ornate gate that visitors drove through to gain access to the ranch. Sadly, today the gate is no longer standing.

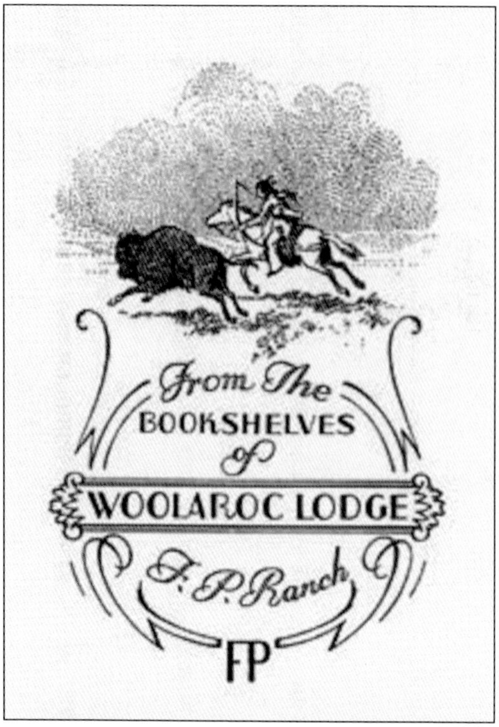

Every detail of life at Woolaroc was important to Frank and Jane Phillips. In addition to a fine art collection housed in the lodge in the early years, Frank and Jane were the owners of a fine library. Every book was marked with the Woolaroc Lodge bookplate.

Stepping through the front door of the lodge at Woolaroc was a magical experience for Frank's visitors, especially those from back east who had never traveled west of the Mississippi. Wild, rough-hewn, and rustic, the lodge boasted a diverse assemblage of art, artifacts, and a veritable zoo of taxidermy specimens.

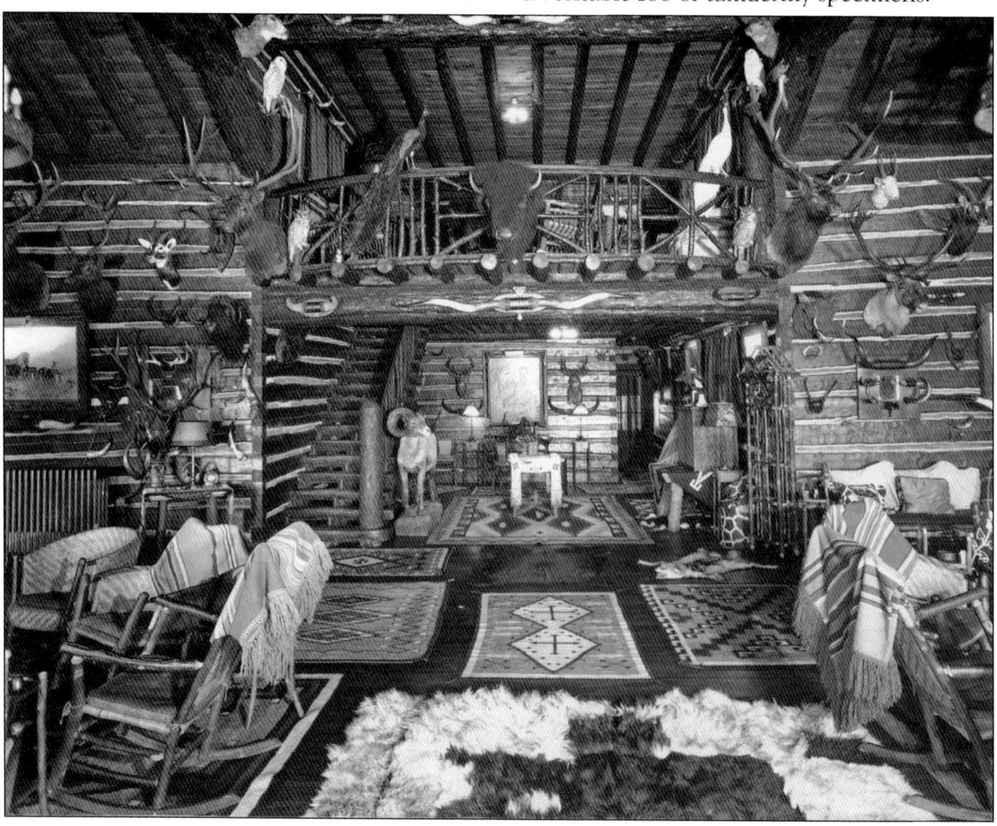

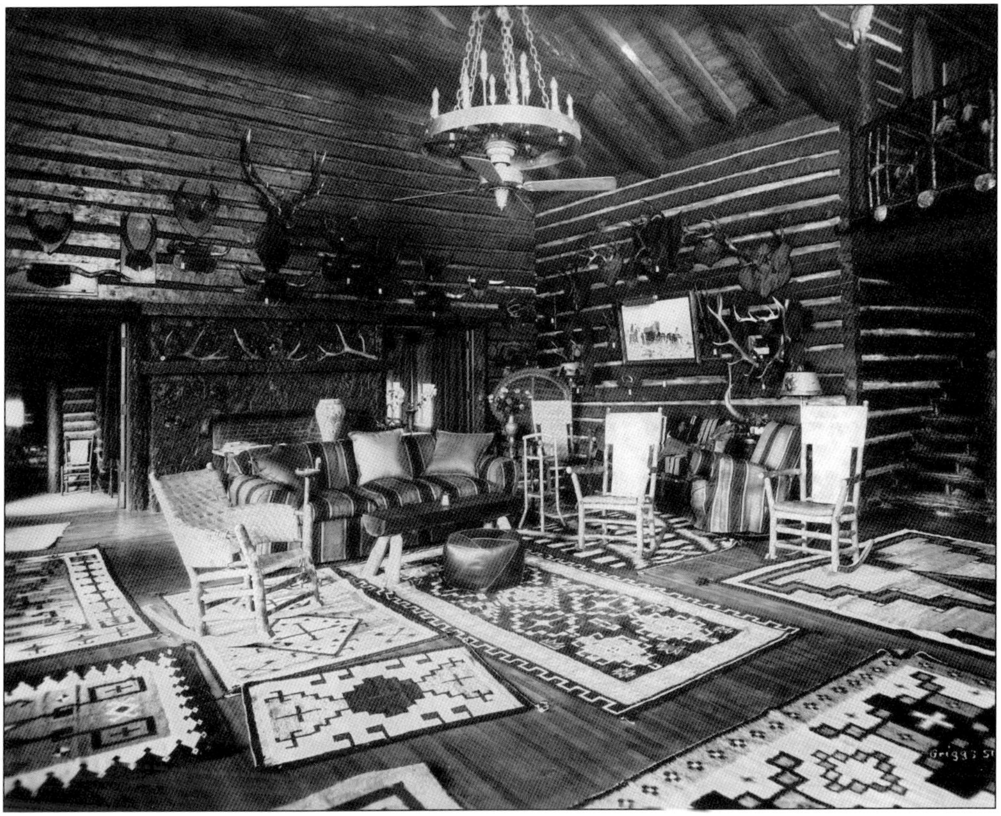

Much inspiration for the layout and decor of the lodge came from a trip Frank Phillips took to the Grand Canyon. In 1925, while on business in California, Phillips and engineer Paul Endacott visited the El-Tovar Lodge near Williams, Arizona.

To continue on his mission to decorate and outfit the lodge, Frank Phillips called upon the expertise and services of Emil W. Lenders. German-born Lenders was an artist, Wild West Show performer (with the incomparable Col. William F. Cody), and arbiter of Western taste. Phillips wished to decorate the lodge in a style that evoked memories of the West.

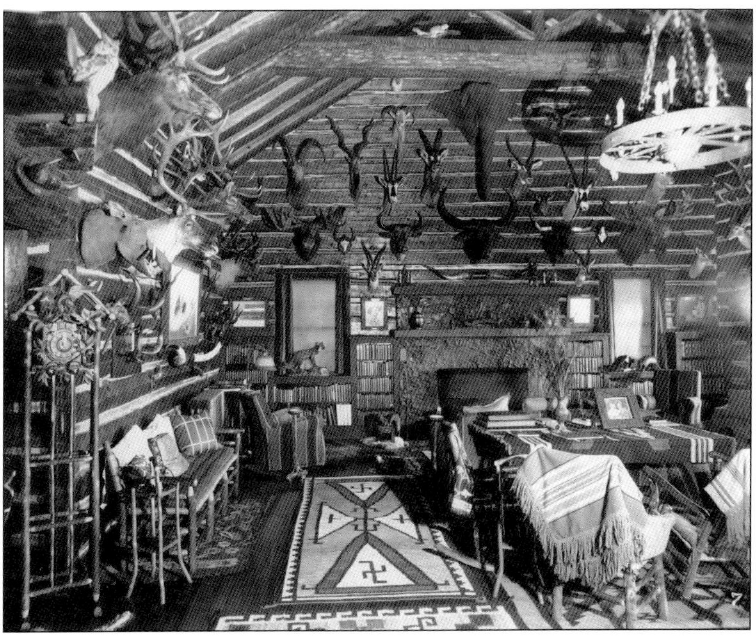

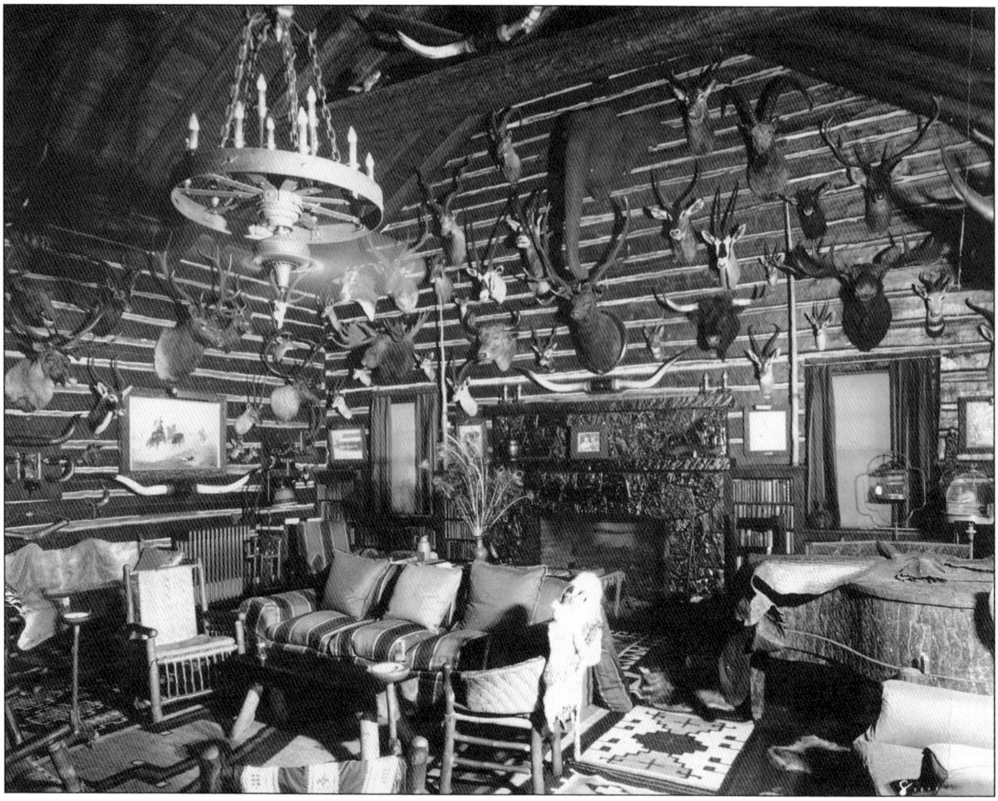

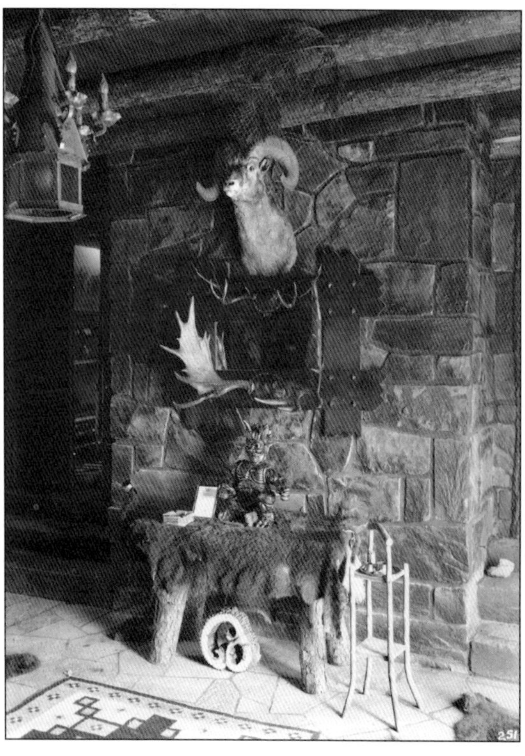

This view of the lodge showcases the variety of decorative objects—art, animal heads, horns, artifacts, rugs, rustic furnishings, and a very special grand piano (right front corner). In August 1926, Phillips ordered a Steinway Duo-Art grand piano. Light-colored unfinished walnut, the piano is the stuff of Woolaroc legend. Once installed in the lodge, the piano was a gathering place for sing-alongs. Horrified guests at the lodge watched one evening as Phillips, with a showman's flair, struck a match on its surface. Little did they know that Phillips planned to have Art Gorman cover the piano with Woolaroc veneer made of bark. Today, the piano still fascinates visitors to the lodge.

Rustic hanging lanterns, a ram's head, antlers, and furnishings made from logs obtained on the grounds create a Western decor to fascinate lodge visitors. This breezeway connects the great room and dining area of the lodge.

This mounted Rocky Mountain big horn ram found its final resting place in the living room at lodge. Many of the animal specimens mounted died on the ranch, were memorialized, and became decor. Friends of Frank and Jane Phillips, including Martin and Osa Johnson, the famed safari filmmakers and game hunters, sent exotics like elephants for Frank to adorn the walls.

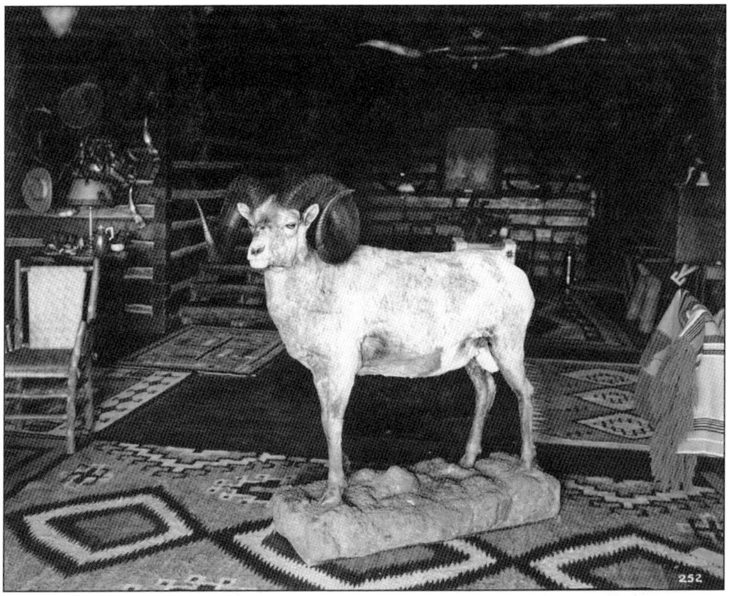

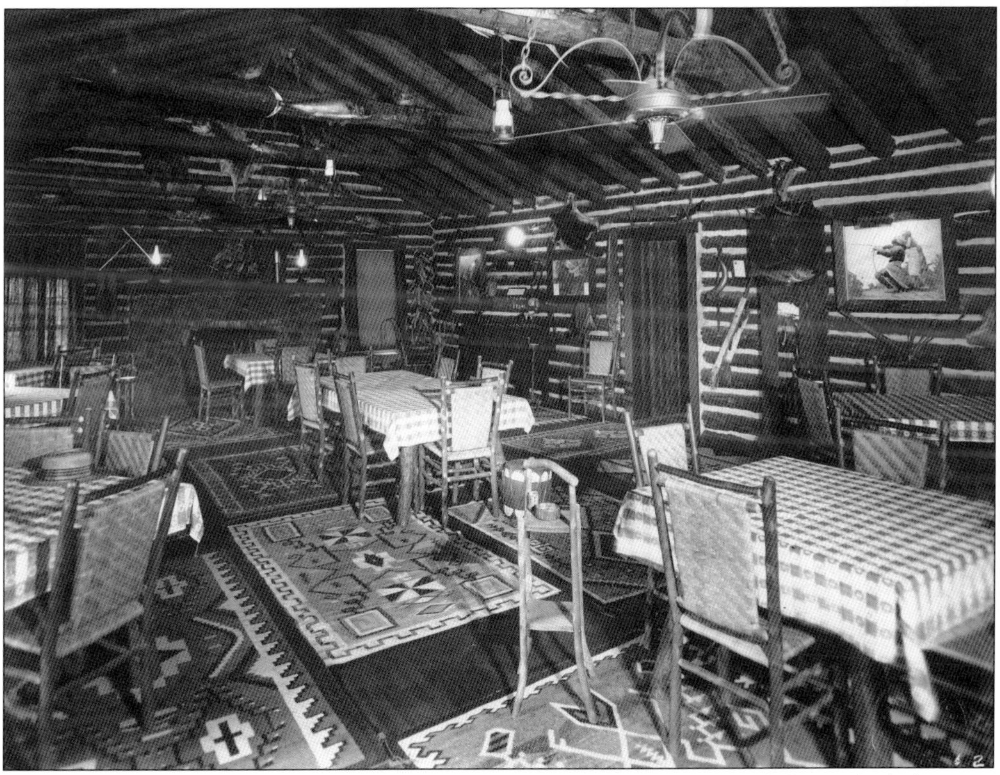

Entertaining, dining, and socializing were important to Frank and Jane Phillips. The lodge gave them a place to escape, relax, and entertain business associates, family, and friends. The dining room was built to resemble the Phillips family log home in Nebraska and was the first section of the lodge to be constructed. On a visit in November 1926 for a Phillips family reunion, Lucinda, the family matriarch, attested that the lodge and dining room strongly resembled the family homestead in Nebraska they left for greener pastures in Iowa.

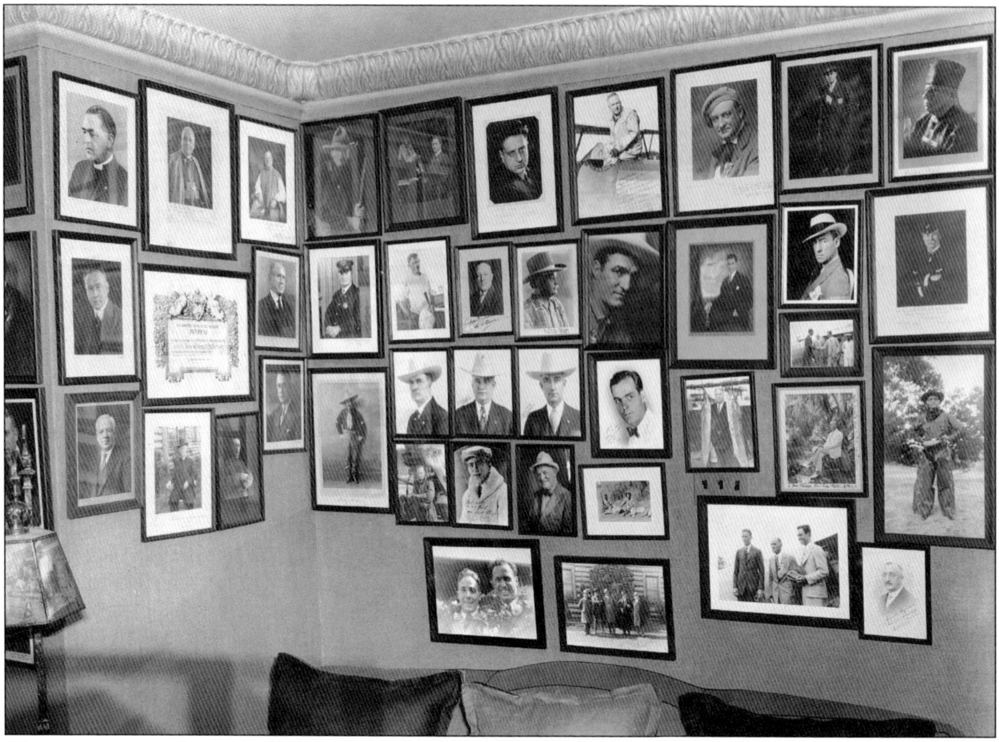

The private family spaces at the lodge gave Frank, Jane, John, Mary, and Sarah Jane a place to unwind. One of the most interesting features of Jane Phillips's private quarters is the extensive photograph collection on her wall affectionately known as her "rouges gallery." With the exception of her daughters and one famous explorer/big-game huntress, all the photographs on the wall are of men. Young Phillips Petroleum executives, actors, politicians, religious figures, classical musicians, aviators, and other notable men signed photographs to Jane, and they were hung on her walls. A sure sign that someone had fallen out of favor was the removal of his or her photograph from the wall.

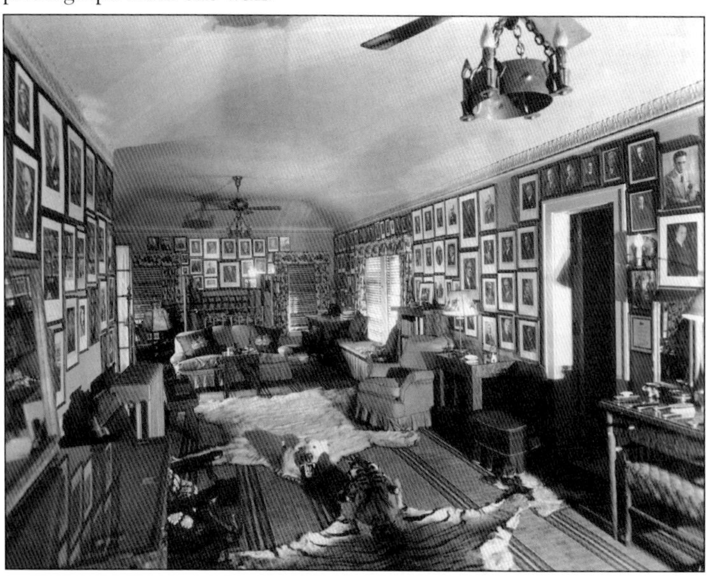

This wide view of Jane's bedroom shows the extensive photograph collection that grew to encompass the hallway that connected her bedroom to Frank's. Each bedroom in the lodge had its own private bath, a luxury to be certain. Animal skins, Navajo rugs, and a mix of rustic and upscale furnishings made Jane's bedroom a comfortable retreat.

In stark contrast, Frank's bedroom on the second floor of the lodge was more rustic and reflected his love of all things Western. Indian rugs, animal skins, and artwork framed with Woolaroc bark, a process developed by Gorman, surrounded Frank when he retreated for the evening. His private bath boasted a sauna.

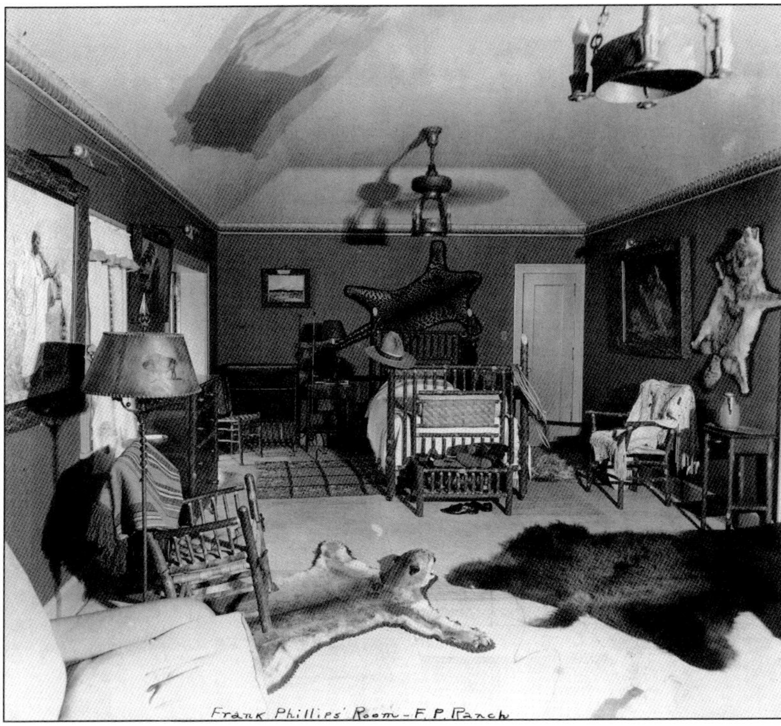

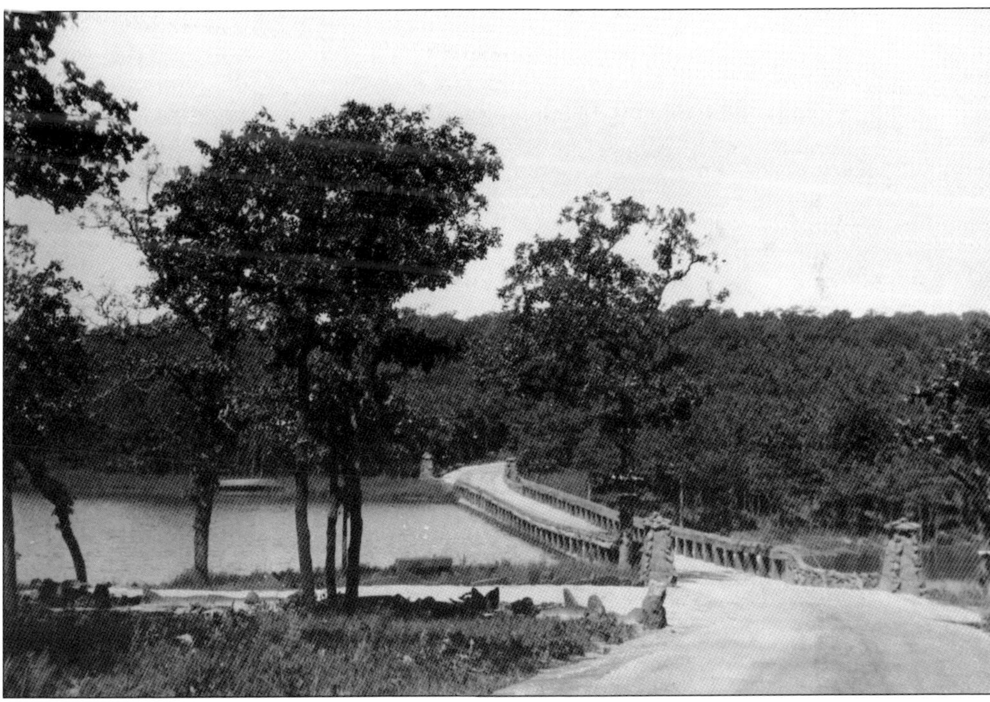

For Frank and Jane, the woods, lakes, and rocks were the true heart of Woolaroc. To ensure that guests could traverse the grounds, Phillips had his engineers from Phillips Petroleum devise a system of roads, bridges, dams, and spillways to control flooding and keep roads passable. These roads are still in use today, and visitors drive along two miles of roadway to reach the lodge and museum.

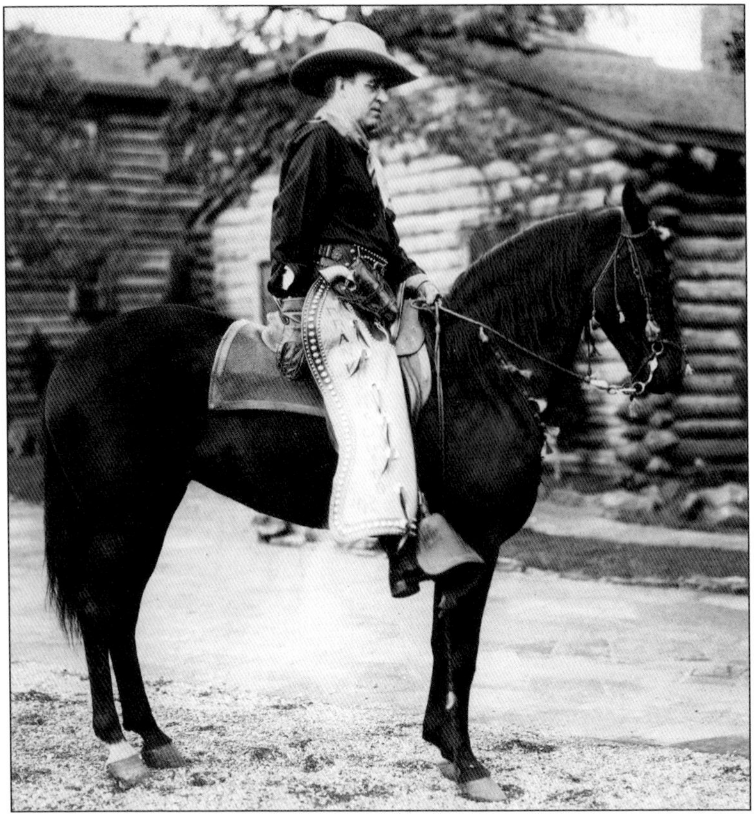

With a flair for showmanship, Frank Phillips played the part of the cowboy when at Woolaroc. He encouraged guests to join in and embrace the spirit of the Old West when visiting. His love of horses and riding brought him many hours of enjoyment while at Woolaroc. Here, Frank dons a cowboy suit given to him by Phillips Petroleum employees at the 1928 Cow Thieves and Outlaws Reunion held at Clyde Lake. In truth, Frank disliked the cowboy regalia and only wore it for photographs and special occasions.

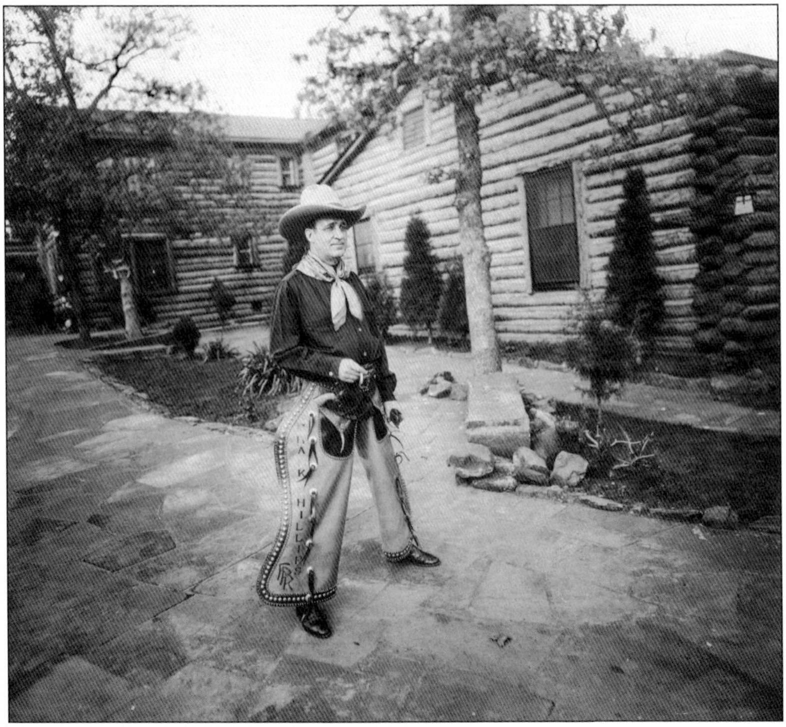

Posing in his new cowboy suit, one that he did not care to wear often, Phillips looks as if he is readying for a gunfight. The stone walkways and rustic lodge construction can be seen. Landscaping is also evident as the lodge progresses from its barren beginnings to the showplace Frank and Jane loved.

When not roaming the grounds in his cowboy attire, Phillips preferred his business attire with pant legs tucked into his cowboy boots. This was considered the mark of a cowman, and with herds of cattle, bison, elk, deer, and other exotic animals on his growing ranch, Phillips considered himself a cattleman.

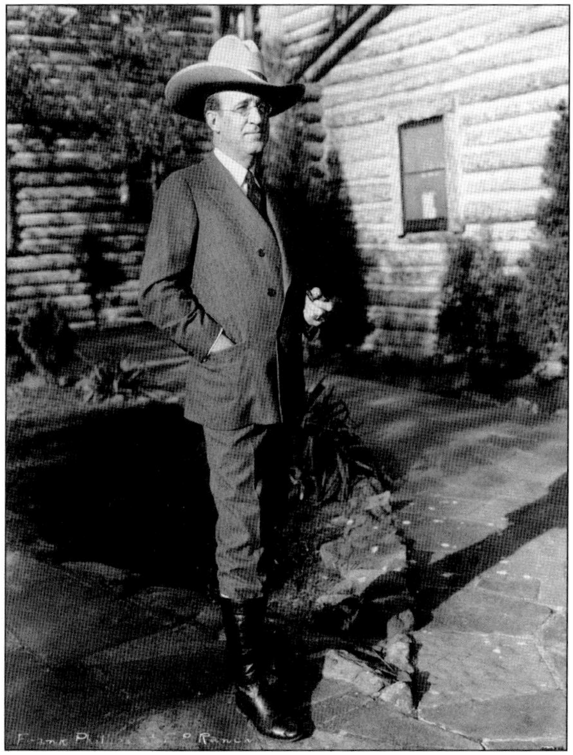

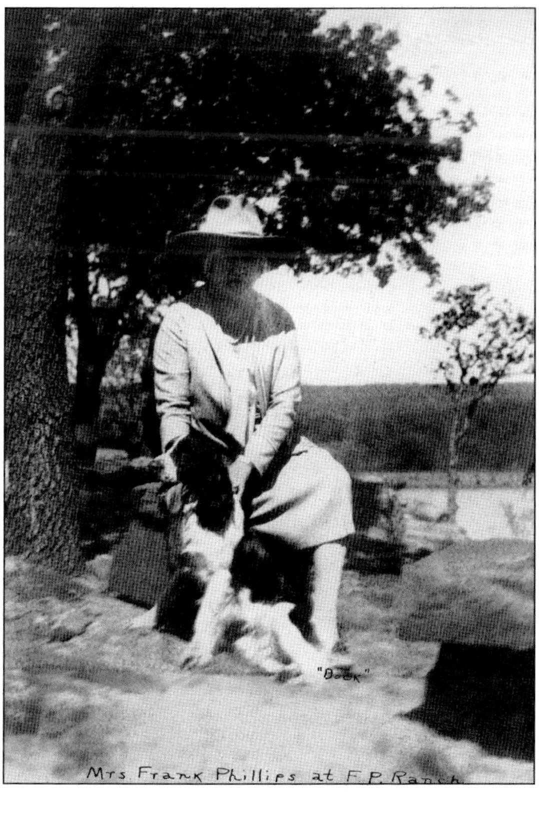

Jane Phillips also enjoyed her time at Woolaroc. The family's large mansion on Cherokee Avenue in Bartlesville was her special domain, but afternoons on the porch at the lodge with family, friends, and pets also appealed to Jane. Sporting a large cowgirl hat, Jane posed for a candid snapshot in front of the lodge with one of the many family pets. Dogs were special favorites of the family. Woolaroc scrapbooks oftentimes contain portraits of their beloved animals.

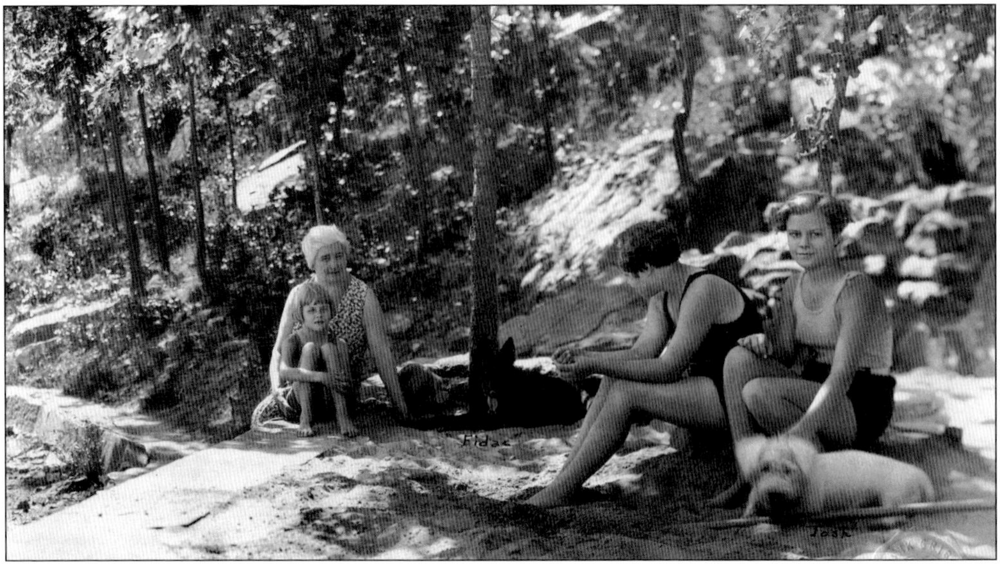

A summer afternoon brought the Phillips women to the lodge. Relaxing under the shade of the trees on the rocks in front of the lodge, Jane (far left), her granddaughter Betty (in front of her), and foster daughters Mary (dark swimsuit) and Sarah Jane, and dogs Josh and Fidac pose for a photograph. In one of the lodge guest registers, granddaughter Betty signed her name and added the following in the comment section: "I don't ever want to leave." The lodge was above and beyond all a home for a family.

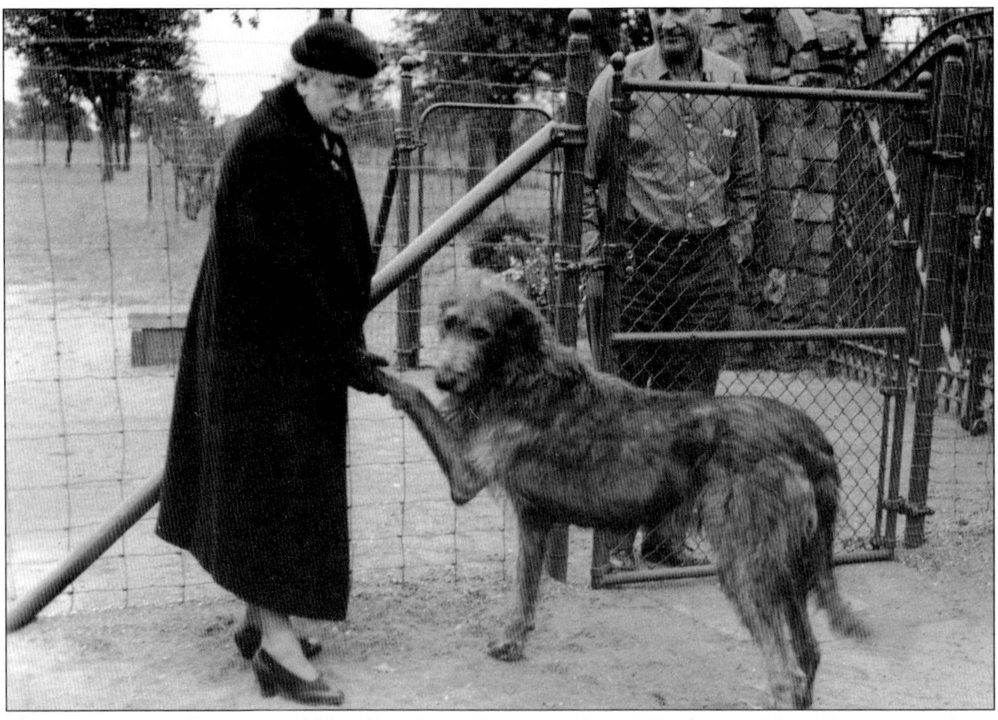

Numerous animal pens could be found on the grounds at Woolaroc. Here, Jane poses for a photograph with Pat the Irish wolfhound. Jane had most likely arrived from town as her stylish hat and fur coat seem out of place in the rough-and-tumble Osage Hills.

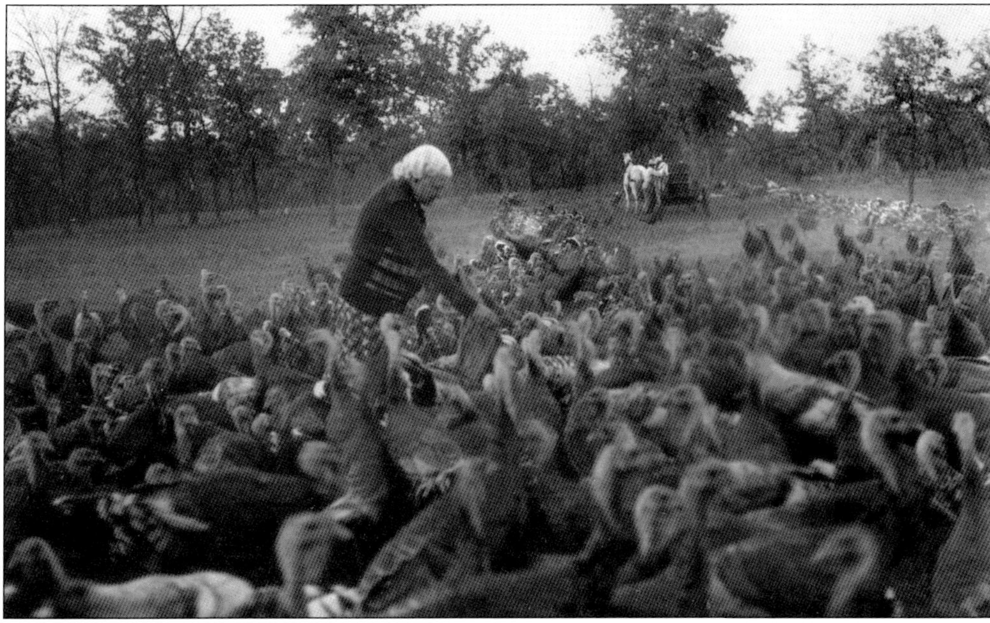

Dressed down and not anticipating a photograph session, Jane takes to the grounds at Woolaroc and feeds a flock of turkeys. Turkey was just one of the many animals that could be found on the ranch.

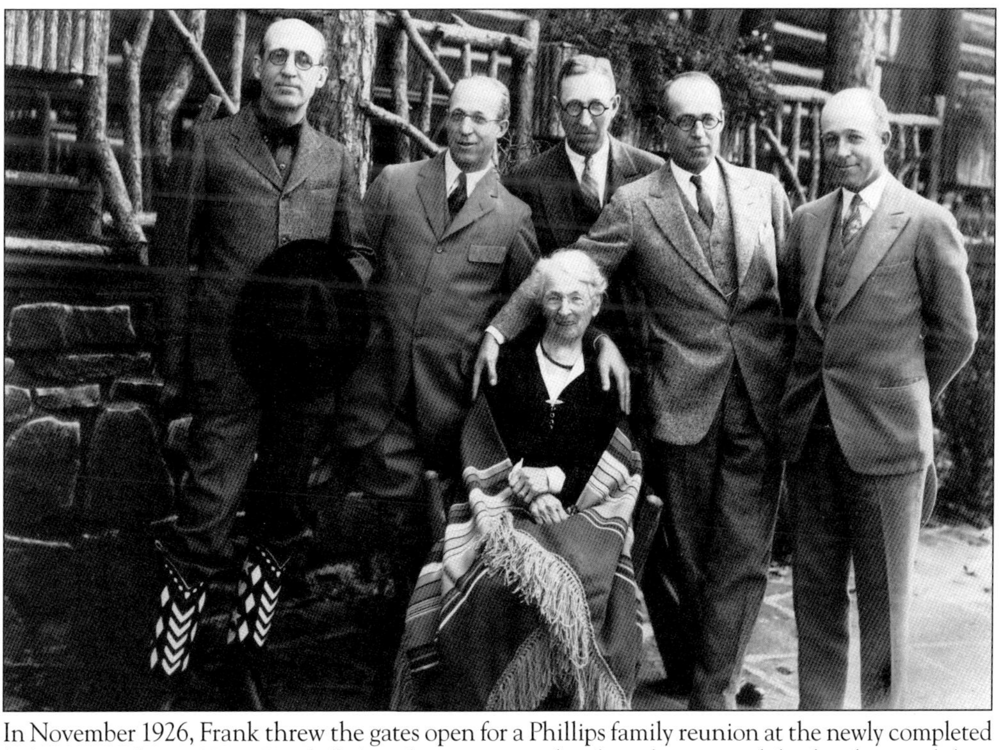

In November 1926, Frank threw the gates open for a Phillips family reunion at the newly completed lodge at Woolaroc. Here, Frank (left in distinctive cowboy boots) poses with his brothers and their mother, Lucinda. She is wrapped in one of many American Indian blankets found in the lodge. From left to right, Frank, L.E., Edd, Waite, and Fred Phillips pose with their mother.

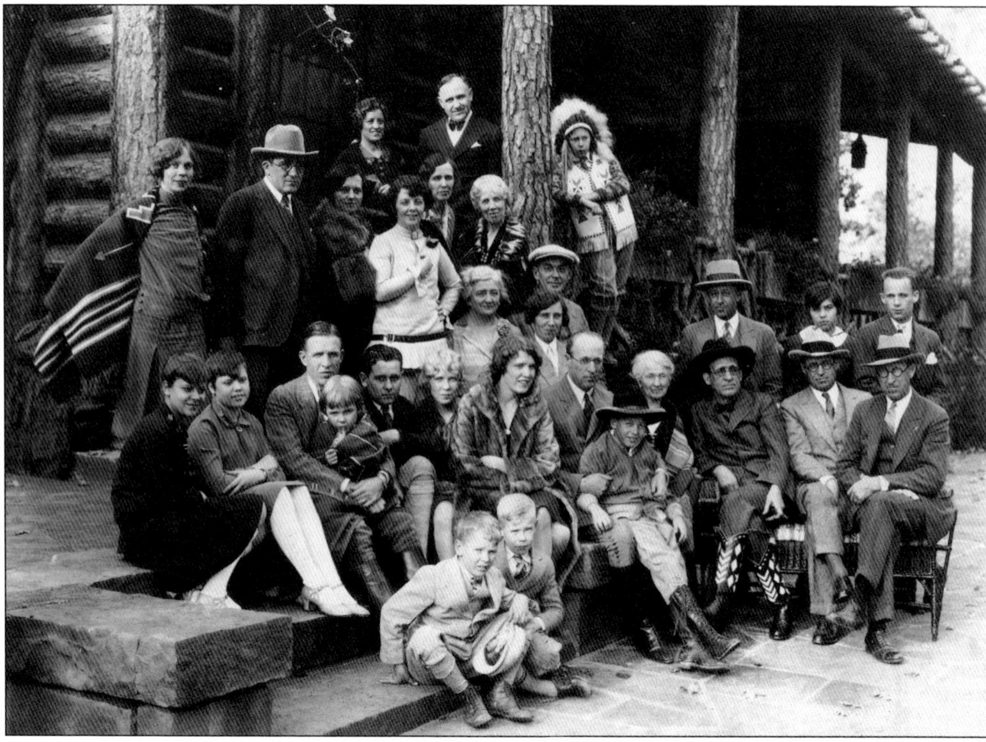

On the porch and steps of the lodge at Woolaroc, the Phillips family gathered for this portrait in November 1926. Frank Phillips is easily spotted with his distinctive boots. Here, the brothers, their wives, and children gathered for the only documented family reunion at the lodge. In later years, Frank and L.E. would travel to Iowa to visit their mother.

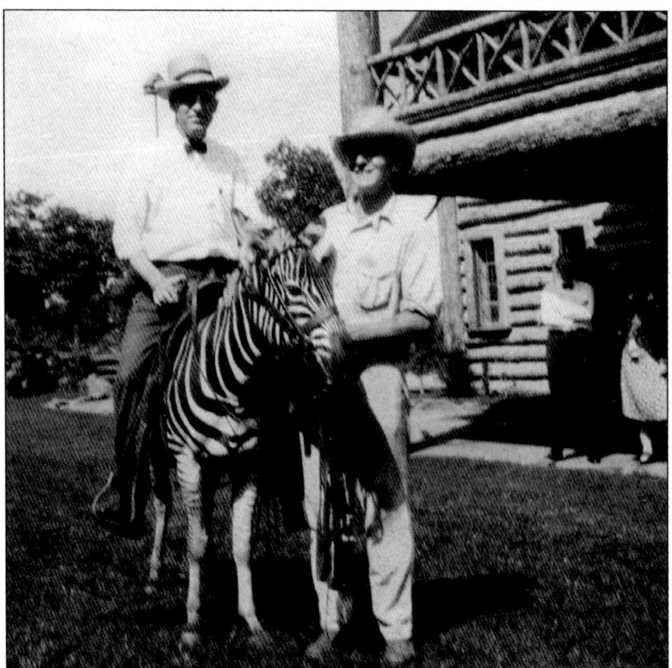

One of the most interesting features of life at Woolaroc was the ever-growing exotic animal herd that Phillips cultivated. Pictured here near the lodge atop a zebra, Frank Phillips's sense of humor is evident. Despite his stern business demeanor, he was known for having a ribald sense of humor and enjoyed playing practical jokes on his friends and guests. He often told guests that they milked the buffalo on the ranch at midnight. He most assuredly got a great laugh when visitors from the East took him seriously.

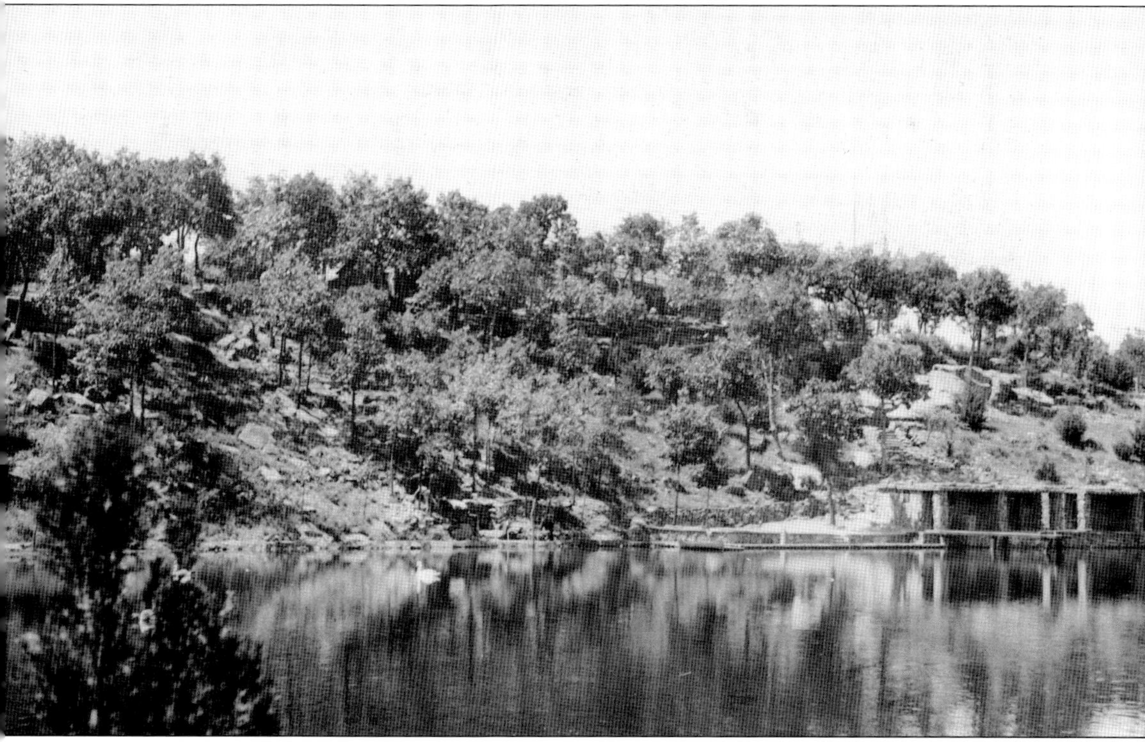

With trees growing and obscuring the lodge on the rocky hillside, this view shows Clyde Lake and the bathhouses that were accessible from the lodge. Visitors could walk down a rocky pathway to the bathhouses and dive into the waters there. The shoreline and bathhouses were the setting for many events at Woolaroc.

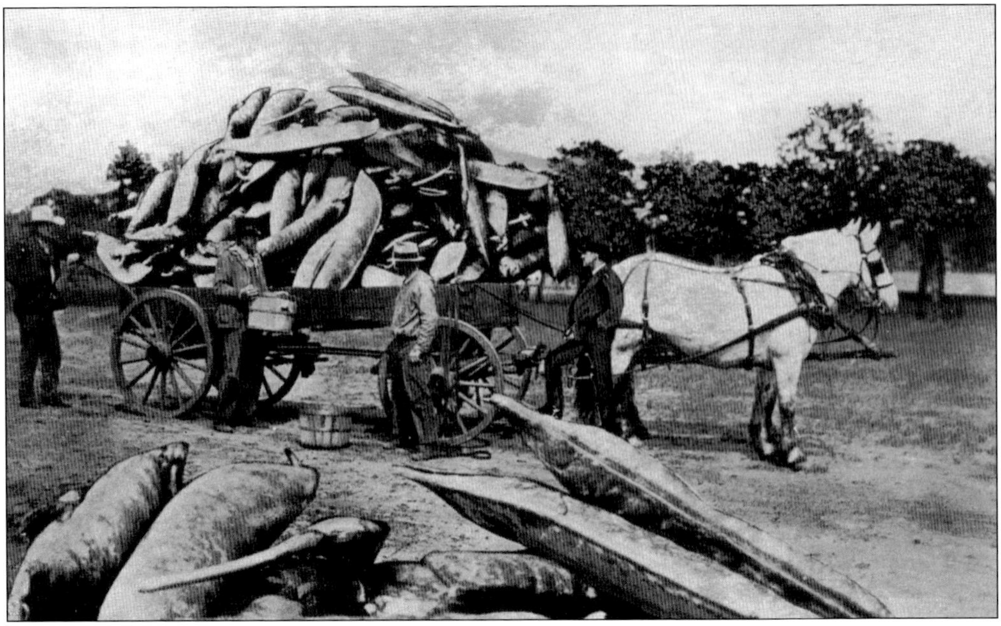

Produced in the early 1930s, taking a cue from the "tall-tale" advertising cards that were popular in the late 19th century, Frank and his brother L.E. (who also boasted a fine farm/ranch in the Bartlesville area) both used photographs of themselves in everyday poses to illustrate the "productivity" of their establishments. Here, a gigantic pea crop is harvested.

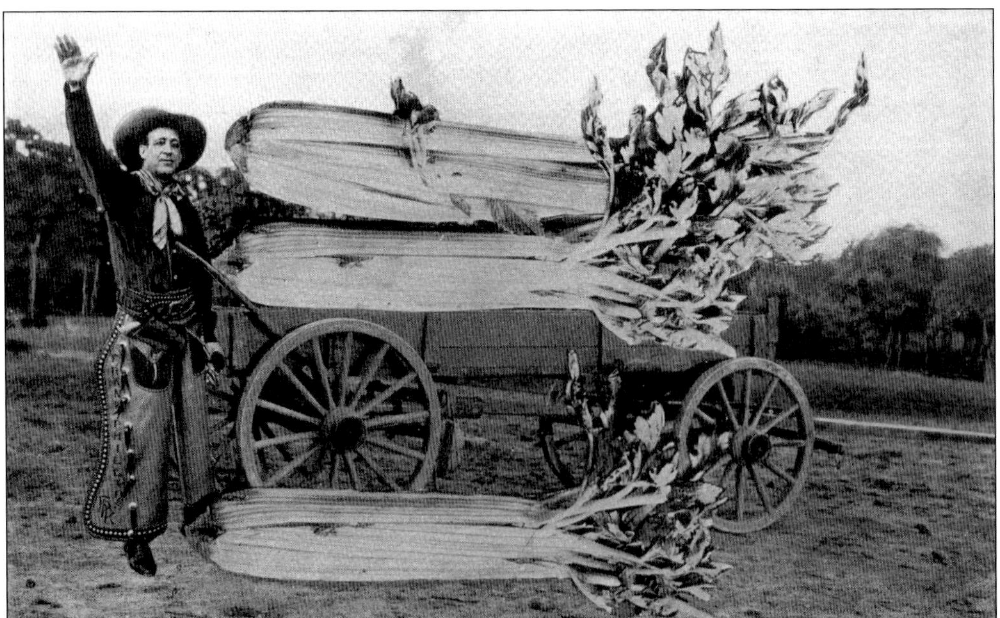

Using a photograph of Frank waving to visitors at the lodge in his cowboy attire, a larger-than-life crop of celery is hauled in from the ranch.

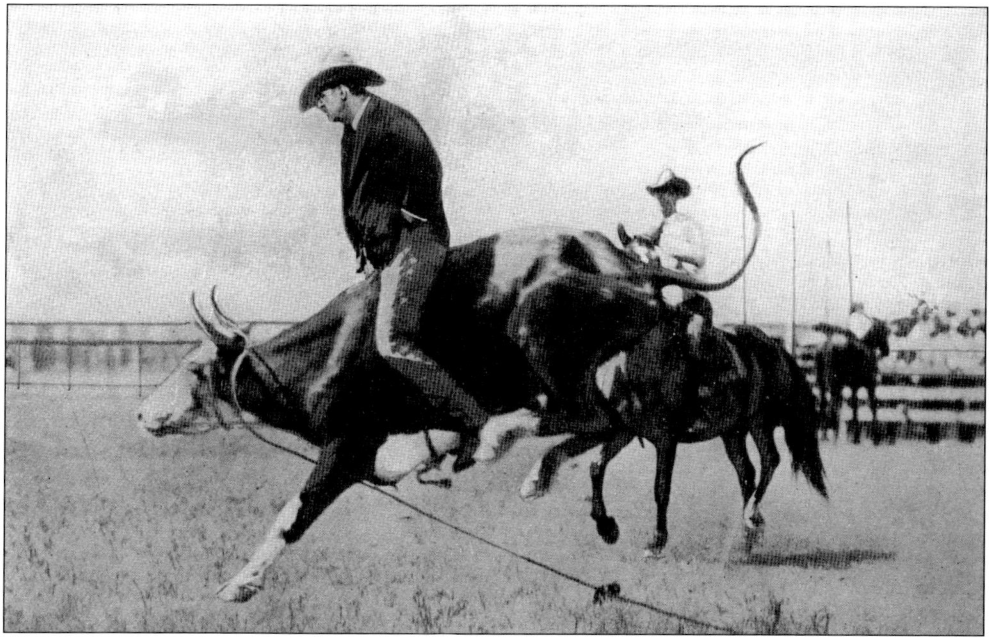

With some trickery and good hand editing, Frank rides a wild steer in a business jacket. There is no evidence that Phillips ever rode a steer or bull; however, he did enjoy riding horses and kept a fine stable of horses for riding at Woolaroc.

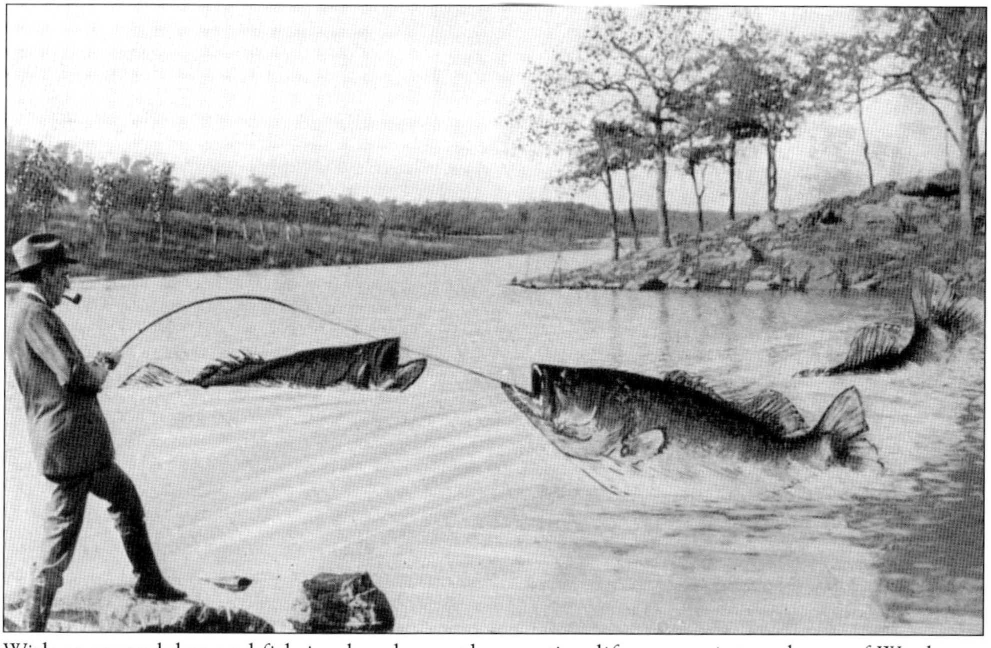

With so many lakes and fish in abundance, the sporting life was an integral part of Woolaroc. Here, a photograph of Frank fishing is meshed with a fish that most certainly would give any sportsman a run for his money.

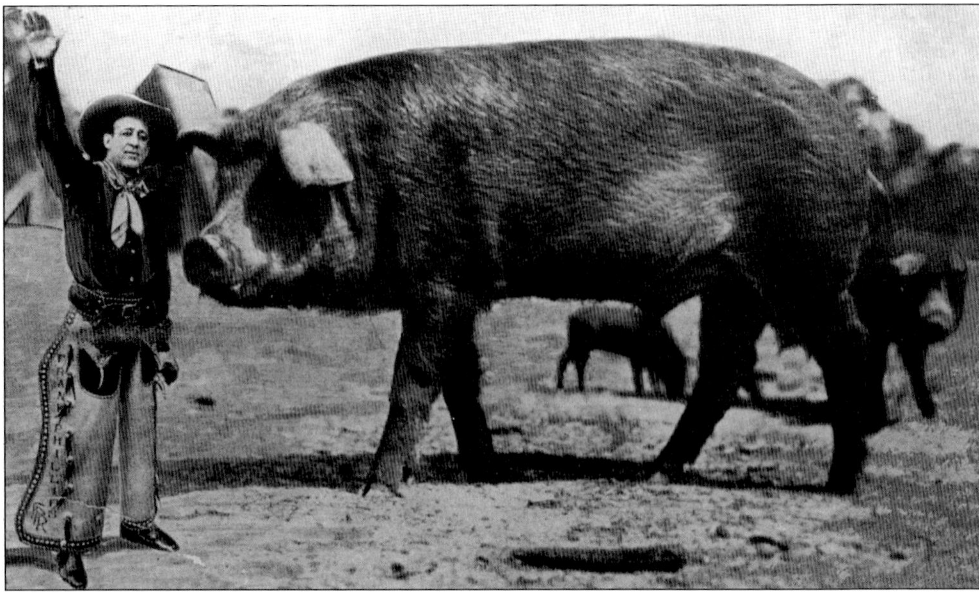

Raising animals was a big part of ranch life at Woolaroc. From exotics to standard breeds, Phillips collected a wide array of animals on the ranch. Frank poses with a larger-than-life pig named Charles Schwab on the ranch. For those that thought Phillips to be a stodgy businessman, the tall-tale cards showcased his sense of humor and playfulness.

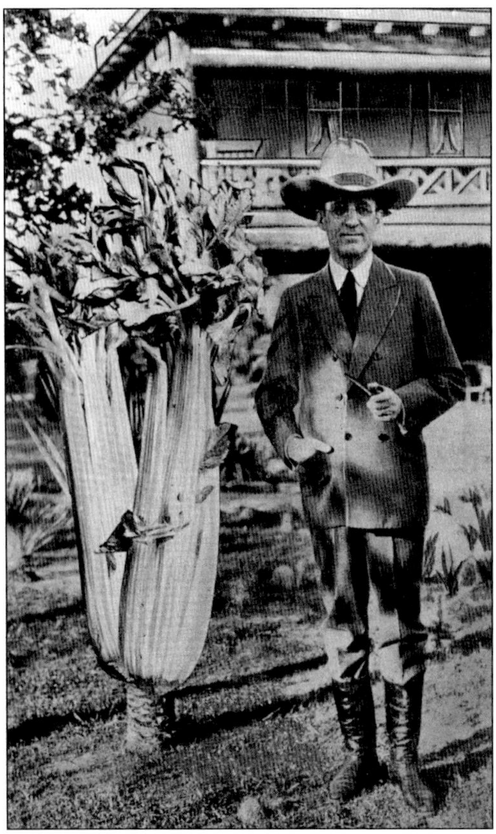

Behind the lodge, Frank poses with celery of monumental proportions. In the original photograph, Phillips, with pants tucked in his boots like any good cattleman, is standing next to a palm tree.

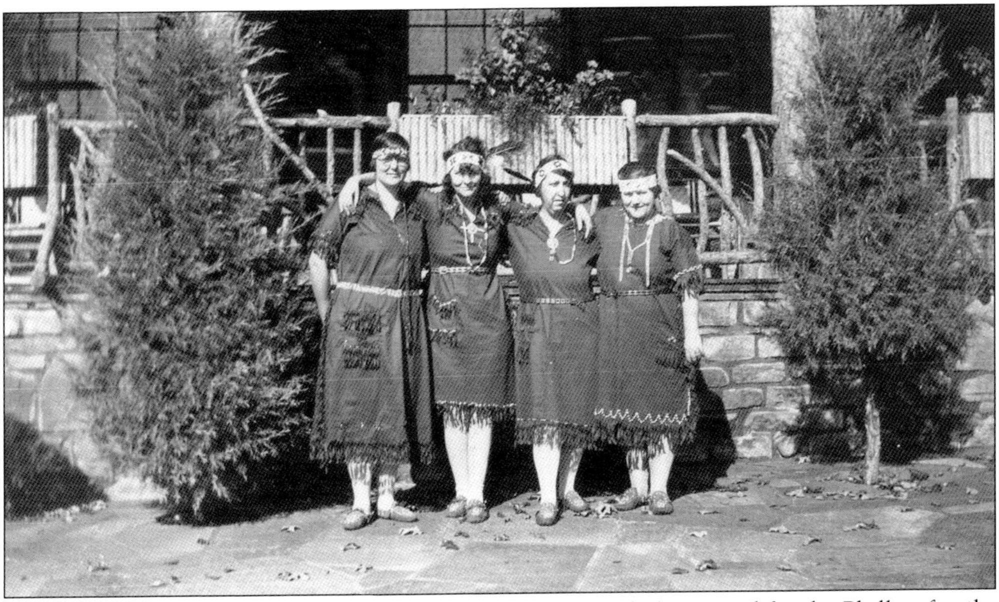

Woolaroc and the lodge were more than just the retreat and playground for the Phillips family. As the years passed, Frank and Jane not only amassed a sizeable collection of American Western art but also began to see that the lodge and museum were of interest to the community. The family employed cooks, maids, butlers, ranch hands, and other staff to make the 3,700-acre establishment run smoothly. Here, four lodge ladies (Fern, Blanche, Mary, and Lola) dressed in American Indian garb pose for a photograph.

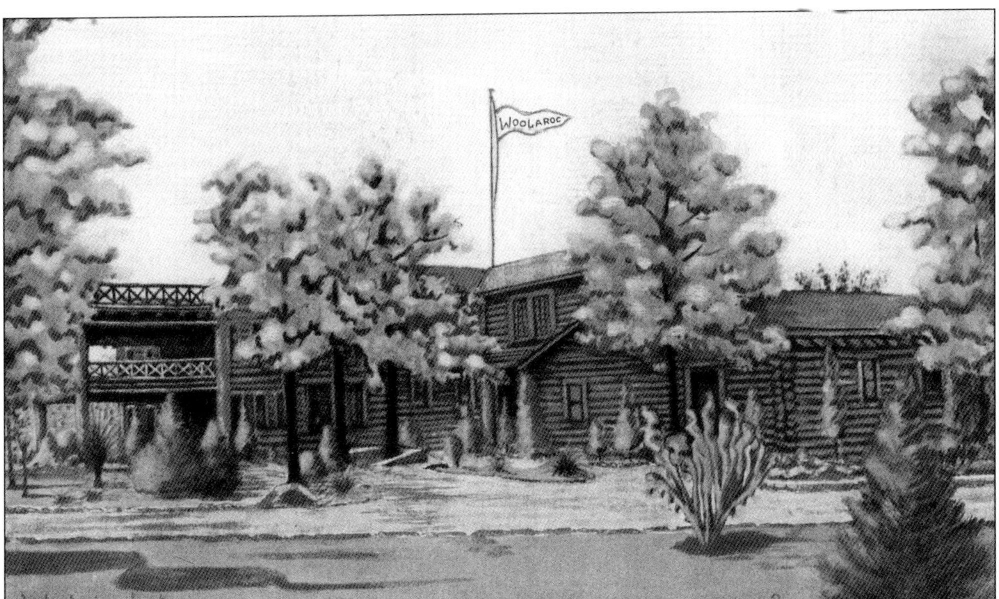

This postcard featuring the lodge shows it in its final form. After years of tweaking, the lodge embodied all that Frank and Jane loved about the West and became the premiere place to entertain in northeast Oklahoma. An invitation from the Phillips family to visit them at Woolaroc and spend time at the lodge was coveted.

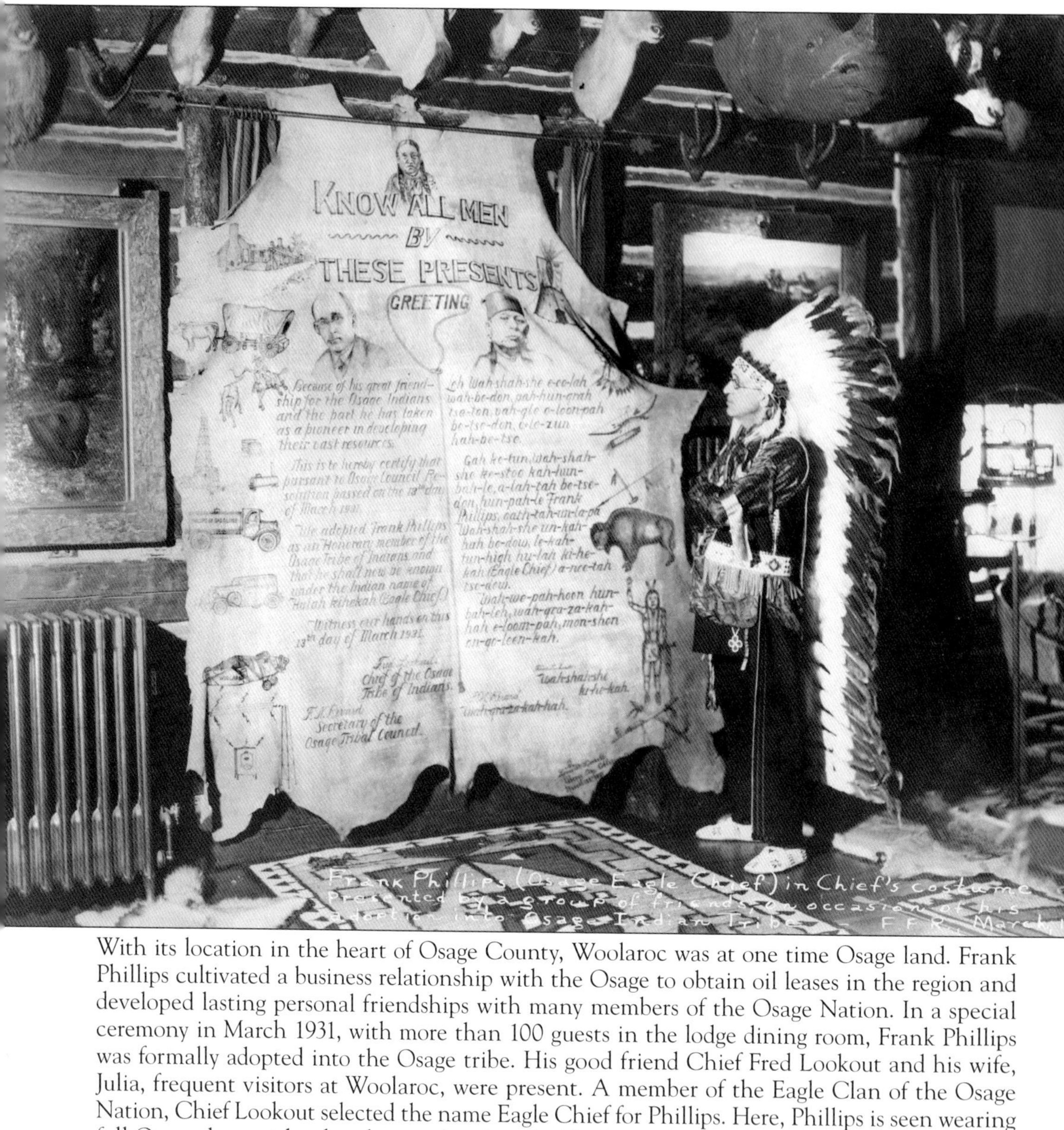

With its location in the heart of Osage County, Woolaroc was at one time Osage land. Frank Phillips cultivated a business relationship with the Osage to obtain oil leases in the region and developed lasting personal friendships with many members of the Osage Nation. In a special ceremony in March 1931, with more than 100 guests in the lodge dining room, Frank Phillips was formally adopted into the Osage tribe. His good friend Chief Fred Lookout and his wife, Julia, frequent visitors at Woolaroc, were present. A member of the Eagle Clan of the Osage Nation, Chief Lookout selected the name Eagle Chief for Phillips. Here, Phillips is seen wearing full Osage dress with a hand-tanned and worked hide proclaiming his new tribal status. Frank remarked the following of his adoption: "I am overwhelmed. I haven't the words to express my appreciation of the honor, which is being conferred. I accept this fellowship with great gratitude . . . I fear I am not worthy and wonder if this wise old tribe is making its first mistake today . . . I shall do my best to be worthy."

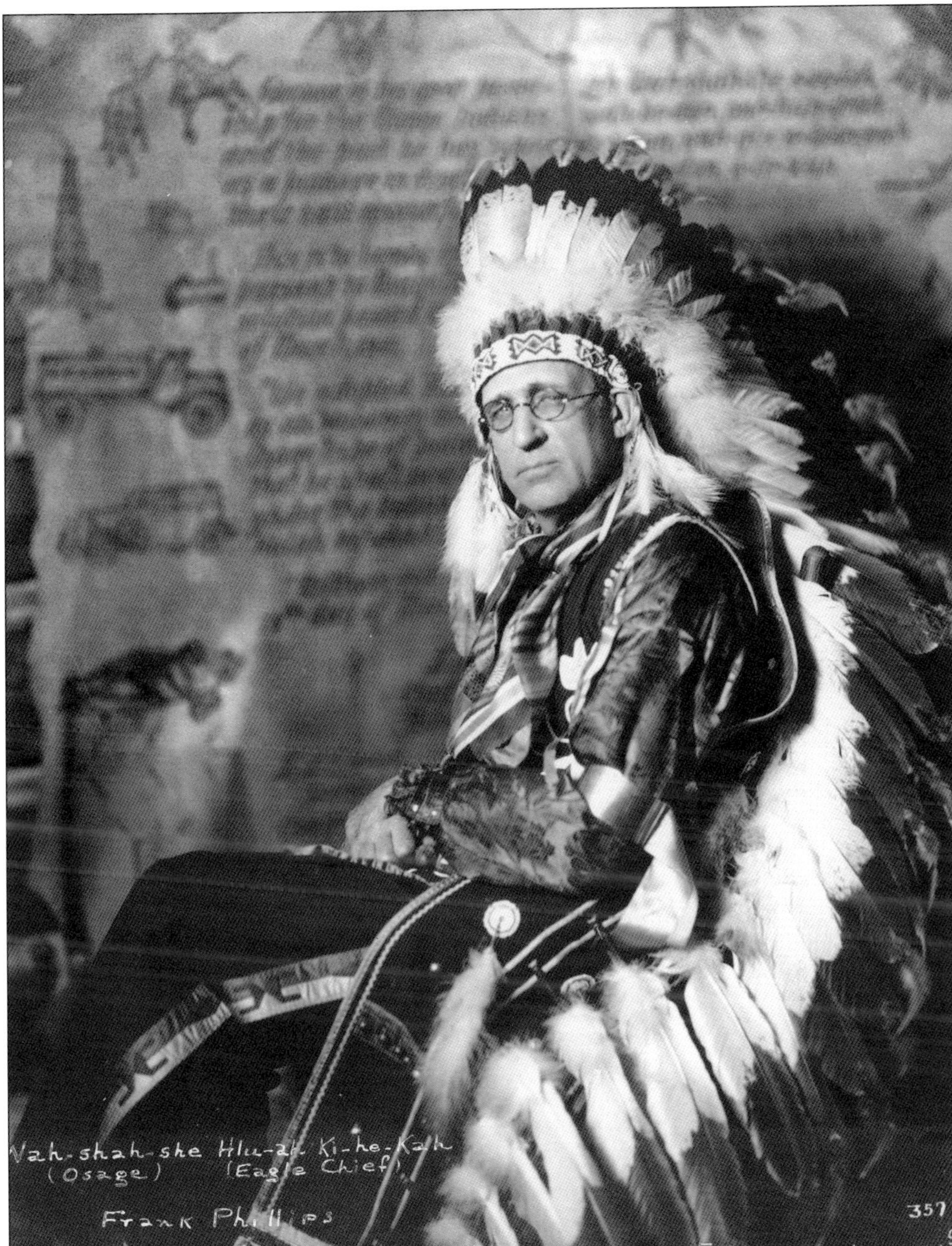

Seated in the lodge in full Osage dress, Frank Phillips poses for Bartlesville photographer Frank Griggs. Griggs captured many important events in the life of the Phillips family at Woolaroc. Many notable individuals were present at this special occasion in March 1931, including Zack Miller of the 101 Ranch and Wild West Show; Col. G.W. Lillie, better known as Pawnee Bill of Pawnee Bill's Wild West Show; oilfield technology pioneer Aramais Artunoff; and family and friends. Those who could not attend sent telegrams with their regrets. William Allen White, Will Rogers, and Charles Curtis (the only American Indian vice president of the United States) were just a few of the many who wished Frank well on this special day.

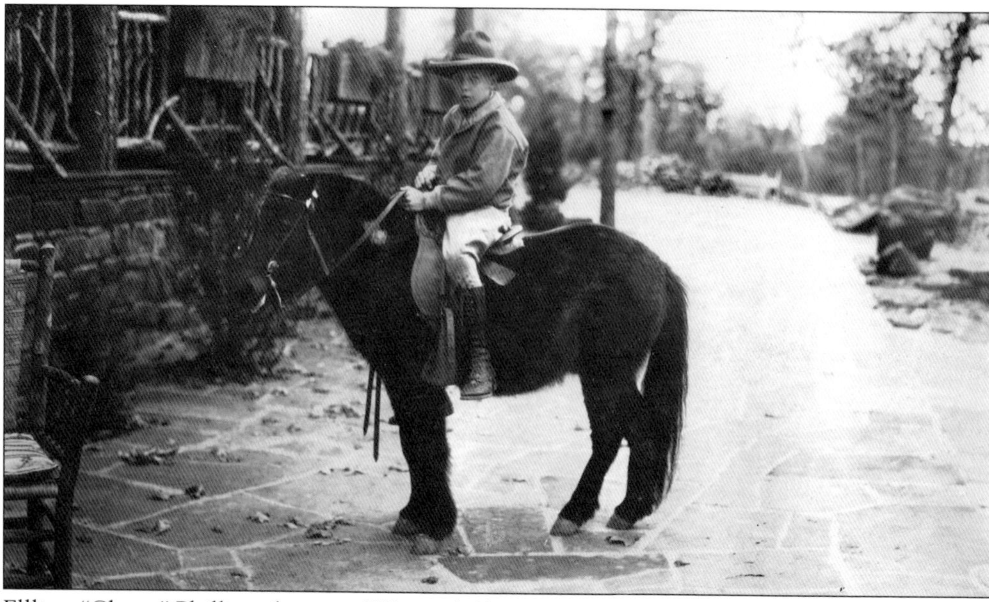

Ellliott "Chope" Phillips, the son of Waite Phillips, sits atop his pony dressed in cowboy garb. He poses for a photograph in front of the lodge during the 1926 family reunion at Woolaroc. For the Phillips children, grandchildren, and friends the ranch was the most wondrous and incredible playground. Parties, picnics, and adventures were to be had when visiting.

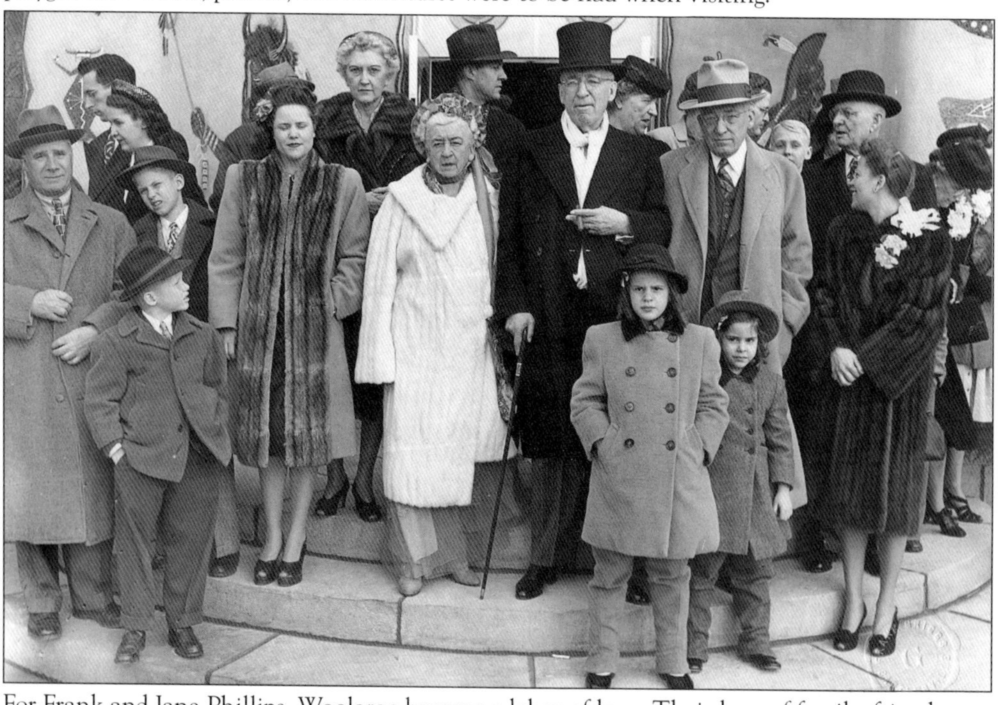

For Frank and Jane Phillips, Woolaroc became a labor of love. Their love of family, friends, art, and sharing their good fortune with the community inspired them to make Woolaroc more than a home but a point of pride for the region. On the occasion of their 50th wedding anniversary, they could have celebrated anywhere but chose to gather at Woolaroc. Here, on the steps of the museum they founded, they posed for a portrait to commemorate the day.

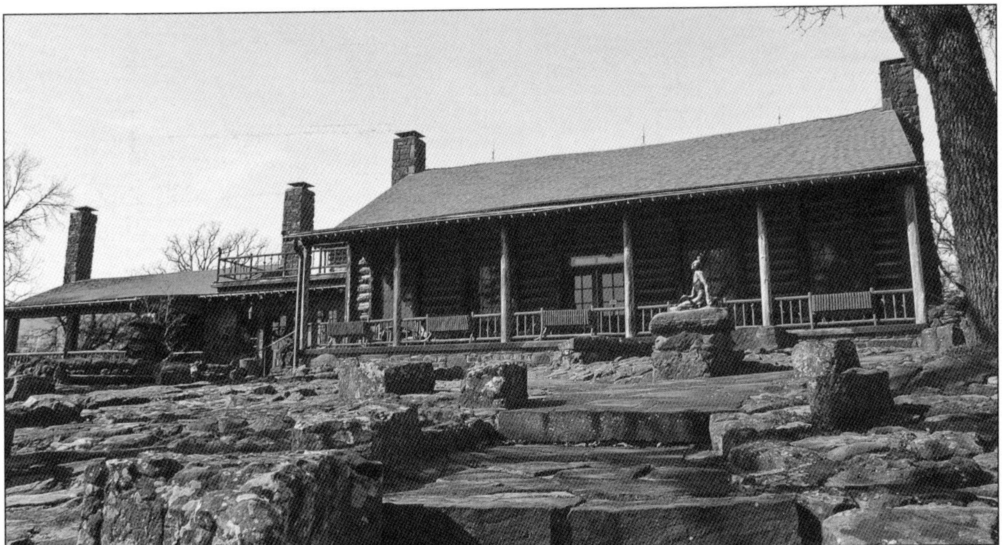

Today, the lodge at Woolaroc sits proudly atop the rocky hillside that afforded Frank and Jane magnificent views of Clyde Lake and the Osage Hills. The native stone walkways, fountains, and landscaping make it a place of beauty. The lodge is cared for and preserved by the Frank Phillips Foundation, Inc., a nonprofit organization that also oversees the ranch and museum. (Author's collection.)

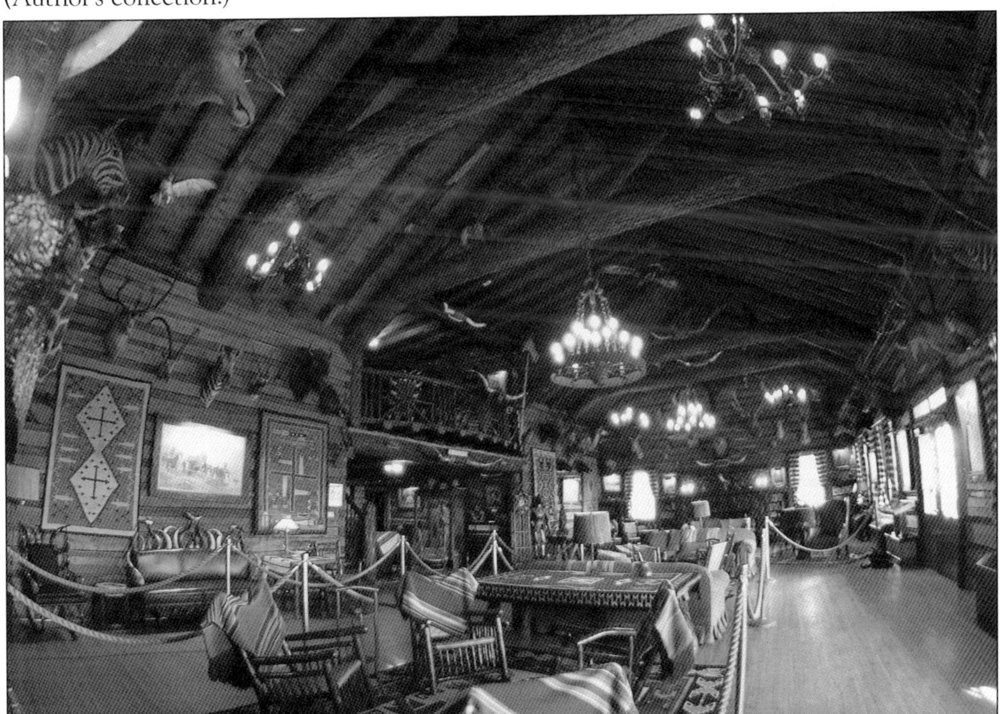

The interior of the lodge looks much today as it did when Frank Phillips passed away in 1950. His artwork, Navajo blankets, animal heads and hides, and artifacts still adorn the walls and tables. The lodge is open to the public and, on special occasions, is used for social functions. (Author's collection.)

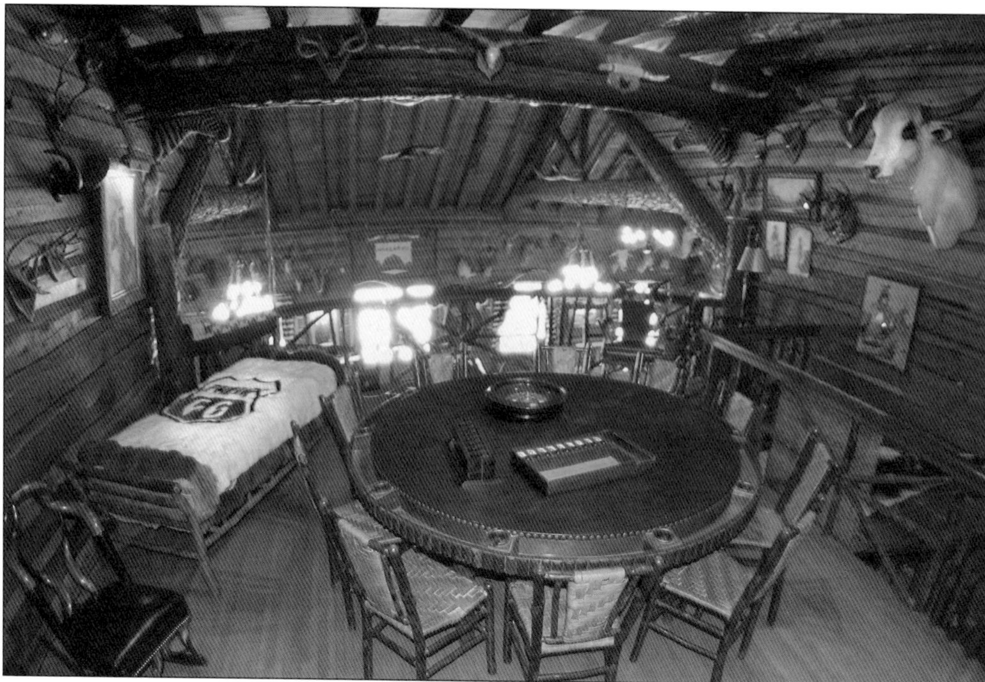

Many an evening was spent around this poker table. One can almost envision Frank and his friends and business associates smoking cigars and playing poker until the wee hours of the morning. To ensure that no one left the poker game, Phillips had a small bed placed in the corner so players could take a brief respite. (Author's collection.)

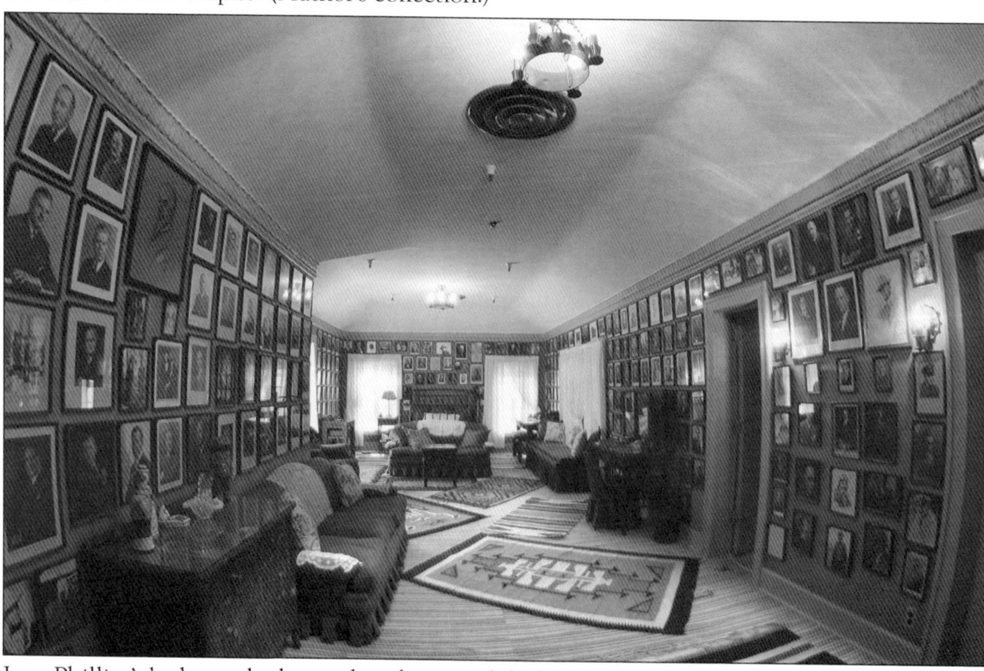

Jane Phillips's bedroom looks much today as it did when she lived at the lodge. Her collection of photographs still graces the walls. To ensure their preservation, the private family bedrooms are not accessible to the public. (Author's collection.)

The only woman to appear on Jane's bedroom walls aside from her daughters is Osa Johnson. The wife of famed pilot and wildlife filmmaker Martin Johnson, Osa was herself a noted photographer and big-game hunter. Osa and Martin presented Frank and Jane with an elephant head for their taxidermy collection that is still at Woolaroc today. Four images of Osa can be found on Jane's walls. (Author's collection.)

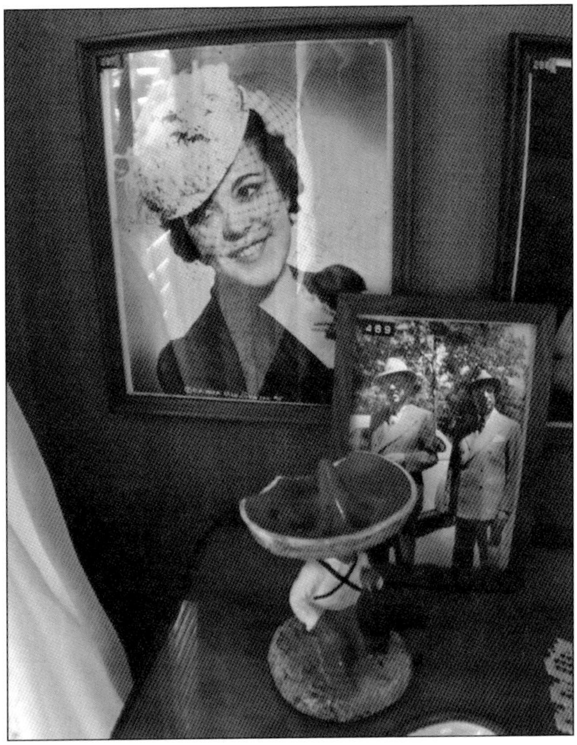

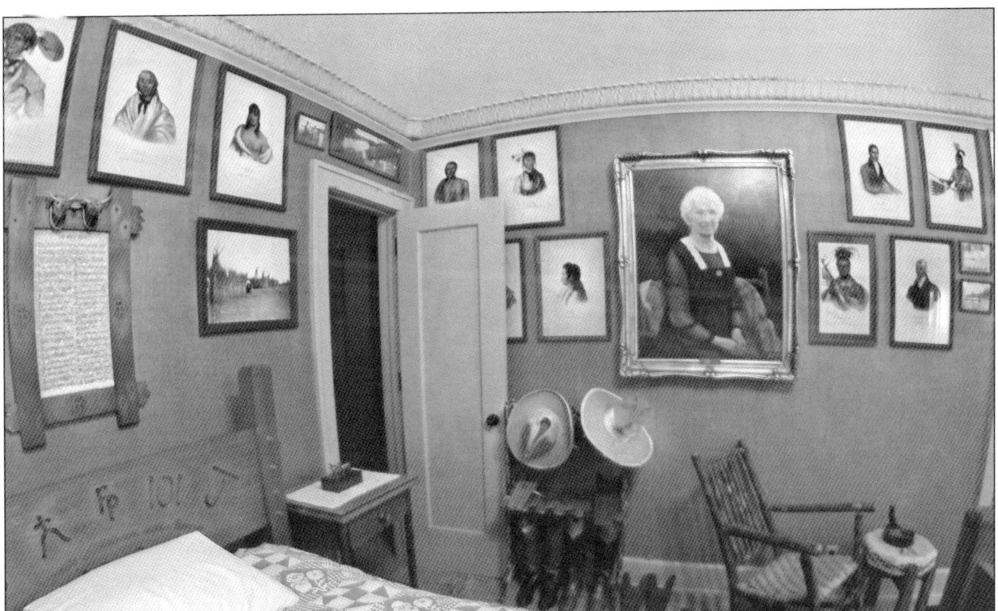

Frank Phillips's somewhat sparsely decorated room contains a fine collection of American Indian prints, from the McKinney and Hall folio, depicting various famous tribal leaders, orators, and statesmen. A large portrait of Frank's mother, Lucinda, is also seen on the wall here. His boots and hats are also visible. His bed, simple and rustic, was fashioned by the ranch hands at Woolaroc. The brands of various famous cattle ranches were branded into the wooden bed frame. (Author's collection.)

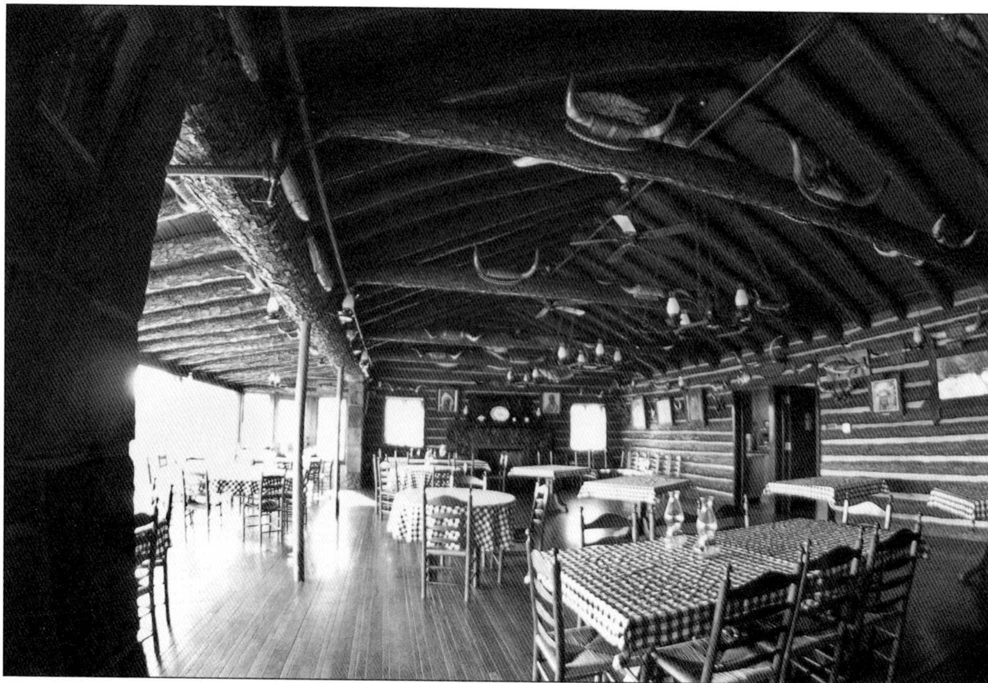

The dining room at the lodge is much as it appeared in Frank and Jane's day. Special events like the annual Valentine's Dinner are held at the lodge, and participants can take in the marvelous scenery. (Author's collection.)

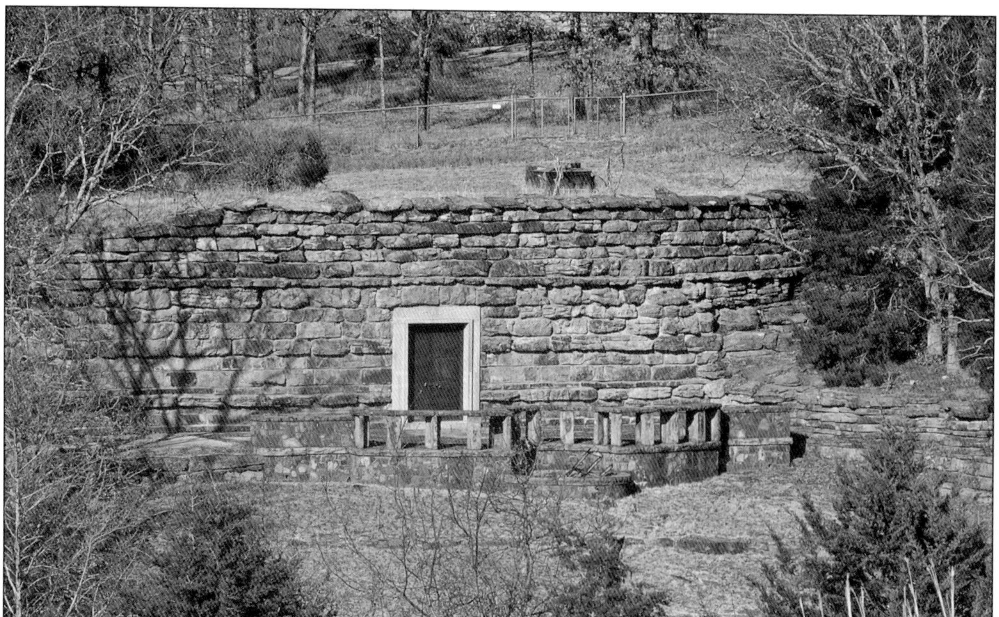

With the death of his beloved Jane in 1948, Frank continued work on a mausoleum that was initiated in 1948. This would become the final resting place for Frank and his beloved Jane. Located on the ranch, the mausoleum is built into a hillside and is visible from the road. Here, Frank and Jane Phillips were interred. Frank died in 1950. Their only son, John, died in 1953 and he also rests there with his parents in the Osage Hills they loved. (Author's collection.)

Two

The Woolaroc Takes Flight

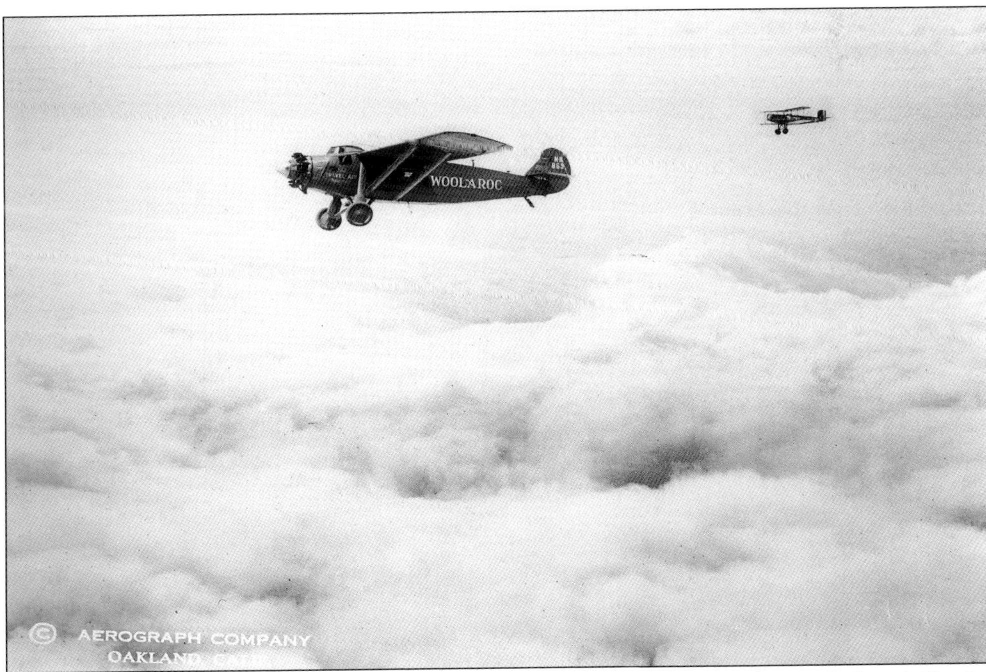

In the 1920s, aviation became a national obsession. With the transatlantic flight of Charles Lindbergh piloting the *Spirit of St. Louis* in 1927, Americans became enamored with aviation. Aviators were the rock stars of their day. Never one to miss a great business opportunity, Frank and L.E. Phillips urged their chemists at Phillips Petroleum to work on new formulations for aviation fuel. To promote Phillips Petroleum's NuAviation fuel, Frank Phillips would enter the world of aviation. It was a relationship that would bring much attention to the company and Bartlesville. Seen here high above the earth in flight, the *Woolaroc*—a Travel Air 5000 monoplane piloted by Arthur Goebel Jr.—carried the name of Frank and Jane Phillips's beloved ranch.

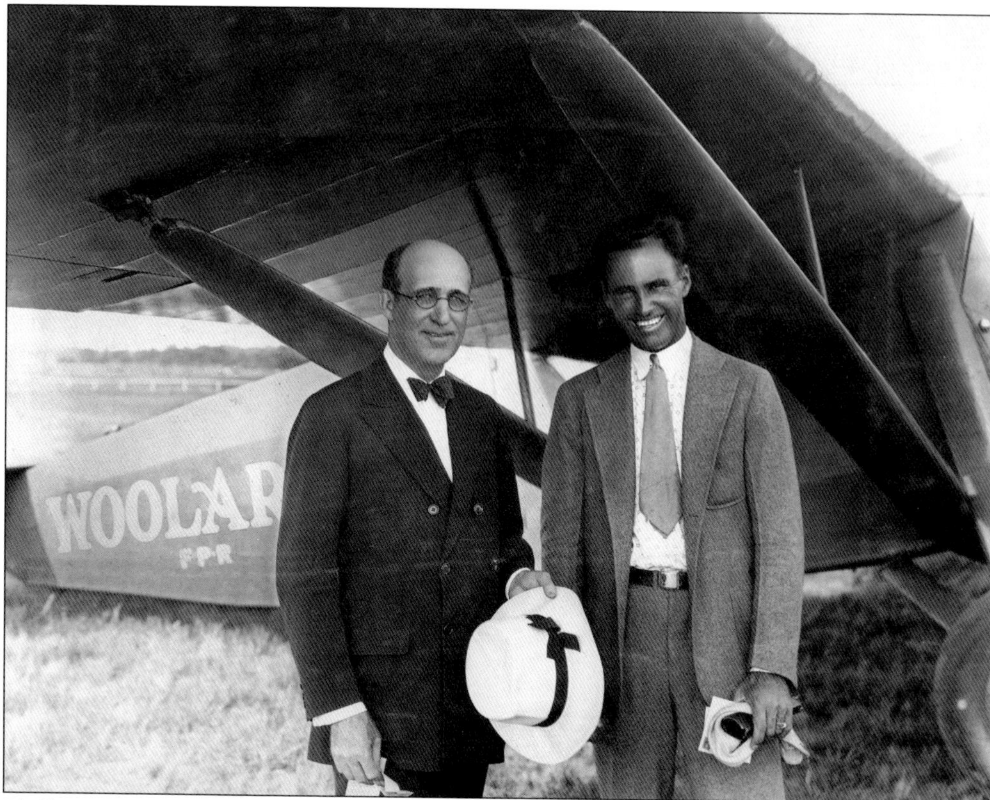

Phillips Petroleum was developing an aviation fuel division under the direction of W.D. "Billy" Parker, an experienced pilot who served during World War I with the British Royal Flying Corps. Under Parker's directive, a Travel Air plane named the *Oklahoma* was purchased by Phillips and used to promote NuAviation fuel. In 1927, Phillips would meet Arthur Goebel Jr. and hedge his bets and enter two planes in the dangerous Dole Race from California to Hawaii. Phillips placed his faith in Goebel to pilot the *Woolaroc*. Dashing, handsome, and camera friendly, Goebel was a Hollywood stunt pilot from California and had a wealth of aviation experience.

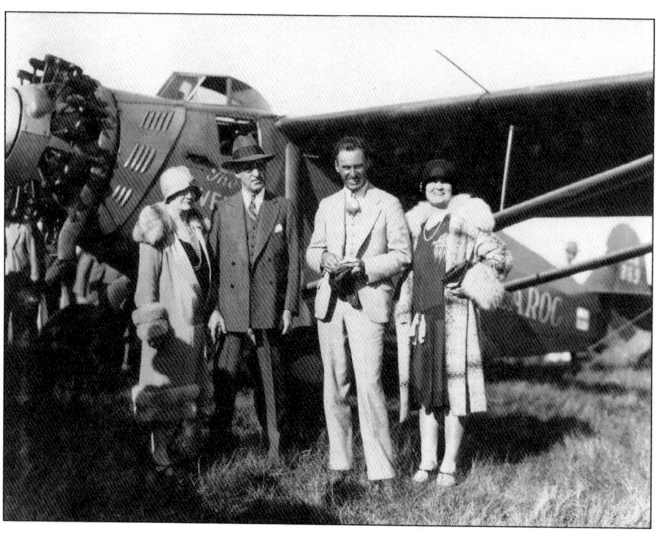

Jane and Frank Phillips pose for a photograph with Arthur "Art" Goebel and a visitor in front of the *Woolaroc*. Goebel began his quest to enter the Dole Race independently. Only when he was unable to raise the last $15,000 payment to Travel Air of Wichita, Kansas, to purchase the Travel Air 5000 monoplane did he approach Frank Phillips and his petroleum company for financial support. It was a relationship that went on to serve both men well.

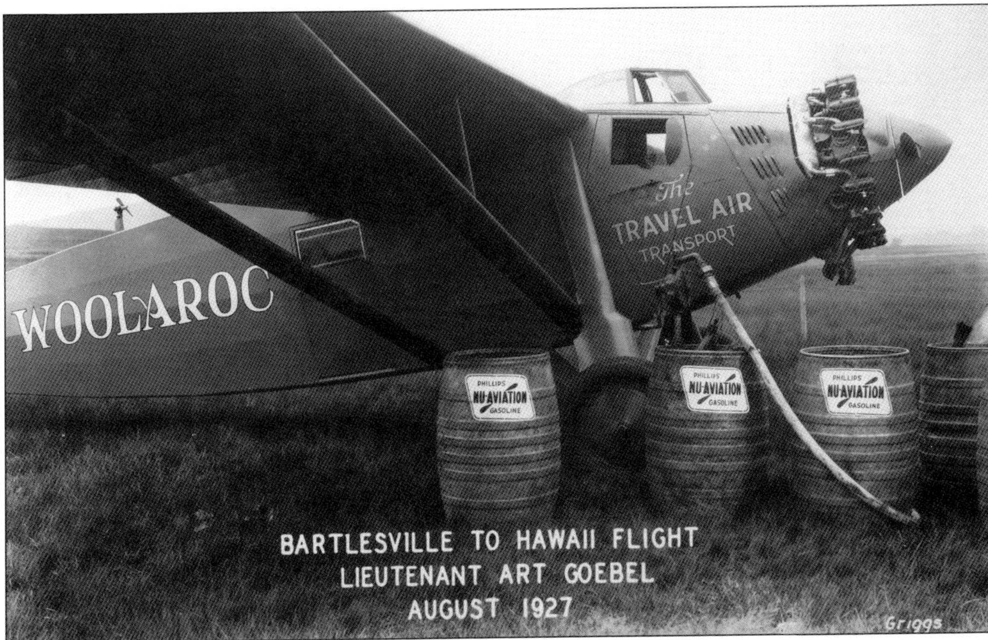

Nearly every photograph of the *Woolaroc* in the collection of the Woolaroc Museum comes from the period leading up to and immediately after the Dole Race in August 1927. Here, the plane is positioned so drums of Phillips Petroleum NuAviation fuel are prominent in the photographs for publicity and promotional purposes. Even though Phillips was keenly interested in aviation, the plane and its participation in the Dole Race was a carefully planned event to promote aviation fuel and cement Phillips Petroleum's position as the prime producer of fuel.

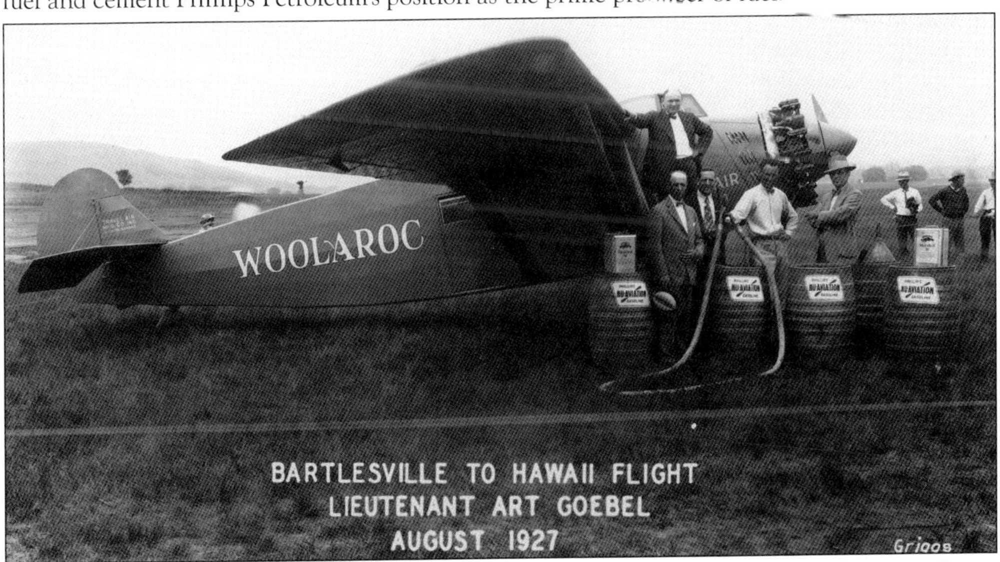

In preparation for the Dole Race, Frank Phillips, Art Goebel, and other men on the ground pose for a photograph as the plane is fueled and readied for the race. The *Woolaroc*, once loaded with fuel, carried 417 gallons of NuAviation fuel and 17 gallons of oil. The plane weighed in at 5,520 pounds. This weight included the plane, fuel, equipment, and crew. A collapsible life raft, paddles, emergency flares, and navigation equipment were packed for the dangerous flight. Art Goebel would attempt to do what Charles Lindbergh would not—fly from the US mainland to Hawaii.

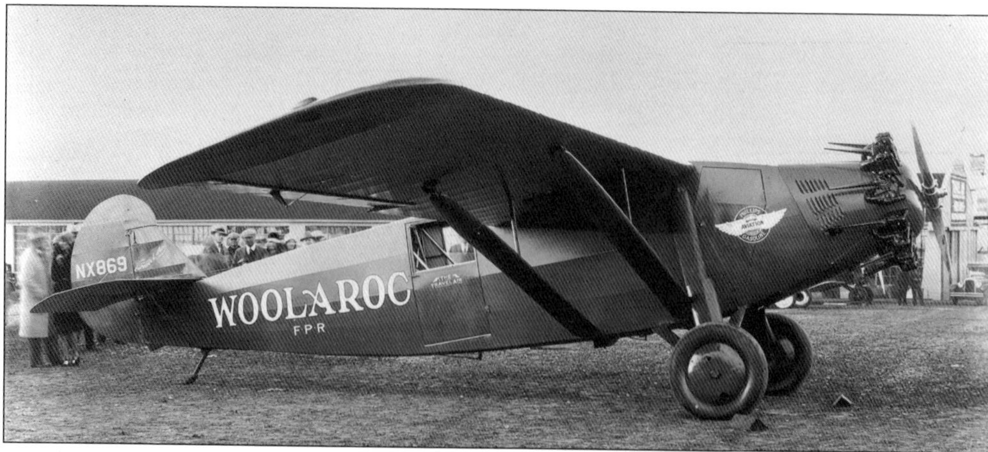

On the morning of August 16, 1927, Frank Phillips nervously waited as his planes the *Oklahoma* and *Woolaroc* readied for takeoff in the Dole Race. The *Oklahoma* took off in position No. 1, while Goebel waited in the *Woolaroc* in position No. 7. After one plane crashed on takeoff, others made their way skyward. Goebel broke the bonds of the earth and was skyward heading west to Hawaii. Soon after takeoff, the *Oklahoma* returned leaving the *Woolaroc* carrying the Phillips banner. Averaging 96 miles per hour and covering 2,400 miles in 26 hours, Art Goebel won the Dole Race and made the *Woolaroc* world famous.

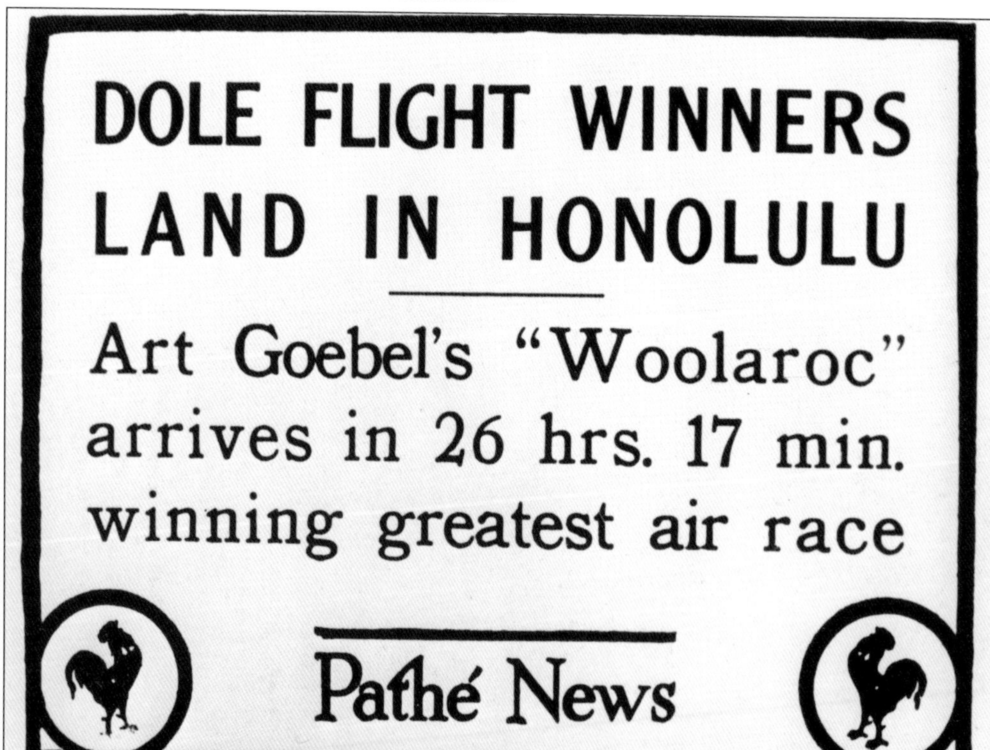

News of Art Goebel's heroic triumph in the daring Dole Race ran on the headlines of every major newspaper in the United States. Moviegoers nationwide learned of Goebel's Pacific flight in movie newsreels. For Frank Phillips, the placement of the Woolaroc in movie newsreels meant excellent product placement and promotion for Phillips Petroleum.

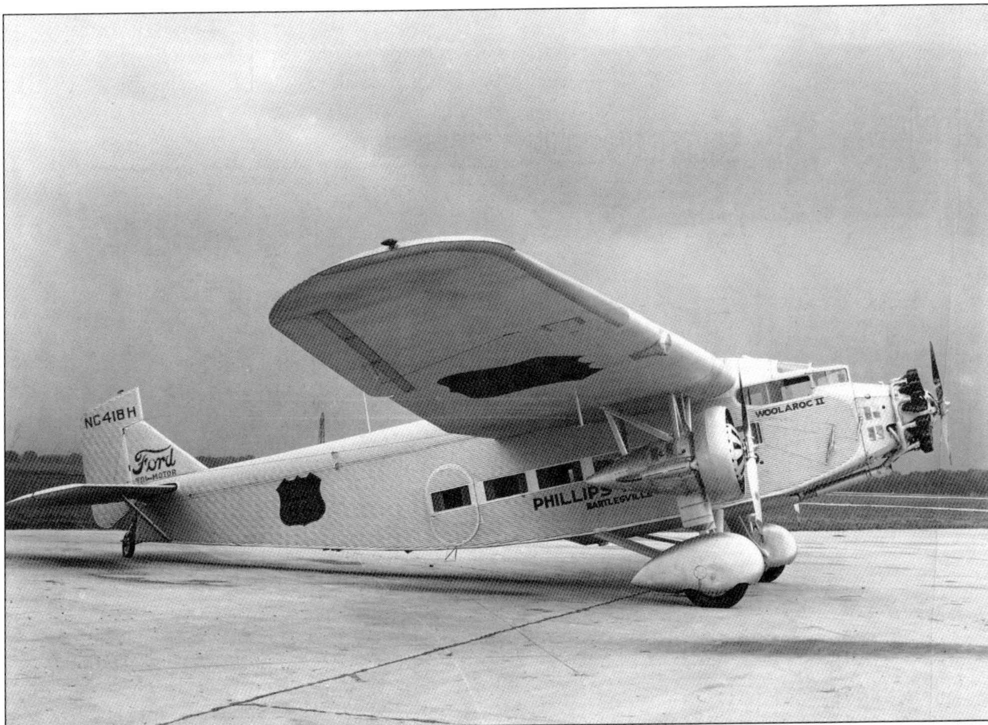

The *Woolaroc II*, a Ford Trimotor, was one of the next planes in the Phillips fleet. Nicknamed the "Tin Goose," the Trimotor was a three-engine plane that was produced by Henry Ford from 1925 to 1933. Less than 200 of the distinctive planes were produced. The plane bore not only the name *Woolaroc II* but also the Phillips 66 insignia, as seen here.

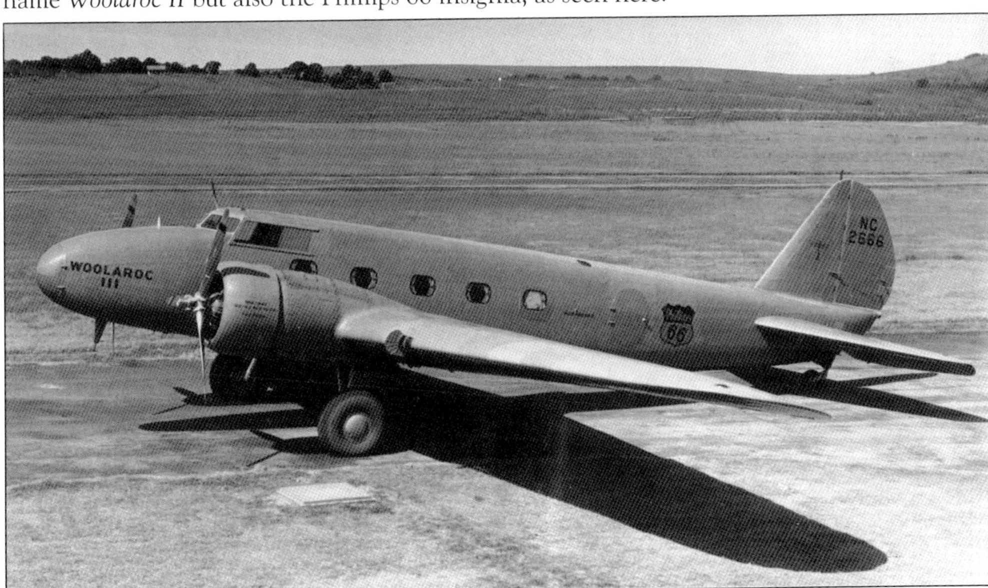

Continuing to promote NuAviation fuel and provide transportation for Phillips employees and crews, the *Woolaroc III*, seen here, bore the name of Frank and Jane's beloved ranch. The *Woolaroc III* was a Boeing 247D and was state of the art. Today, the *Woolaroc II* and *Woolaroc III* no longer exist. Only the *Woolaroc* is preserved for posterity.

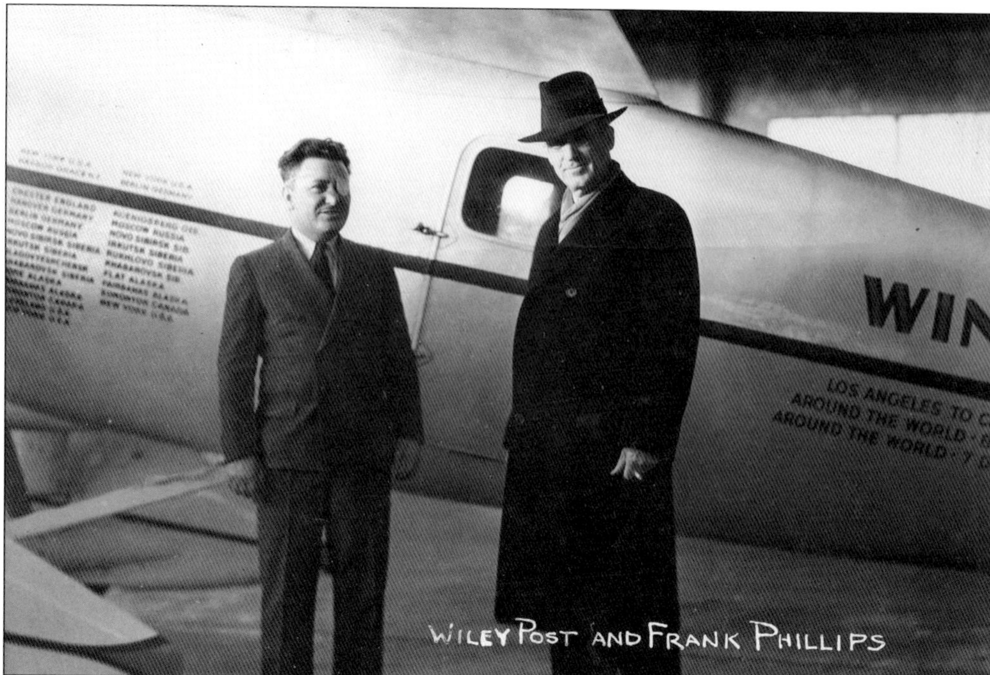

Frank Phillips's interest in aviation allowed him to cultivate an interesting and talented set of friends and business associates. One such individual was Wiley Post. Pictured here with Phillips in front of the *Winnie Mae*, Post's life read like an adventure novel. Born in 1898 in Texas, Post's family moved to a farm near Maysville, Oklahoma, when he was four. At the age of 13, he saw the power and beauty of aviation at a county fair. From then on, he was smitten. During World War I, he joined the US Air Service and learned radio communications. After a stint as a roughneck and a carjacking incident that landed him in reformatory school, Post set his sights at becoming a pilot. In 1926, an oilfield accident left him without the use of his left eye. With settlement money, he bought his first plane. A personal pilot for Powell Briscoe and F.C. Hall, Oklahoma oilmen, Post was the recipient of Hall's favor when he purchased a Lockheed Vega in 1930.

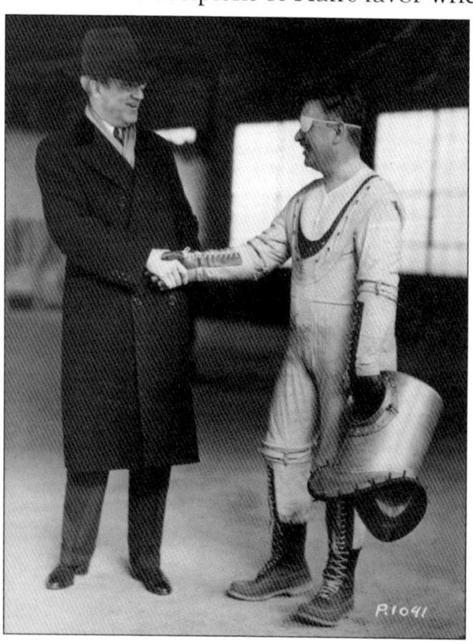

Post pushed the limits of aviation technology every time he flew. In the *Winnie Mae*, he would fly solo around the world in 1931 and would later make the perilous flight again to break his own record. In 1934, with backing from Frank Phillips and Phillips Petroleum, Post began experimenting with various pressurized flight suits and aircraft cabins. Pictured here with Phillips, Post dons one of the three suits he developed for high altitude flights. Above the skies over Bartlesville in the *Winnie Mae*, Post would test his suit and discover the jet stream.

Wiley Post and Oklahoma's native son Will Rogers became close friends. Both men spent time at the lodge at Woolaroc and called Frank Phillips their friend. In the summer of 1935, Post and Rogers headed for Alaska with Post in the pilot's seat. Post was looking for mail routes to Russia, and Rogers was searching for interesting material for his syndicated newspaper column. On August 15, 1935, while attempting to fly to Barrow, Alaska, their plane crashed over water killing both men instantly. Out of respect for both men, Art Goebel places a black mourning wreath on the propeller of the *Winnie Mae* in Bartlesville.

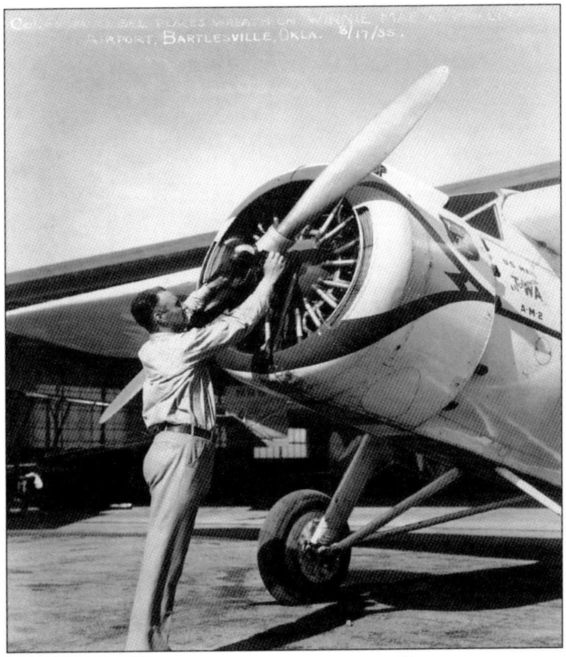

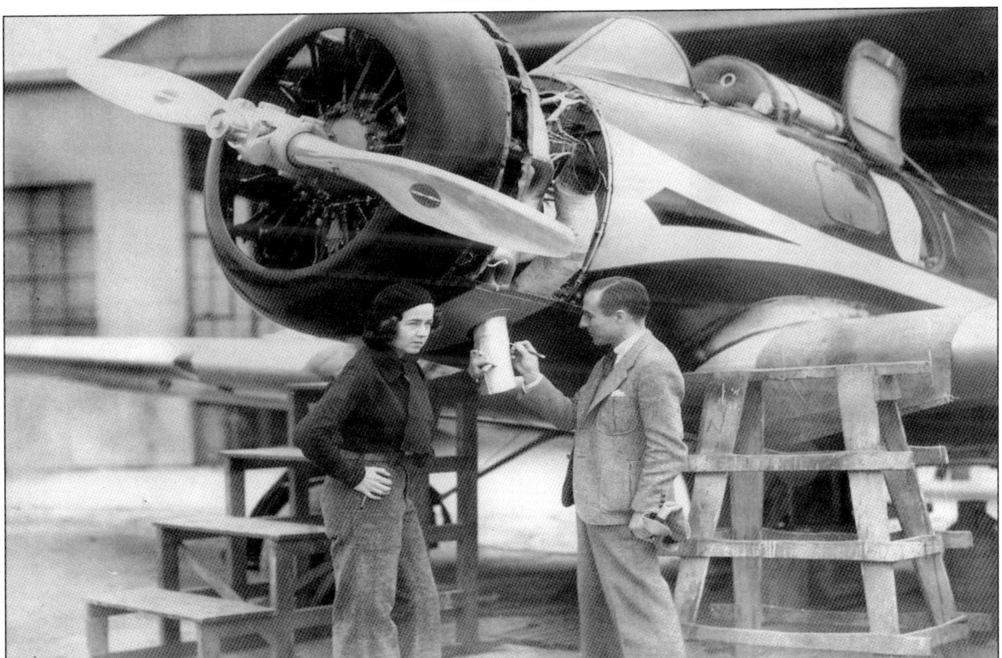

Parker, Goebel, and Post were not the only aviators to visit Frank Phillips in Bartlesville. Laura Ingalls (not to be confused with the children's author) was a pioneering aviatrix. From 1930 to 1934, Ingalls set out to make and break aviation records. She was the first woman to fly solo from North to South America. She became the first pilot (male or female) to fly solo around South America and complete a land flight in South America. She became the first woman to fly solo across the Andes and made the longest solo flight for a woman, which was an amazing 17,000 miles. Here, she is seen with Billy Parker at the airport in Bartlesville.

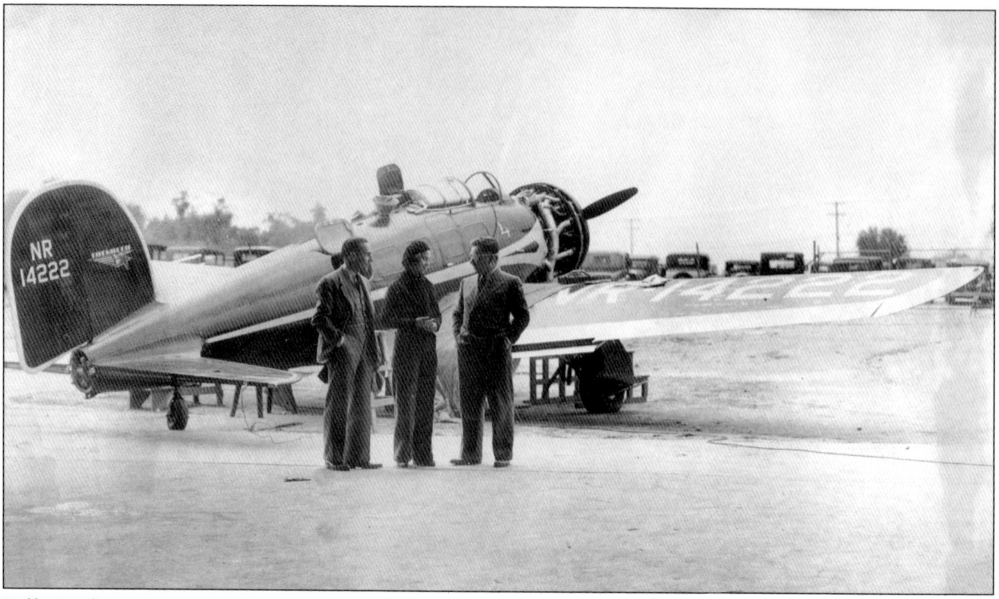

Billy Parker, Laura Ingalls, and Wiley Post inspect Laura's Lockheed Orion in Bartlesville at the municipal airport. Frank Phillips and Phillips Petroleum courted the daring pilots of the 1920s and 1930s as their exploits always garnered headlines. To have Phillips NuAviation fuel a part of record-breaking flights could yield lucrative business deals for the company.

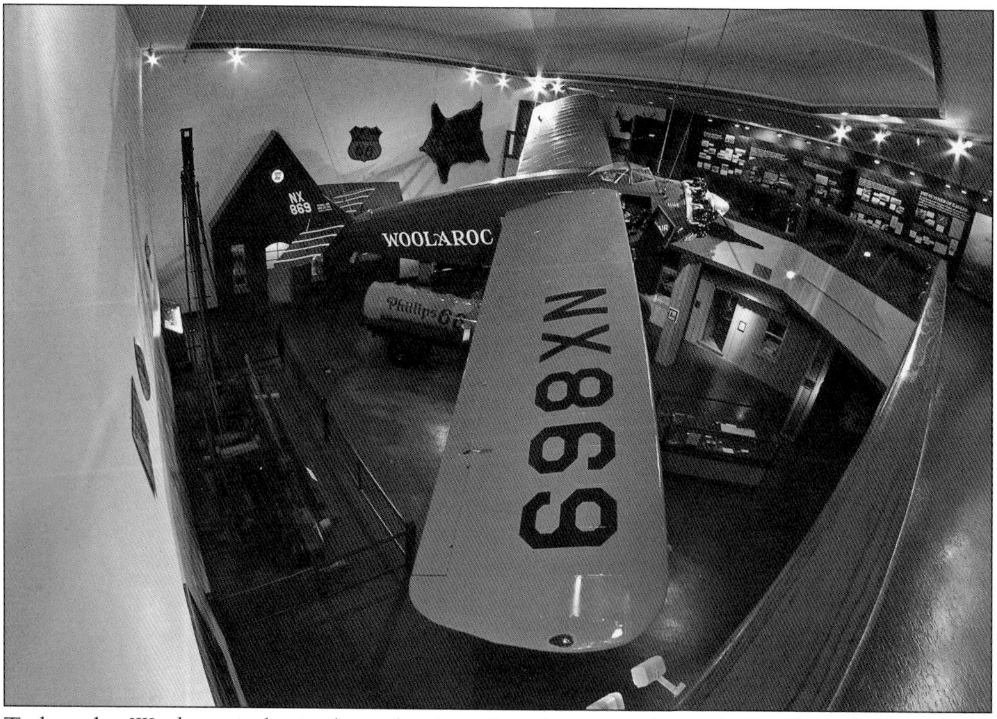

Today, the *Woolaroc* is lovingly and painstakingly restored and housed in the Woolaroc Museum. The original museum building was once the plane's hangar on the ranch. Visitors can see the plane and learn about the daring exploits of Art Goebel in the dangerous Dole Race. (Author's collection.)

Three

The Hangar that Became a Museum

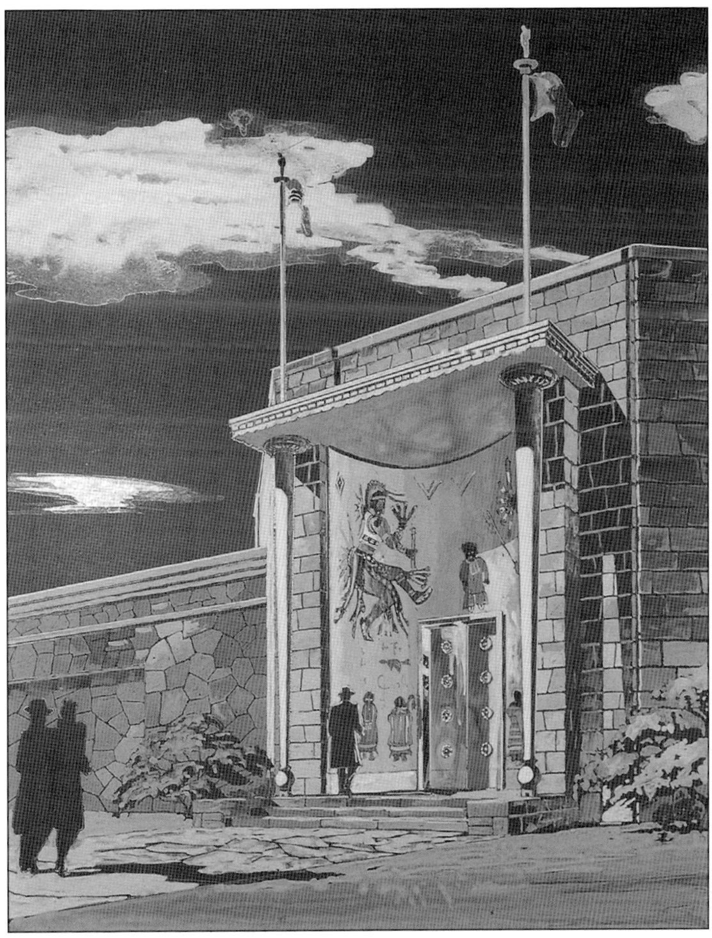

Constructed from hand-quarried stone, the museum at Woolaroc began humbly from this natural material. Today, the museum at Woolaroc houses one of the largest and most diverse collections of American Western and American Indian art in the country. Western enthusiasts make Woolaroc their destination to see Western art from Charles Russell, Frederic Remington, William R. Leigh, Frank Tenney Johnson, and Joe Beeler. A host of American Indian cultural artifacts tell the story of the American Indian in the West. A trip through the galleries of the Woolaroc Museum is a trip back in time and into the amazing collection of one man: Frank Phillips.

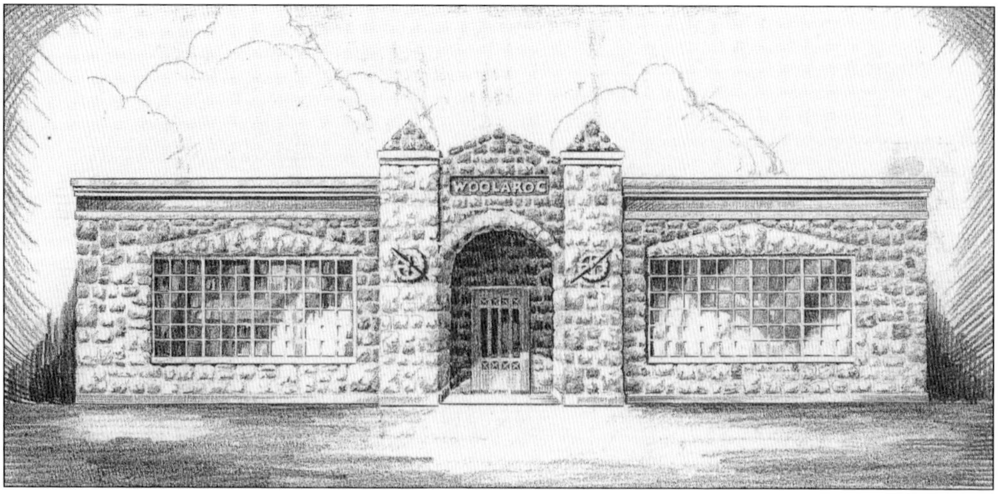

This early sketch shows the genesis of the Woolaroc Museum. Built in 1929 under the supervision of Art Gorman, the original structure that would later become the museum was initially a hangar to house the famed *Woolaroc* Travel Air 5000 monoplane that Art Goebel piloted to victory in the perilous Dole Race from California to Hawaii in 1927.

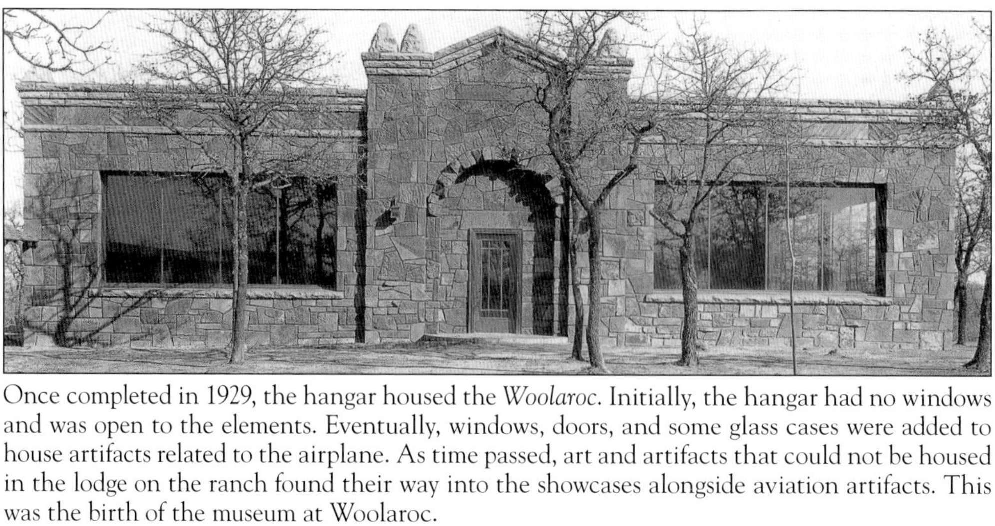

Once completed in 1929, the hangar housed the *Woolaroc*. Initially, the hangar had no windows and was open to the elements. Eventually, windows, doors, and some glass cases were added to house artifacts related to the airplane. As time passed, art and artifacts that could not be housed in the lodge on the ranch found their way into the showcases alongside aviation artifacts. This was the birth of the museum at Woolaroc.

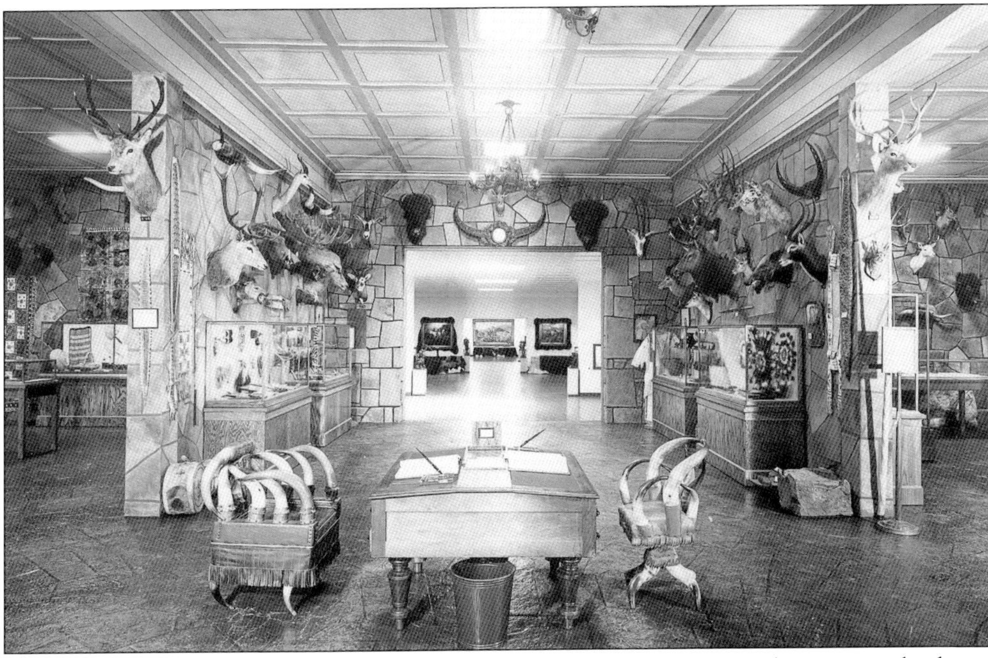

This view of the museum in 1940 shows one of the two original large rooms that were used to house artifacts and art. Toward the back of the photograph, one can see new gallery space. Despite the ravages of the Depression from 1932 to 1939, the museum building would be expanded to house the ever-growing collection of art and artifacts that Frank Phillips amassed.

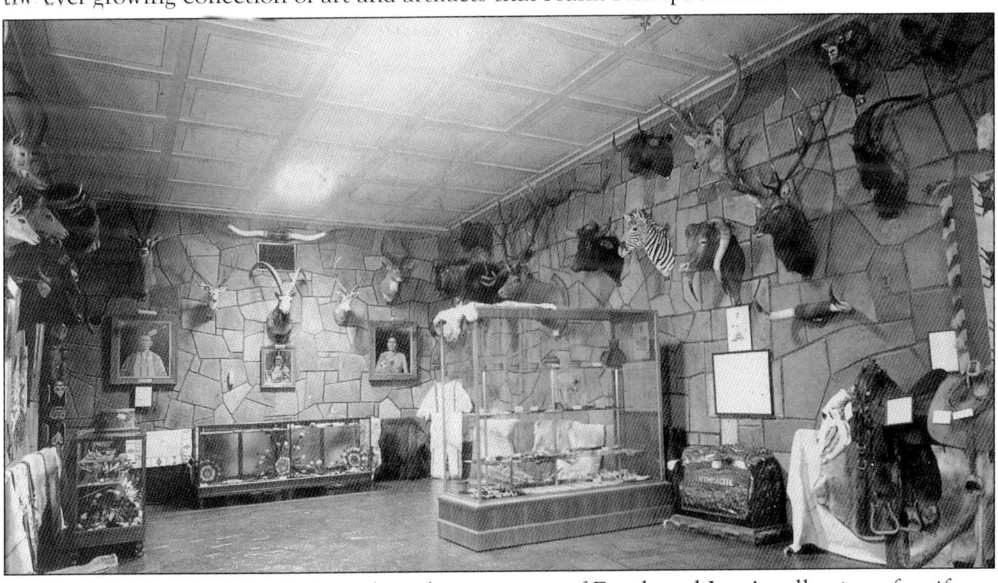

Early images of the museum show the eclectic nature of Frank and Jane's collection of artifacts. This photograph, taken around 1939, showcases the first room of the museum to be utilized. Animal heads, skins, furs, fossils, American Indian relics, and cultural material, art, and items related to the *Woolaroc* all found a home in the museum. According to Phillips himself, the museum originated as a place to safeguard the items given to him by family and friends and the objects he collected. His fondest hope was that his collection would inspire and educate those who came to visit.

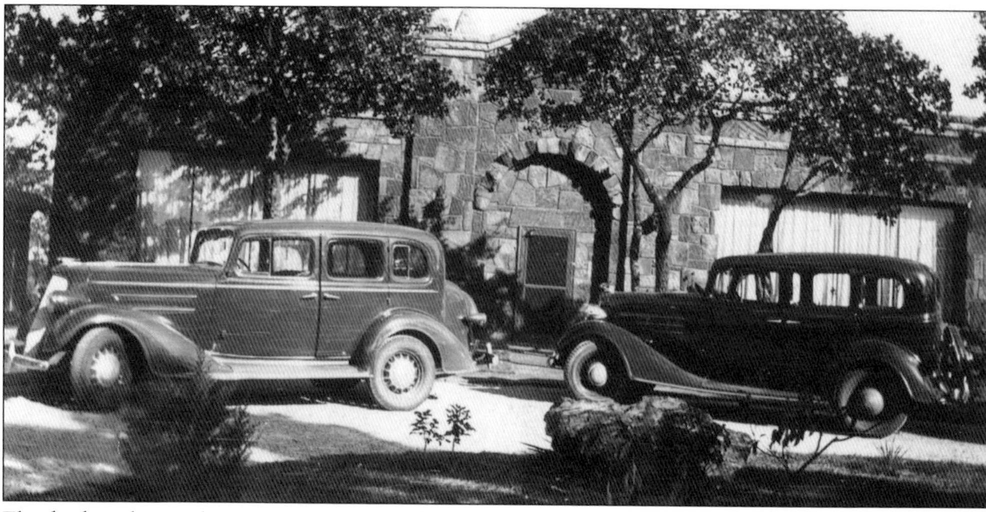

Flanked with two large plate-glass windows, the entrance is simple and unadorned. As their collection enlarged, Frank and Jane threw the doors open to the public. In 1940, limited tours for the public began. Phillips hoped that collecting and preserving art and artifacts that were indicative of the historical struggle between white and Indian peoples in the West would help remind people of the sacrifices of previous generations of Americans.

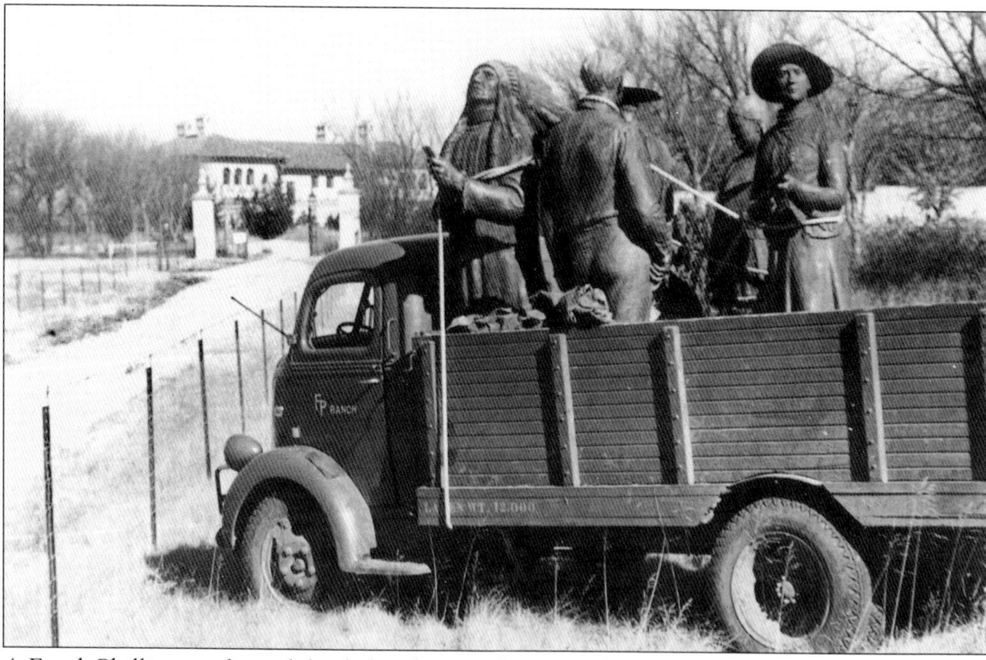

A Frank Phillips ranch truck loaded with several Jo Mora bronze statues makes its way from the Marland Estate in Ponca City to the Woolaroc Museum, where they found a new home. Born in Uruguay in 1876, Mora was a cartoonist, illustrator, and eventual cowboy. Mora lived among the Hopi in the American Southwest and would later become an art historian, sculptor, painter, photographer, and muralist. Given his myriad talents, he was truly a Western Renaissance man. *Belle Starr*, *Indian Maiden*, *The Cowboy*, and *The Indian Chief* by Mora are seen here along with Bryant Baker's *The Plainsman* on their way to their permanent homes in the museum on December 7, 1941.

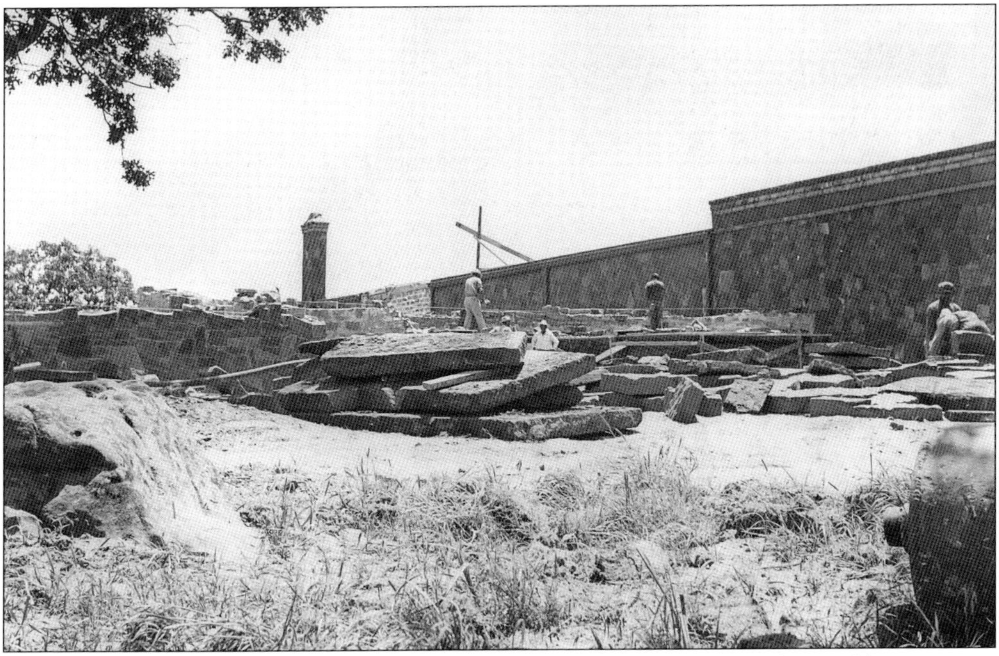

Additional rooms had to be added to the original hangar to accommodate the steadily increasing art collection. Stone was quarried on ranch grounds whenever possible to take advantage of nature's sturdy building material. Expansions to the museum were built in 1932, 1939, 1945–1946, 1979, and 1985 to house the growing art and artifact collection at Woolaroc.

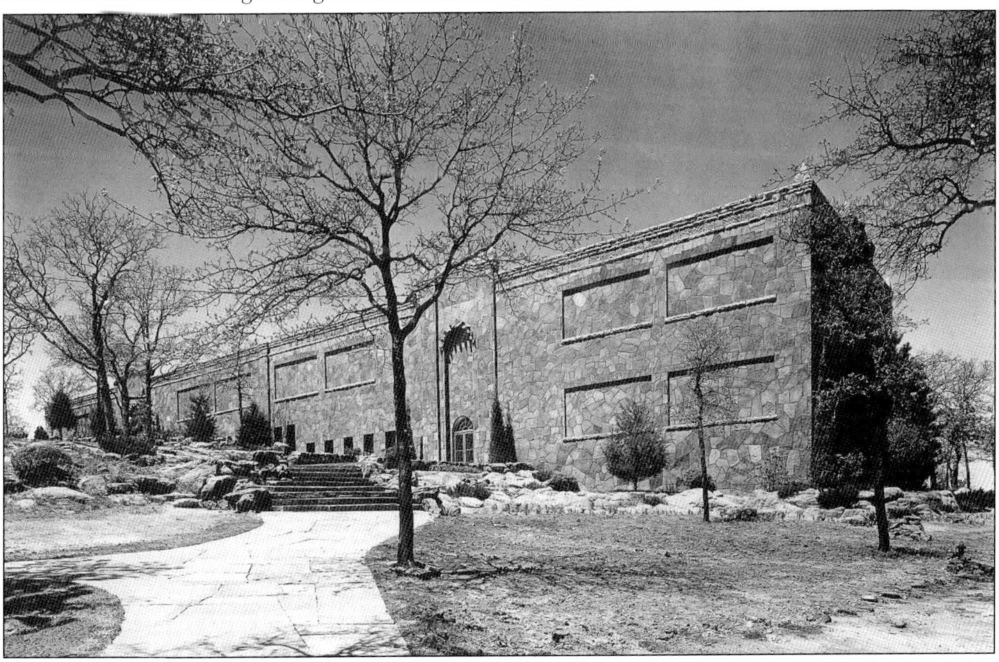

This view of the museum in the late 1930s shows the expansion that has taken place. In this form, the museum more resembles the structure that greets visitors today. A grand entrance would be added along with a magnificent dome room in 1945–1946, just in time for Frank and Jane to celebrate their 50th wedding anniversary.

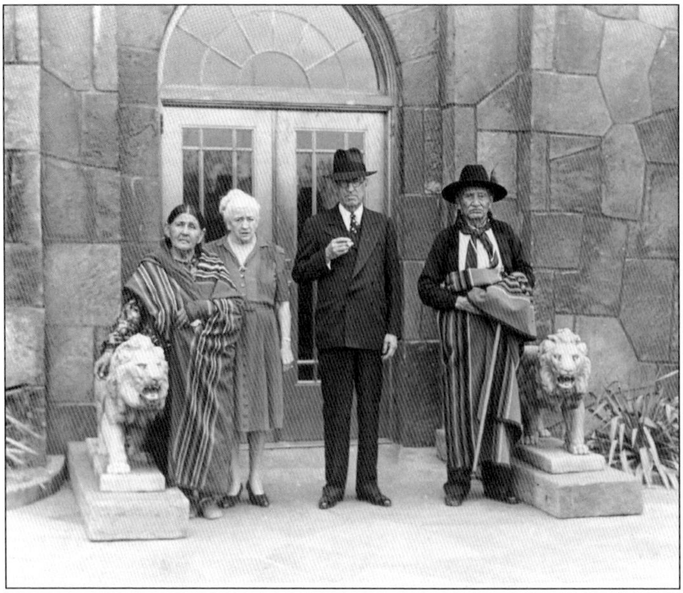

Frank and Jane Phillips (center) take a moment for a photograph with their longtime friends Julia and Fred Lookout. Fred was at one time a principal chief of the Osage. Lookout was responsible for Phillips's adoption into the Osage tribe. The two couples spent many happy hours at Woolaroc and remained lifelong friends. Here, they pose in front of the museum entrance. Many Osage artifacts that tell the story of the tribe and their role in Oklahoma history are contained in the collection at Woolaroc.

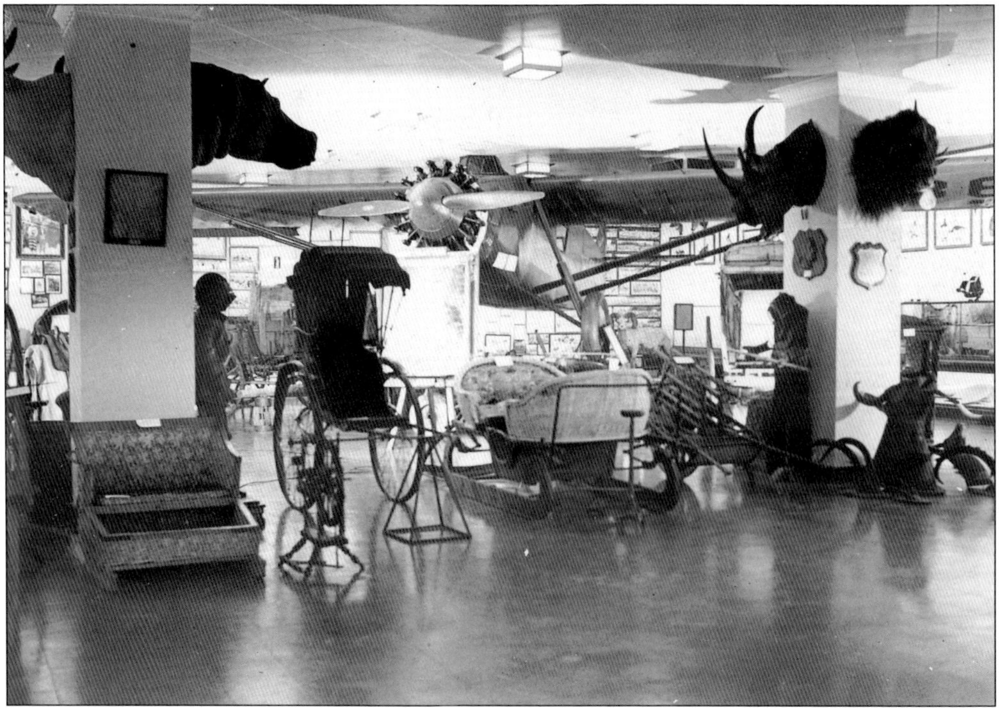

This view of the museum shows the juxtaposition of the *Woolaroc* among the animal horns, hides, skins, and works of art. With rhino and hippo heads on the columns in front of the *Woolaroc*, the museum looks more like a safari expedition than a home for fine art.

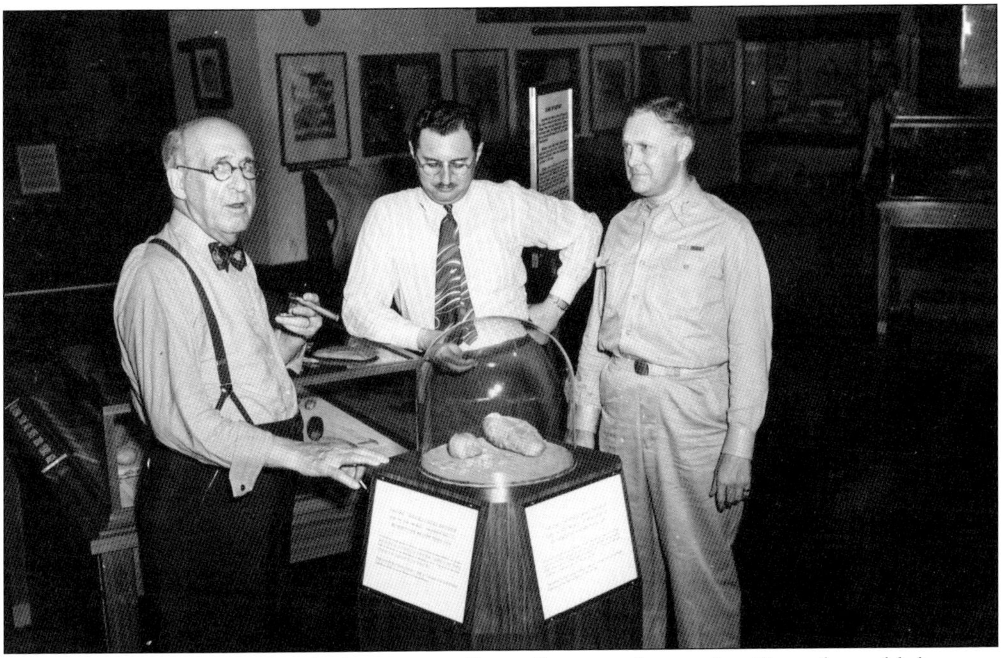

Frank Phillips was pleased with the variety of his collection of art and artifacts that told the story of American history from the dawn of time to the present day. Here, Frank shows off what was then the only privately owned dinosaur egg in the United States.

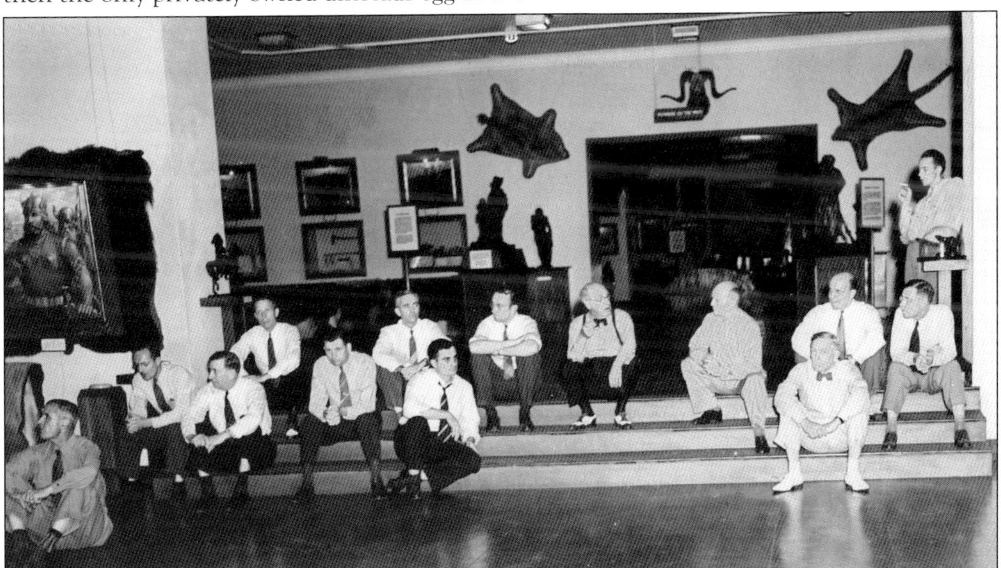

Early in the history of Woolaroc, young Phillips executives and their families would be invited to visit the lodge. Frank Phillips (seated in the center wearing a bow tie) relaxes with a group of Phillips employees as they tour the museum. Frank and Jane both took great pleasure in giving tours of the museum for visitors. Jane herself kept acquisition ledger books by hand, chronicling the collections. Both Frank and Jane were active in the museum and its administration in the early years.

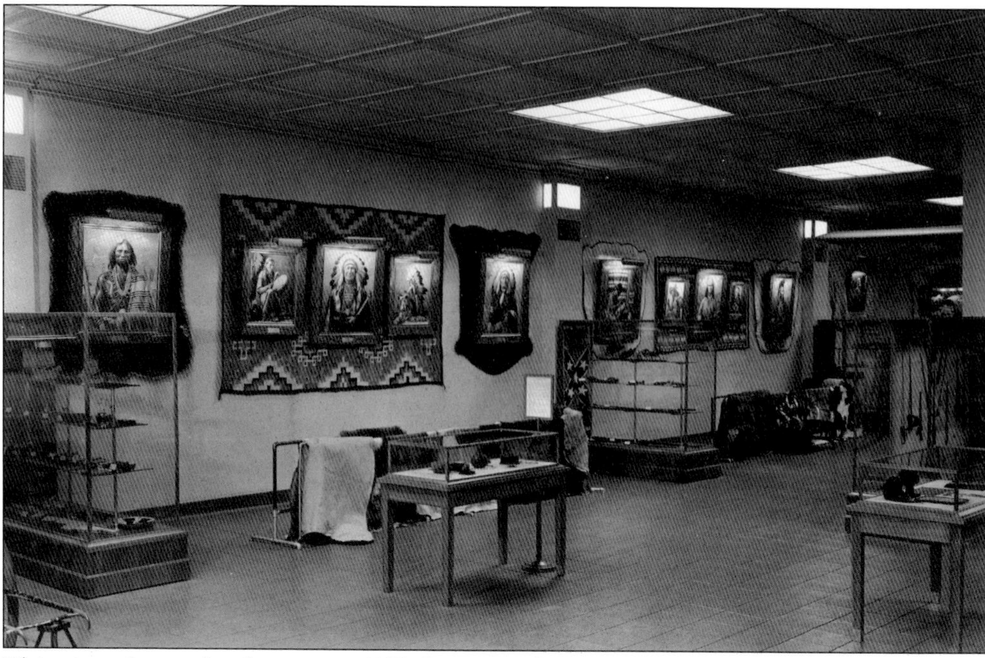

This view of upper-level rooms in 1935 showcases the variety of items collected by the Phillips family. The paintings of famous American Indian chiefs and leaders by Robert Lindeux were framed using Art Gorman's bark process that was used to cover the Steinway in the lodge. Navajo and other American Indian woven blankets adorn the walls as well.

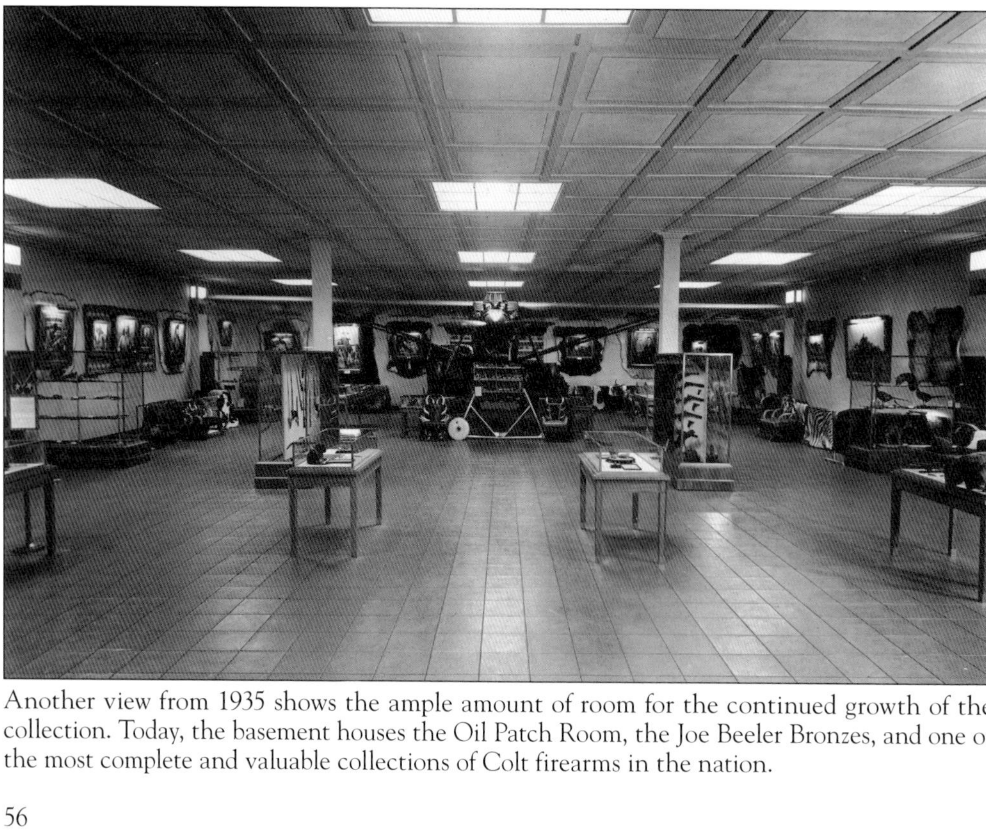

Another view from 1935 shows the ample amount of room for the continued growth of the collection. Today, the basement houses the Oil Patch Room, the Joe Beeler Bronzes, and one of the most complete and valuable collections of Colt firearms in the nation.

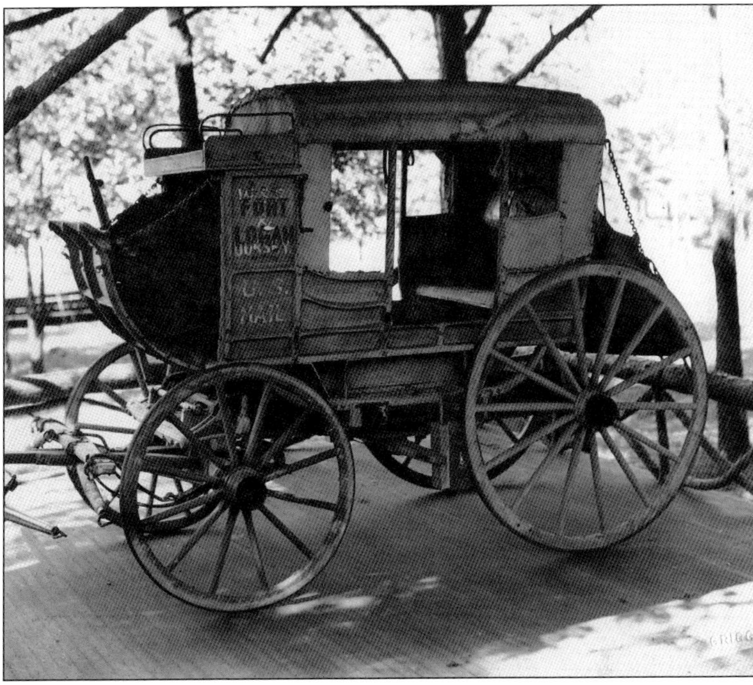

A showpiece of the Woolaroc Museum is the Fort Logan-to-Dorsey Stage. This stage traversed the dusty, dangerous trails of the American West and covered over 600,000 miles in its career from 1869 to the late 1890s. The stagecoach was brought in for the 1928 Cow Thieves and Outlaws gathering. The stage found its final home at Woolaroc as a gift to Frank Phillips.

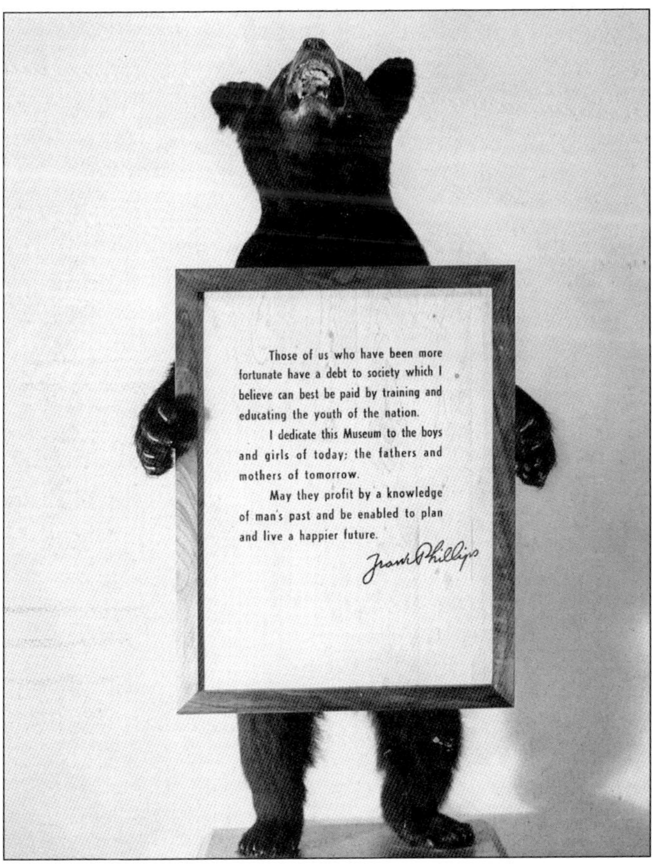

This bear greeted museum visitors for generations. The sign was a message from Frank Phillips to visitors. It stated the following: "Those of us who have been more fortunate have a debt to society which I believe can best be paid by training and educating the youth of the nation. I dedicate this Museum to the boys and girls of today; the mothers and fathers of tomorrow. May they profit by a knowledge of man's past and be enabled to plan and live a happier future."

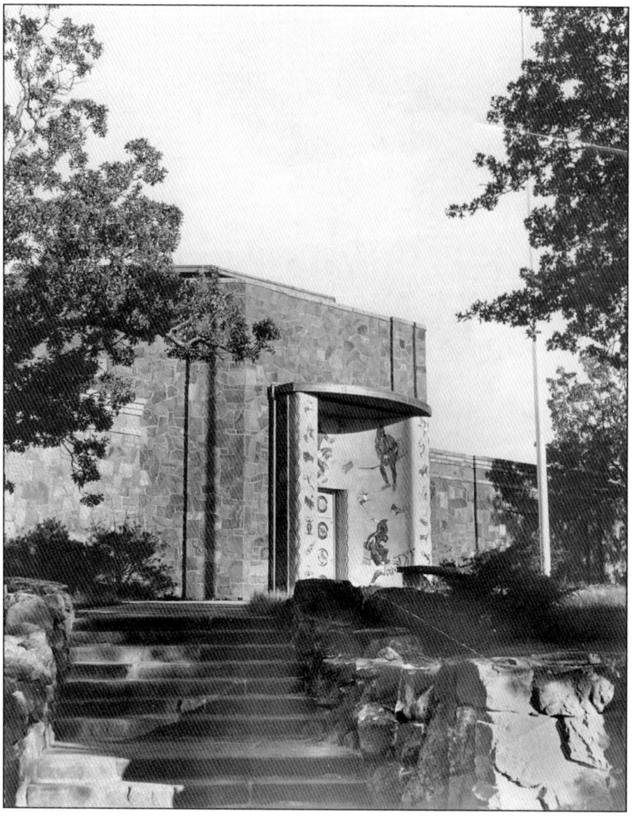

In 1945–1946, a grand new entrance to the museum was constructed along with the dome room and new museum offices. Complete with an eye-popping and intricate mosaic, the new entrance attracted visitors' attention. The mosaic, by artist Winold Reiss, features five American Indian figures from various regions of North America.

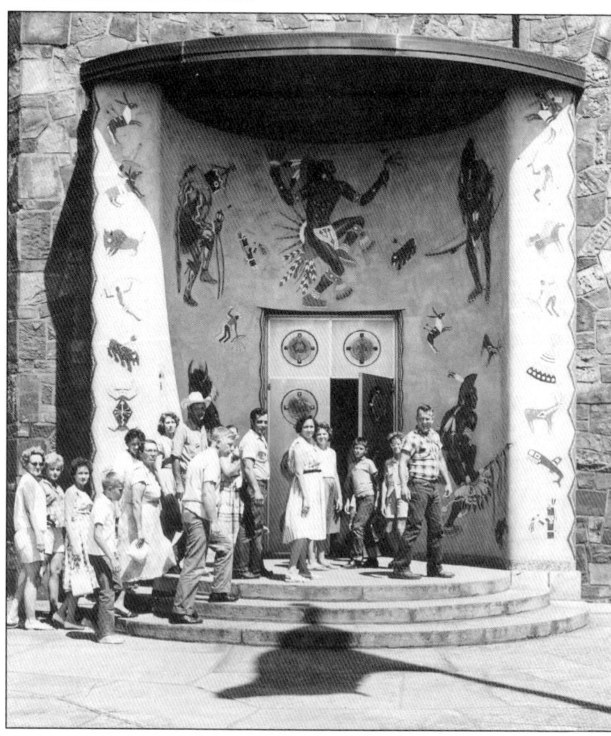

A group of visitors to Woolaroc in 1947 pose for a photograph on the steps of the newly completed museum entrance outside the grand dome room that housed large bronze statues over the years including a plainsman, an American Indian, and Frank Phillips. The massive doors are decorated with eight onyx plaques engraved with designs found on artifacts from Spiro Mound, located near the present-day town of Spiro, Oklahoma.

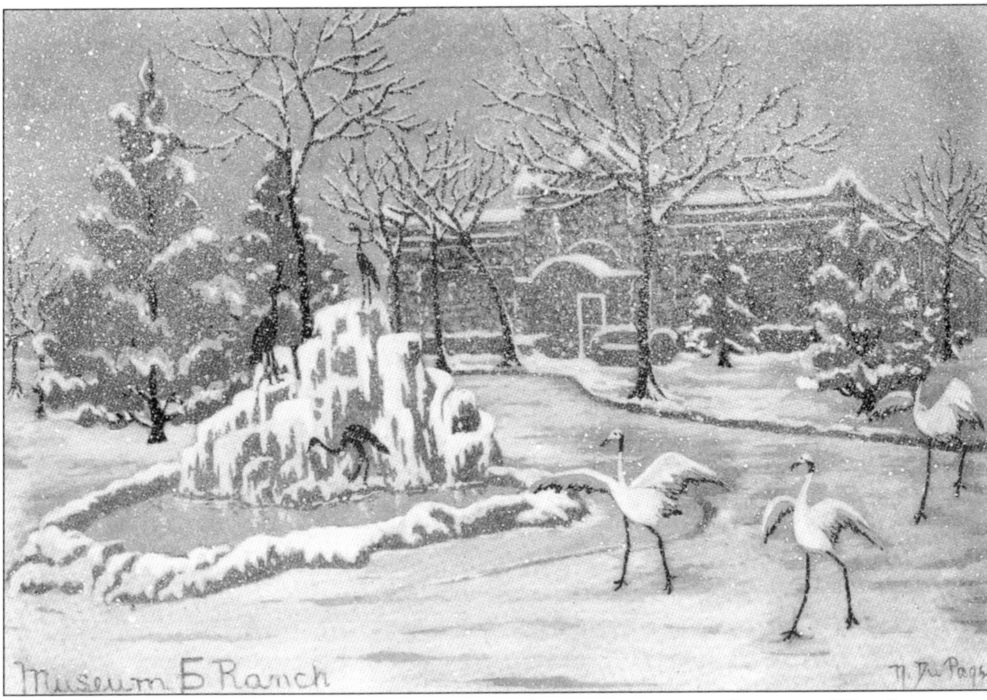

This postcard shows the museum in wintertime with pine trees covered in snow. The flamingoes on the grounds add a touch of frivolity.

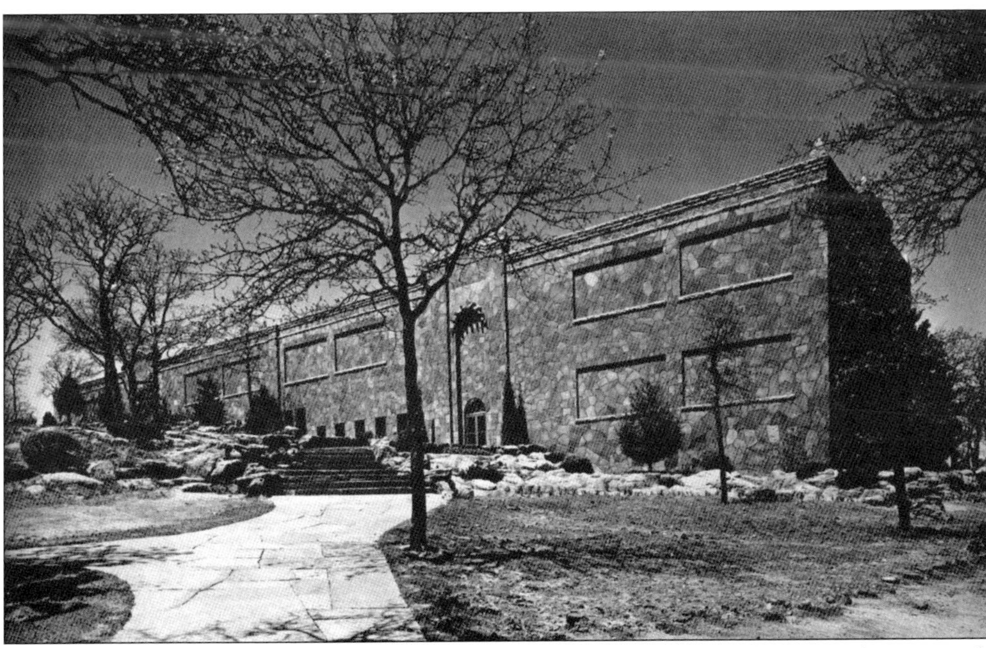

Over the years, several guidebooks to Woolaroc have been produced. This image from an early guidebook shows the museum building before the dome room and new entrance were added.

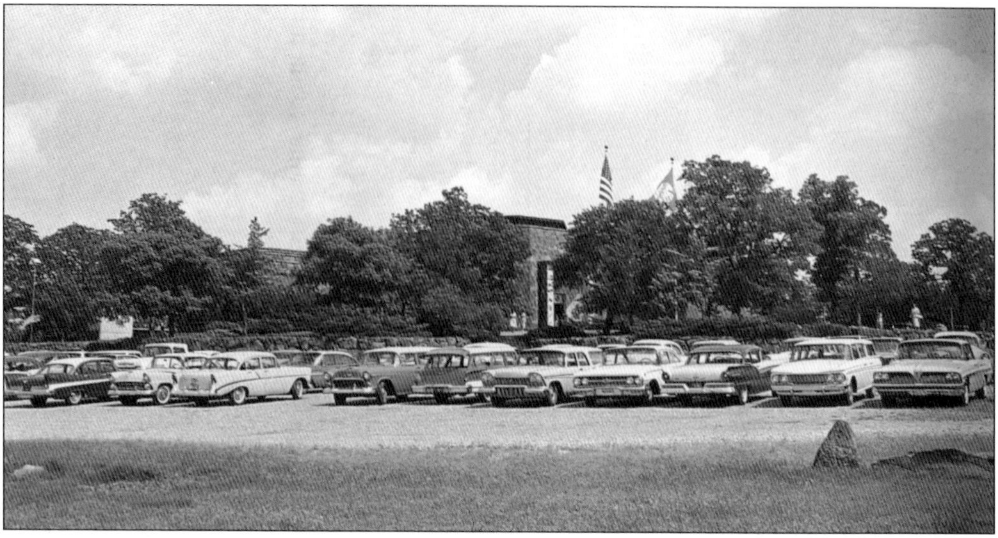

As Americans became more mobile, the automobile allowed families to travel like never before. In the 1950s and 1960s, families took to the open roads, and national parks, museums, and wildlife preserves were popular tourist destinations. For generations, Oklahomans and families from around the nation made Woolaroc a prime vacation stop. This photograph from one of the various Woolaroc guidebooks shows a full parking lot in the 1960s.

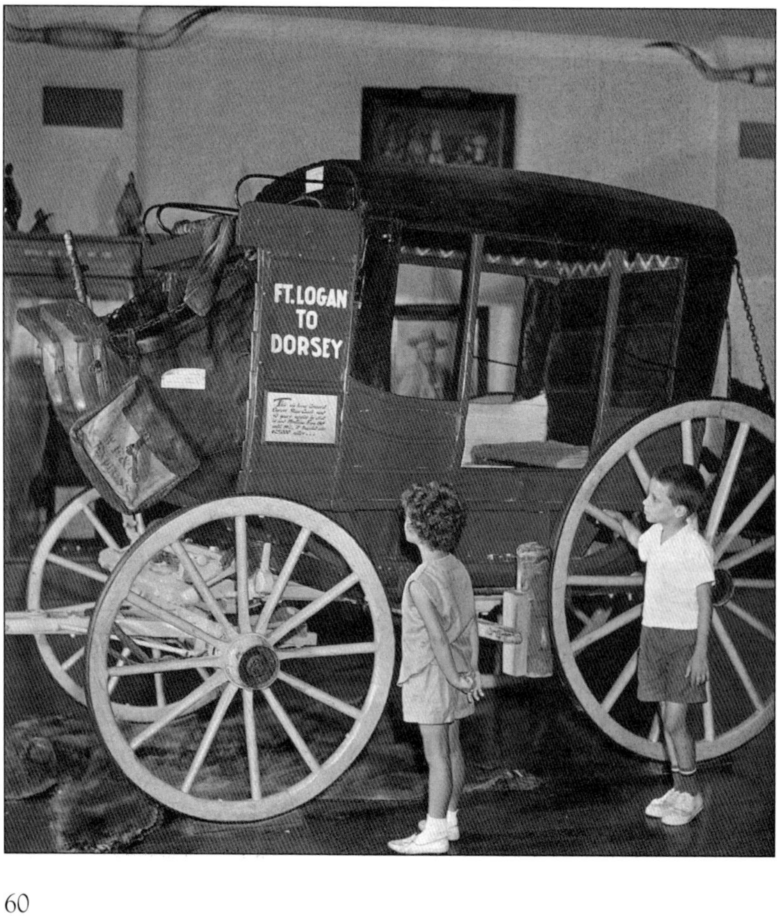

Youngsters were one of Frank Phillips's main reasons for preserving his collection and sharing it with the public. Here, a young boy and girl get up close and personal with the Fort Logan-to-Dorsey stagecoach and ponder the history of the American West. Taken from another Woolaroc guidebook, the photograph shows the realization of Frank's dream to share his good fortune with the youth of America.

Belle Starr, with weapon loaded, stands guard in the museum flanked by the head of big-game animals to her left. The large painting underneath the trophy heads depicts a young Pocahontas (possibly modeled after Osage prima ballerina Maria Tallchief) saving the life of John Smith at Jamestown by noted artist William R. Leigh.

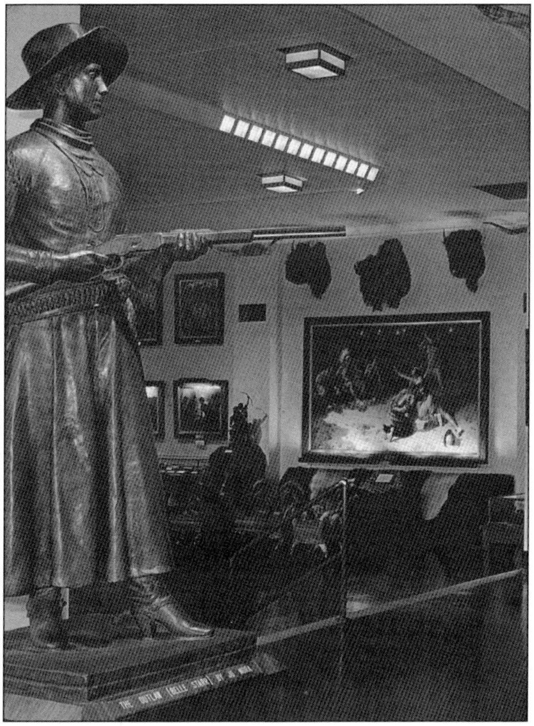

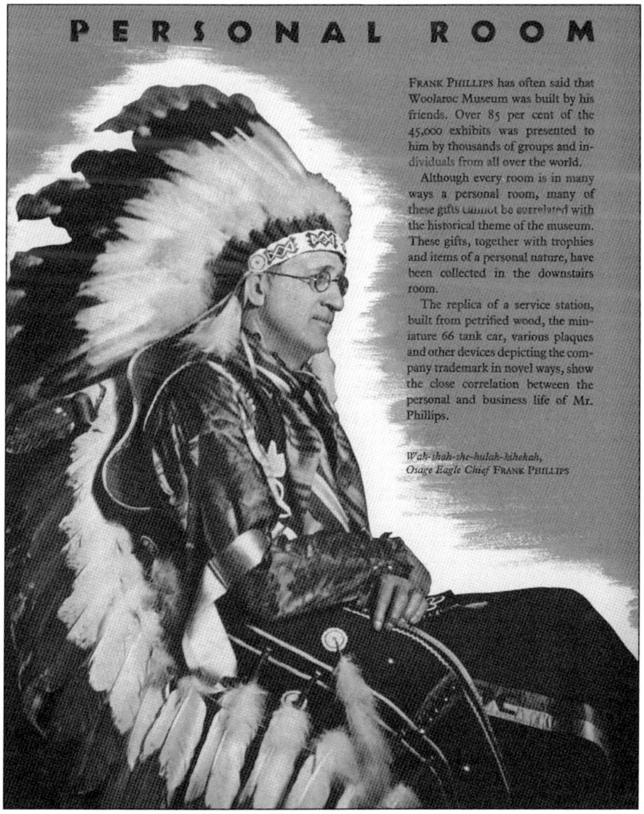

PERSONAL ROOM

FRANK PHILLIPS has often said that Woolaroc Museum was built by his friends. Over 85 per cent of the 45,000 exhibits was presented to him by thousands of groups and individuals from all over the world.

Although every room is in many ways a personal room, many of these gifts cannot be correlated with the historical theme of the museum. These gifts, together with trophies and items of a personal nature, have been collected in the downstairs room.

The replica of a service station, built from petrified wood, the miniature 66 tank car, various plaques and other devices depicting the company trademark in novel ways, show the close correlation between the personal and business life of Mr. Phillips.

Wah-shah-she-hulah-hihekah, Osage Eagle Chief FRANK PHILLIPS

The Personal Room at the Woolaroc Museum displayed personal items that belonged to Frank and Jane Phillips. Among the artifacts displayed were Frank's Osage regalia, headdress, cowboy boots, hat, chaps, and spurs. The Personal Room also contained photographs of the family and their visitors to the lodge and ranch. Visitors had the opportunity to form a bond with the man whose vision made the museum possible.

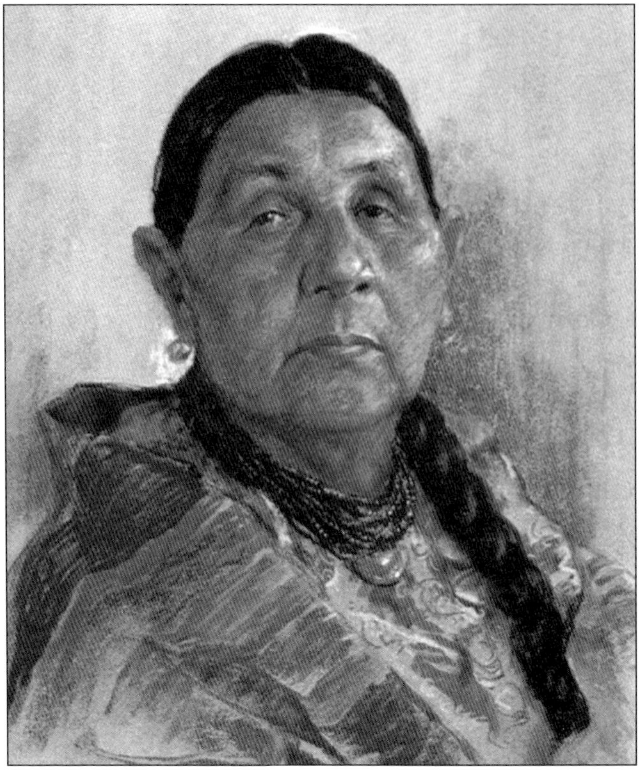

Julia Lookout was a frequent visitor at Woolaroc. A close friend of Frank and Jane Phillips, Julia appears in numerous photographs of events held at the lodge. If Frank and Jane threw a party on the ranch, the Lookouts were most assuredly on the guest list. This drawing of Julia in her later years by artist N. De Grandmaison hangs in the museum.

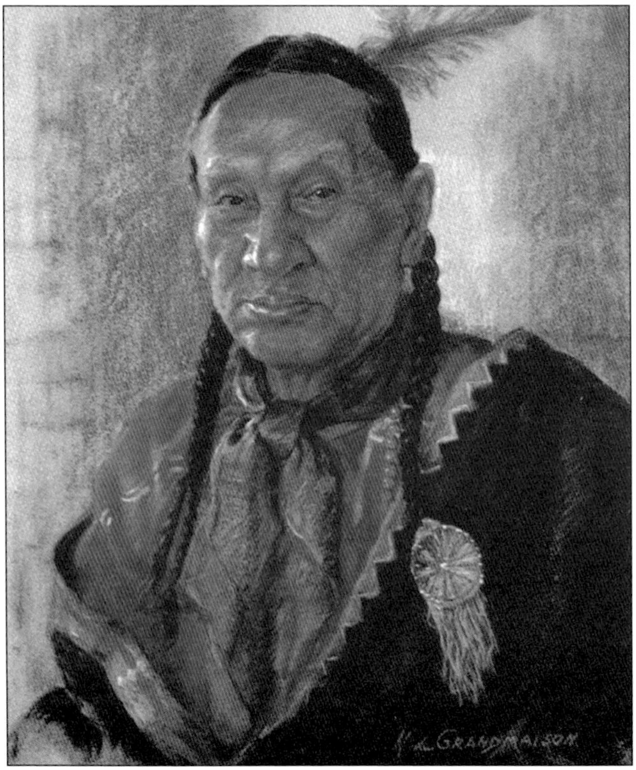

Fred Lookout served as an Osage chief and was a close friend of Frank and Jane Phillips. Fred was the motivating force behind Frank's adoption into the Osage Nation and gave a moving speech at the adoption ceremony. His portrait hangs next to his wife's in the museum.

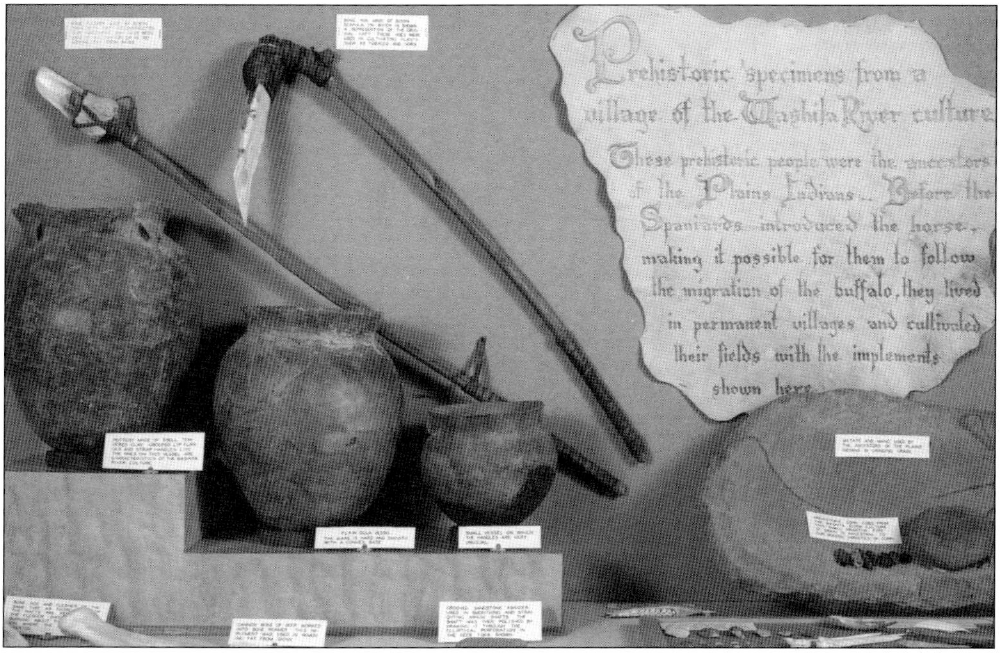

The museum at Woolaroc boasts a collection of ethnographical and archaeological artifacts that cover a wide swath of history in North America. This display in the museum showcases artifacts from the Washita River Indian cultural group that called central and western Oklahoma its home over 1,000 years ago.

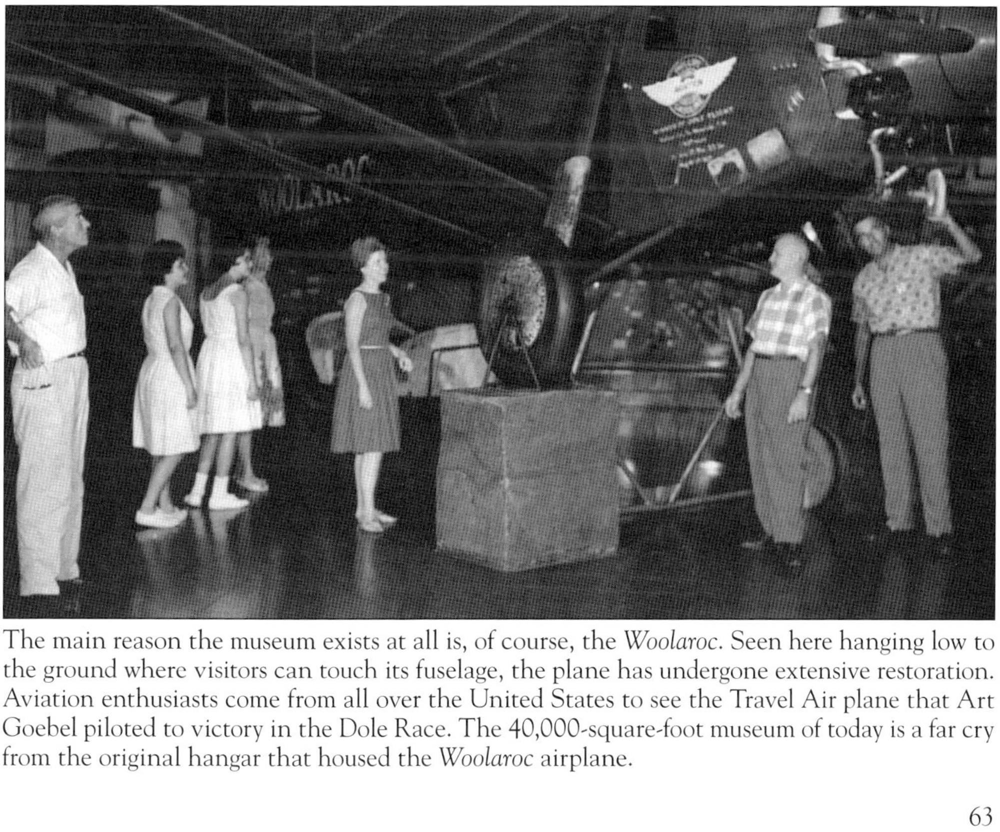

The main reason the museum exists at all is, of course, the *Woolaroc*. Seen here hanging low to the ground where visitors can touch its fuselage, the plane has undergone extensive restoration. Aviation enthusiasts come from all over the United States to see the Travel Air plane that Art Goebel piloted to victory in the Dole Race. The 40,000-square-foot museum of today is a far cry from the original hangar that housed the *Woolaroc* airplane.

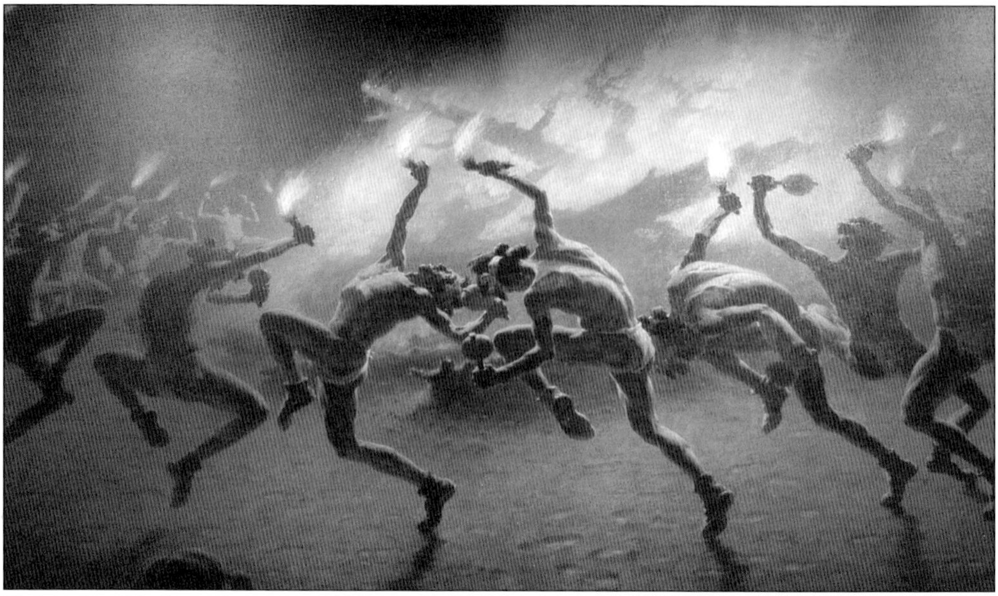

Today, the Woolaroc Museum is home to a diverse collection of art that showcases the American West and American Indian culture. Charles M. Russell, Frederic Remington, William R. Leigh, and Frank Tenney Johnson are just a few of the illustrious names whose works hang upon the gallery walls. Known as the "Sagebrush Rembrandt," Leigh's works are noted for their sheer size. *Navajo Fire Dancer* by Leigh is one of many paintings that depict American Indian culture. (Author's collection.)

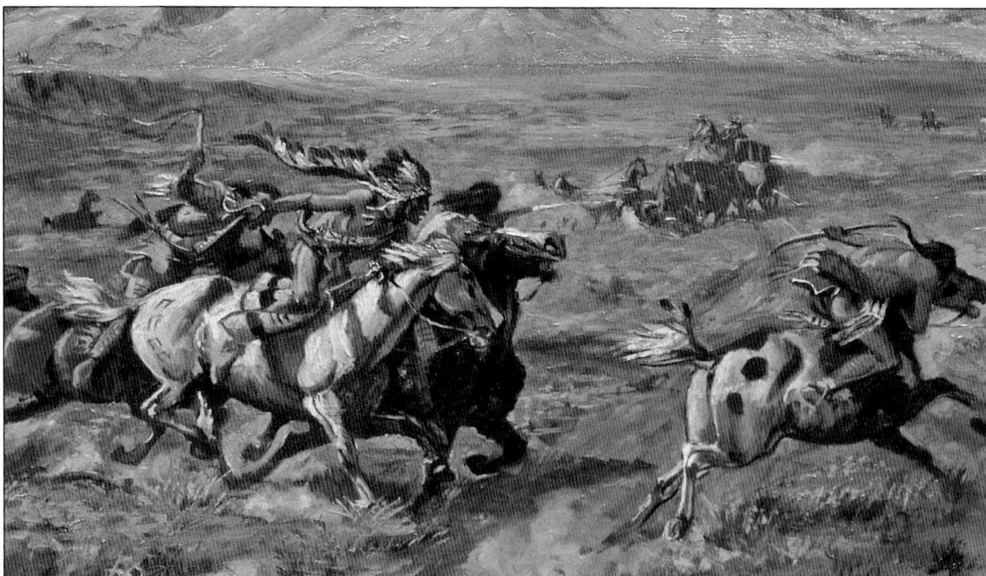

Cowboy, painter, writer, historian, and American Indian advocate Charles Marion Russell was one of American's foremost and renown Western artists. Frank Phillips admired Russell's art and several of his works grace the walls of the museum. In this work, a group of American Indians raids a stagecoach. Russell greatly admired the Northern Plains tribes, and they oftentimes were depicted in his works. In *The Stagecoach Attack*, a group of plains warriors wreak havoc on a stagecoach traversing open ground. (Author's collection.)

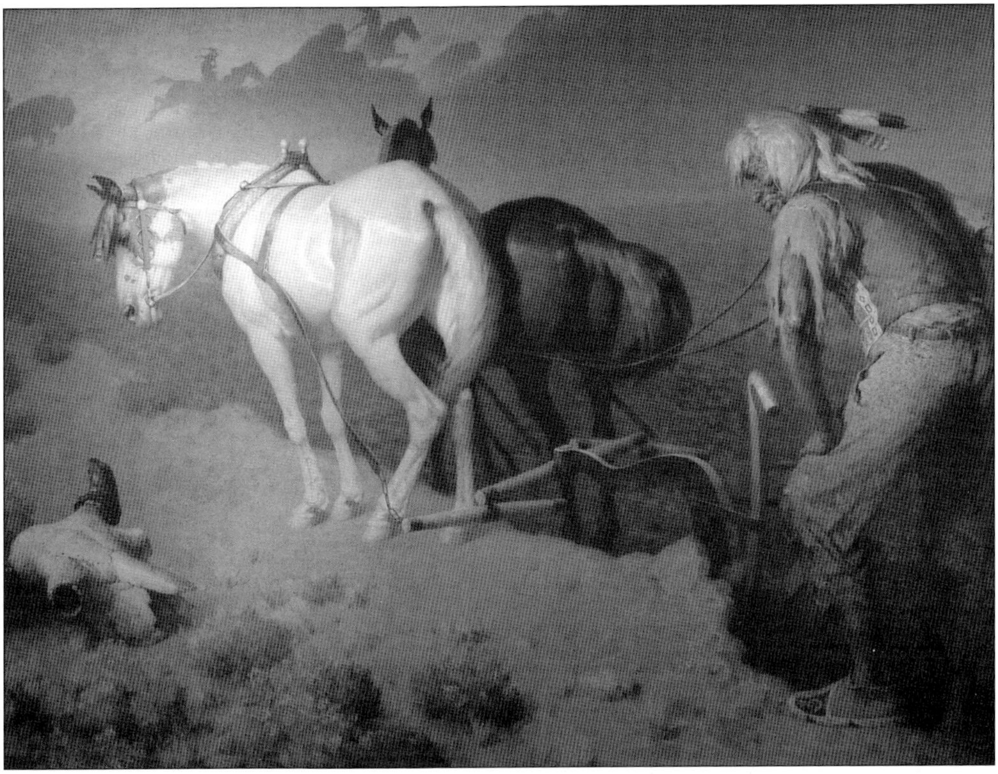

Another massive canvas from William R. Leigh depicts the downfall and state of American Indian life as the Old West passed from existence into mere memory. In *Visions of Yesterday*, an elderly American Indian man hitches what may have been his war pony to a plow while visions of his youth and a better life for his people are mere visions in the clouds. (Author's collection.)

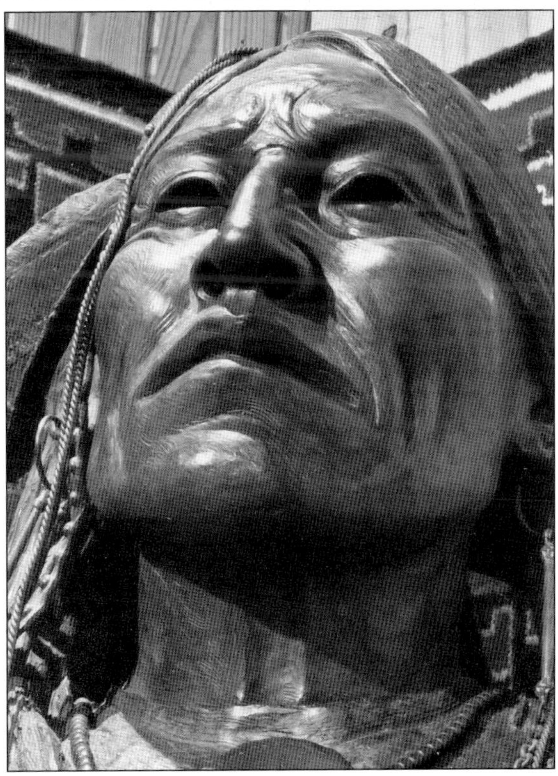

Some artists are blessed to work in more than one medium. Joe Beeler is one such artist, and his work can be found in almost every gallery in the museum as well as the grounds outside. This intricate and emotional bronze is the artist's depiction of the American Indian leader Crazy Horse. (Author's collection.)

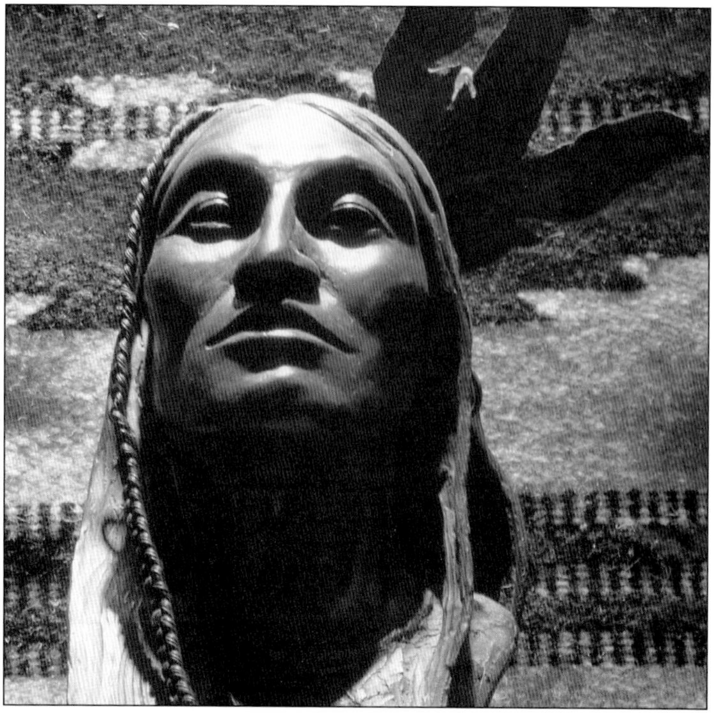

Another example of Joe Beeler's work is juxtaposed next to a woven blanket. The museum is home to a diverse collection of American Indian blankets, baskets, pottery, and other handmade items. The museum's collection also includes sculptures from Jo Mora and Frederic Remington. (Author's collection.)

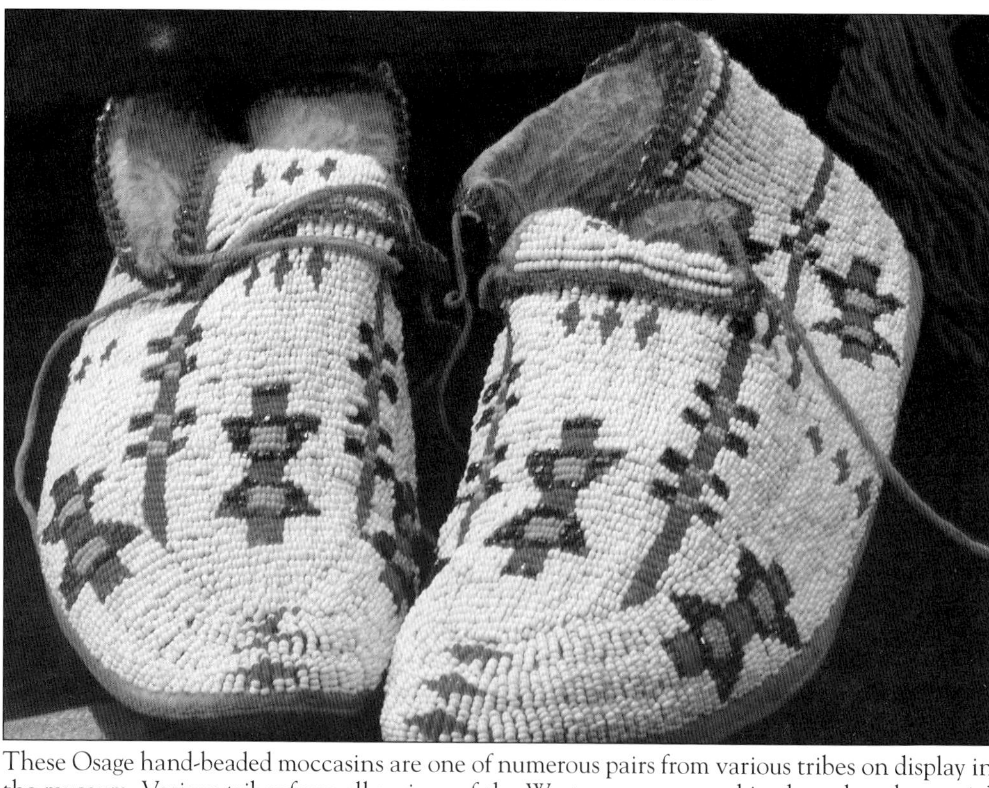

These Osage hand-beaded moccasins are one of numerous pairs from various tribes on display in the museum. Various tribes from all regions of the West are represented in the cultural material collections at the museum. (Author's collection.)

Preserved for future generations, the Fort Logan-to-Dorsey stagecoach is featured prominently in the museum. Unlike many stagecoaches that became scrap, this lucky artifact from the past inspires and teaches museum visitors about the dangers of life in the American West. (Author's collection.)

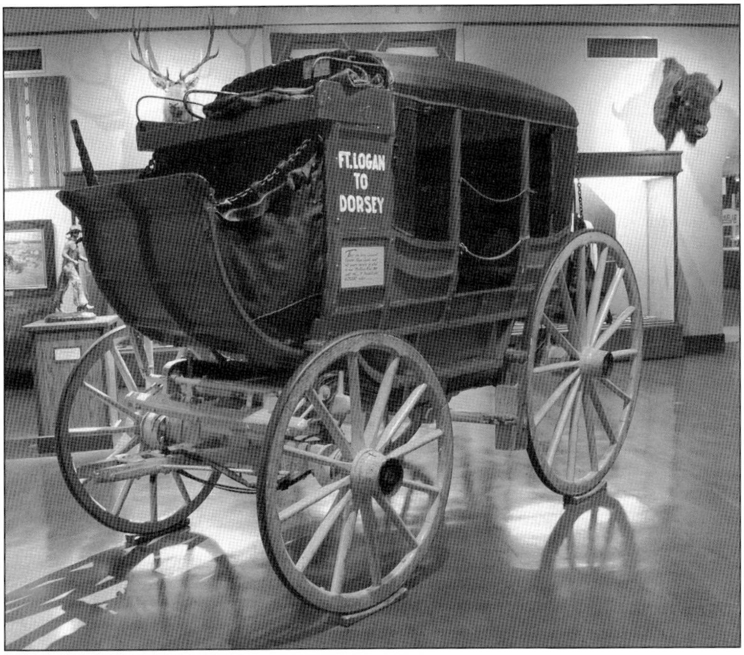

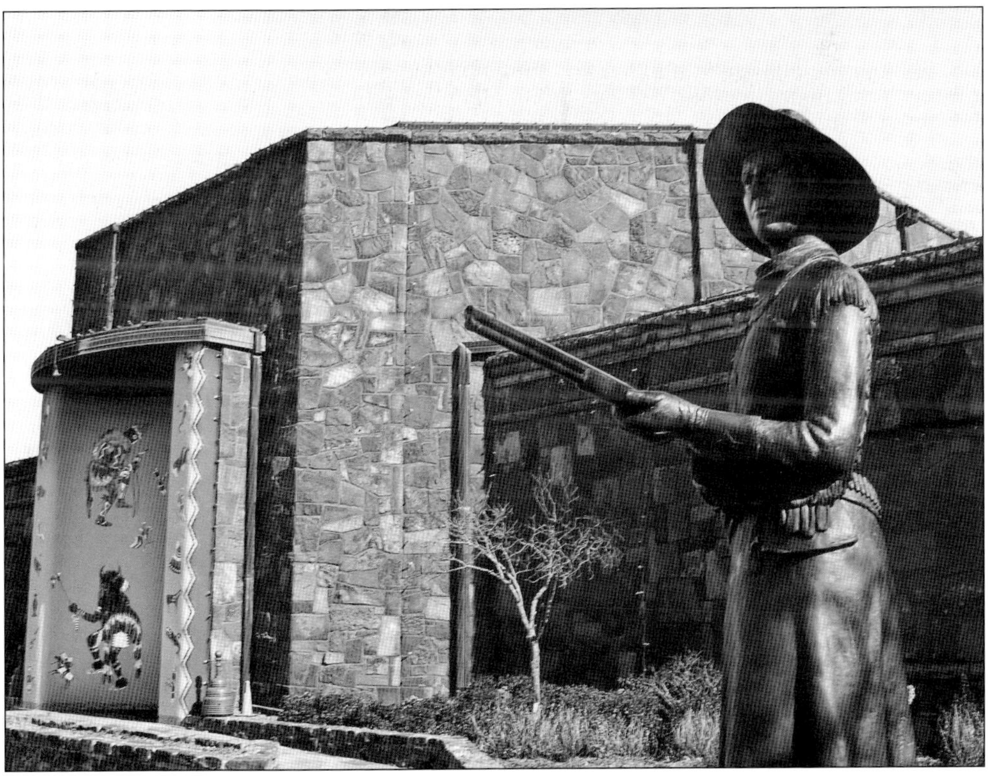

Standing guard outside the museum this statue of Belle Starr, the outlaw bandit queen, greets visitors as they enter the facility. Comprised of native stone from the ranch, the museum today is home to not only Frank Phillips's original art collection but also many other gifts of American Western art from Phillips family members. (Author's collection.)

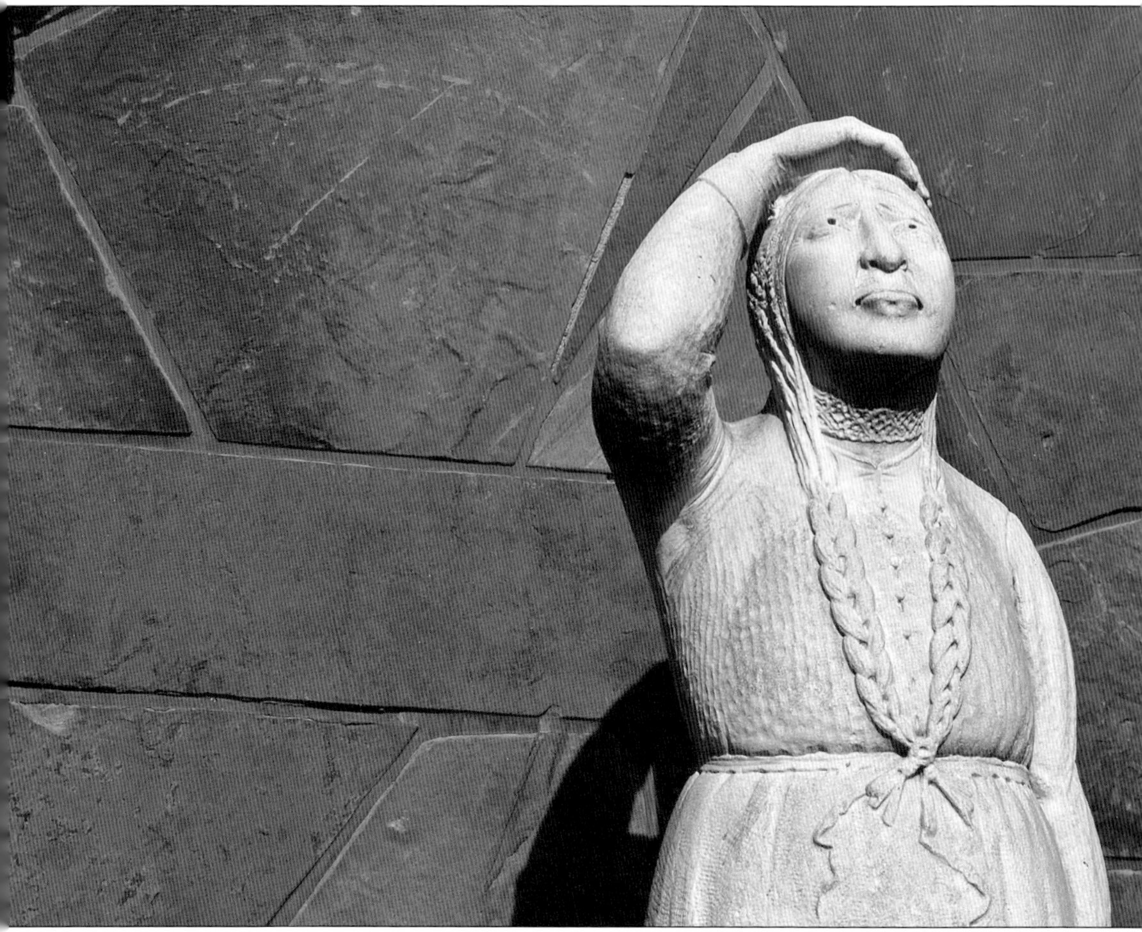

This statue of Ekalaka, a relative of Sitting Bull, stands watch outside the museum. The grounds of the museum feature fine sculptures. Frank Phillips wanted his museum to help educate America's youth about the history of the American West that he so loved and admired. Today, the Woolaroc museum continues the mission that Phillips set forth. Various educational programs bring the museum collections to life for a new generation of youngsters. (Author's collection.)

Four

The Rolling Osage Hills

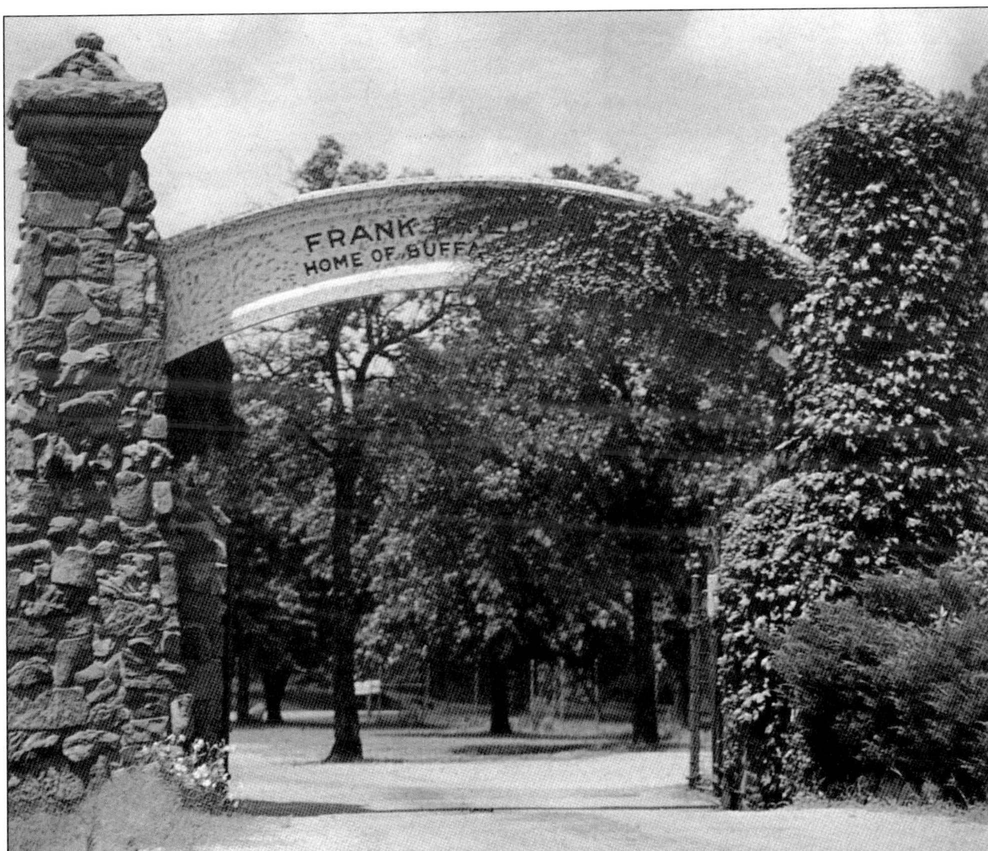

After Frank Phillips purchased his 3,700-acre ranch in Osage County, Oklahoma, he set forth not only building himself a retreat but also began to assemble a diverse collection of animals that would come to call the ranch their home. The original gate at Woolaroc was comprised of native stone and was manned by Grif Graham and his wife, Orpha. A new entrance has long since replaced the original gate and gatehouse. Taken from the pages of the museum's earliest guidebook, the gate is shown as it looked early in Woolaroc's history.

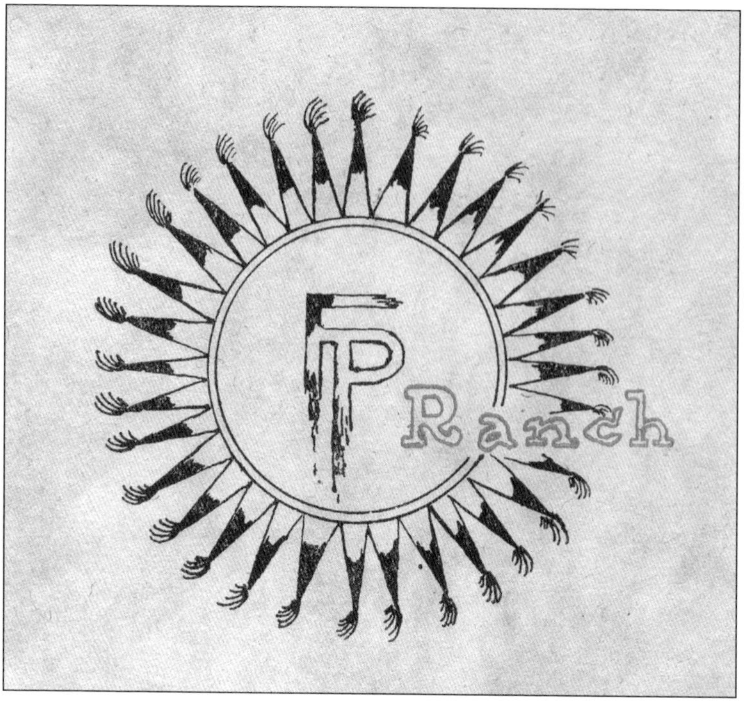

Every cattleman and rancher adopted a brand and logo to represent their establishment. The FP brand was placed on all cattle on the Phillips ranch. The logo features a circle of tepees surrounding his brand.

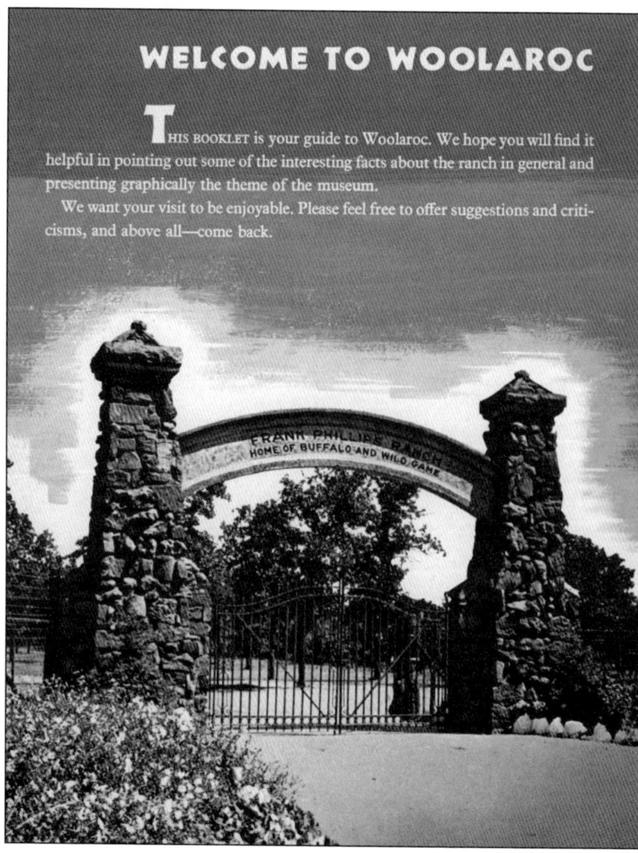

WELCOME TO WOOLAROC

This booklet is your guide to Woolaroc. We hope you will find it helpful in pointing out some of the interesting facts about the ranch in general and presenting graphically the theme of the museum.

We want your visit to be enjoyable. Please feel free to offer suggestions and criticisms, and above all—come back.

During Woolaroc's early years, the ranch was not open to the public, with the exception of the famed Cow Thieves and Outlaws events that were by invitation only. The original gate at Woolaroc was closed, and admission was by invitation only. One of the jobs of Grif Graham and his wife, Orpha, was to ensure that individuals did not pass through the gates without invitation or approval.

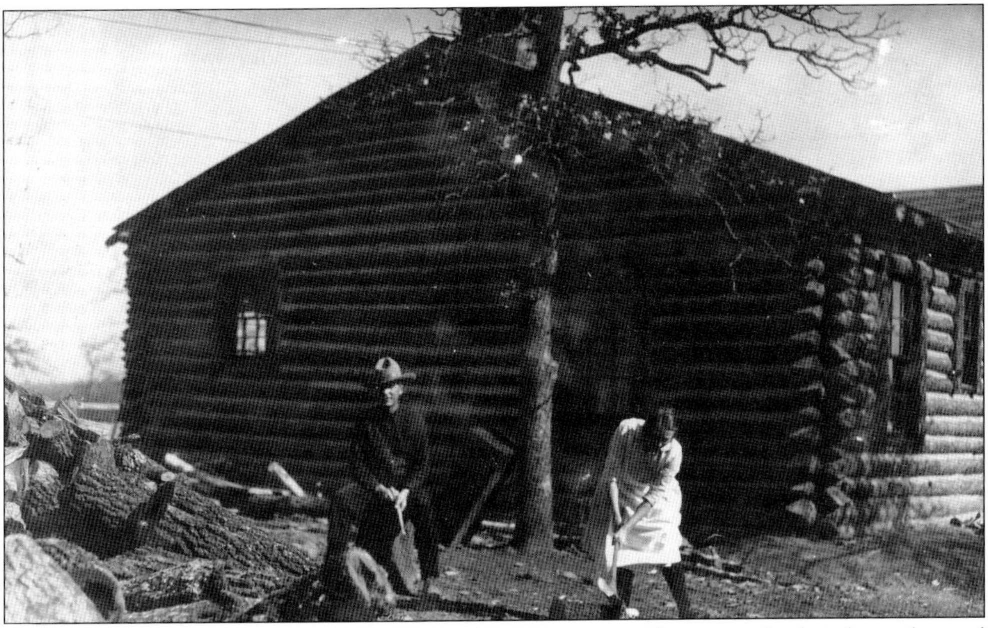

In this early photograph, Grif and Orpha Graham are seen working outside their home located within the boundaries of the ranch. Grif was a former Washington County, Oklahoma, sheriff and served as the ranch manager for Frank Phillips at Woolaroc. He and Orpha were an important part of the social life at Woolaroc as well.

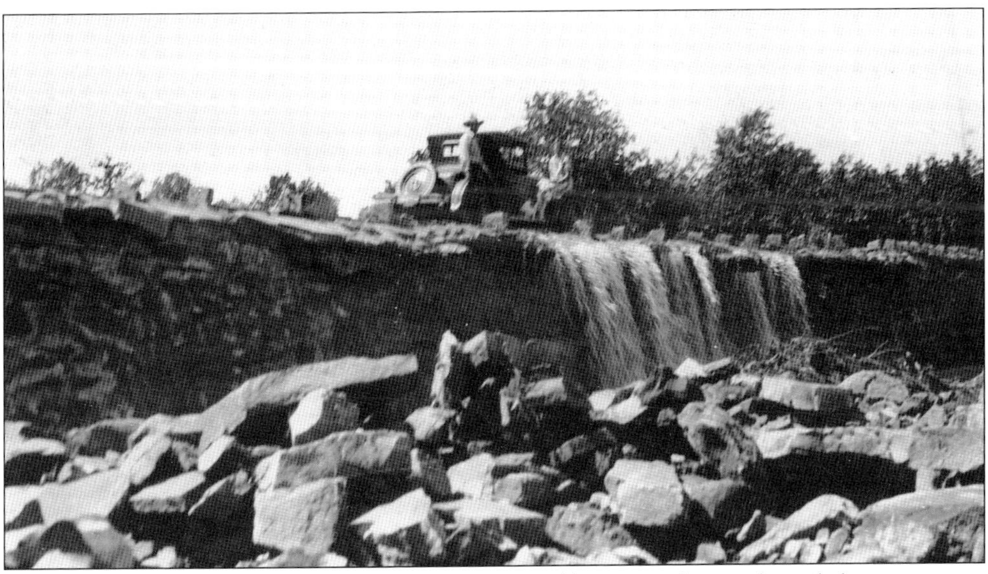

To ensure that the Phillips family and their guests could traverse the ranch easily by motorcar, a series of roads were engineered and built. With the unpredictable Oklahoma weather, especially in spring storm and fall rainy seasons, a series of dams and spillways were constructed to keep roads from flooding and stranding people at the ranch.

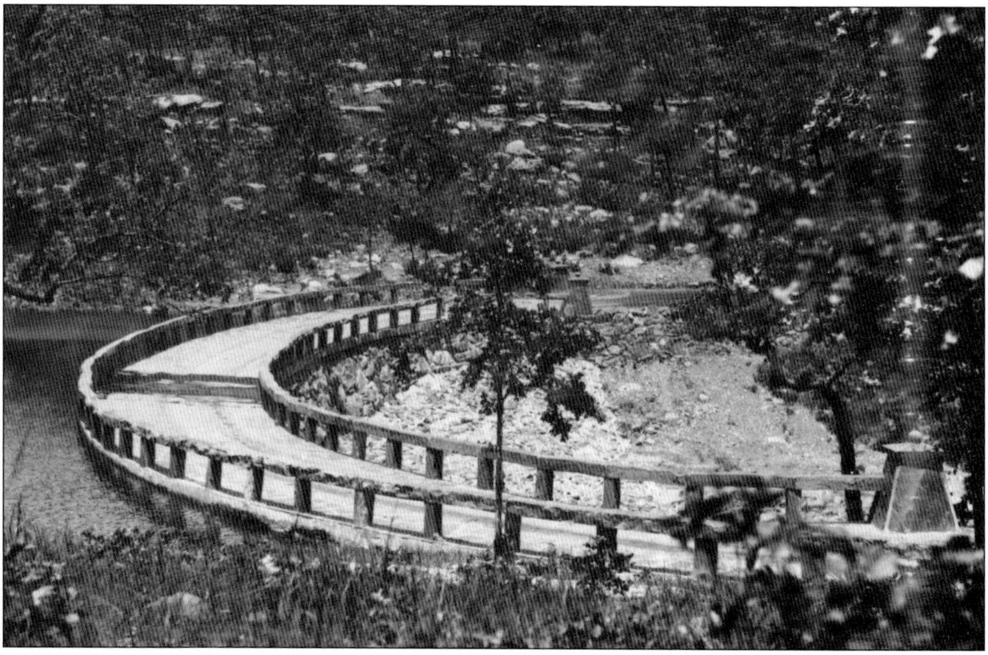

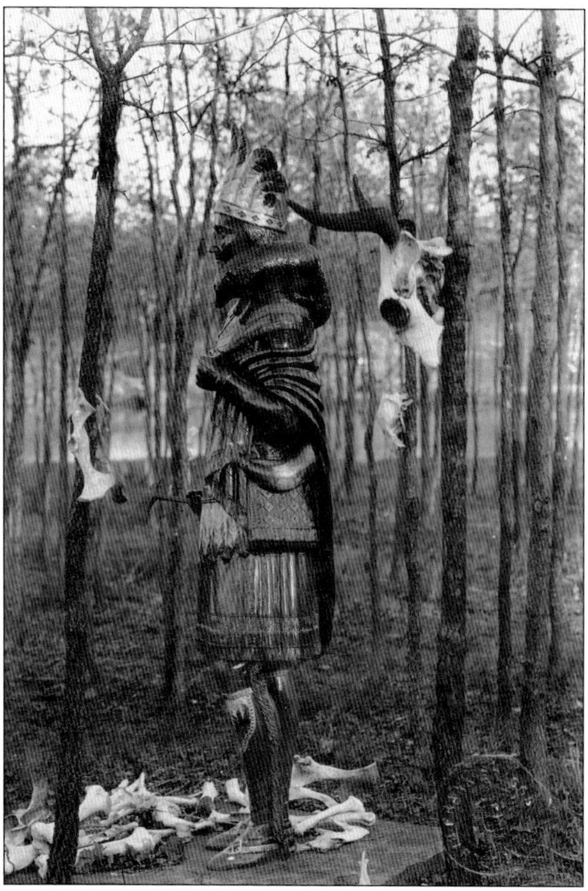

The roads through Woolaroc utilized a natural building material in abundance—stone. Bridges, guardrails, and other ornamental features along the roadways through the ranch were made from stone quarried right on the ranch. Today, many of these features are still in existence on the ranch and can be seen along the two-mile drive from the front gate to the museum.

As the ranch road snakes and winds its way through the blackjack oaks and other trees, a Haunted Grove was created. In this early photograph from the late 1920s, animal bones flank a tall Indian chief. As visitors drive through the grounds today, the Haunted Grove is still there with animal bones littering the ground. The area is a wonderful place to watch deer.

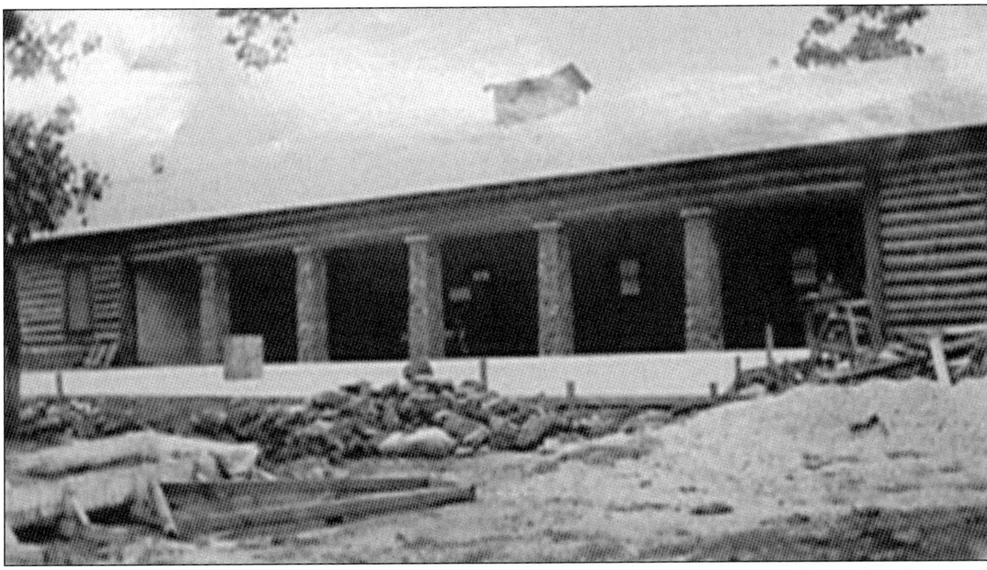

On any ranch, a number of ranch hands are needed to ensure that things run efficiently. The Frank Phillips Ranch was no exception. Built in 1926, the bunkhouse, pictured here, was constructed from Arkansas pine at the same time the lodge was being built. A center portion served as a garage for Frank Phillips's automobiles. For a little over $12,000, the bunkhouse was an important structure on the grounds. Later in its life, the bunkhouse was used as storage, and at one time, the *Woolaroc* airplane was housed in the structure. Today, the bunkhouse is 20 by 60 feet of exhibition space and is the location for temporary exhibitions.

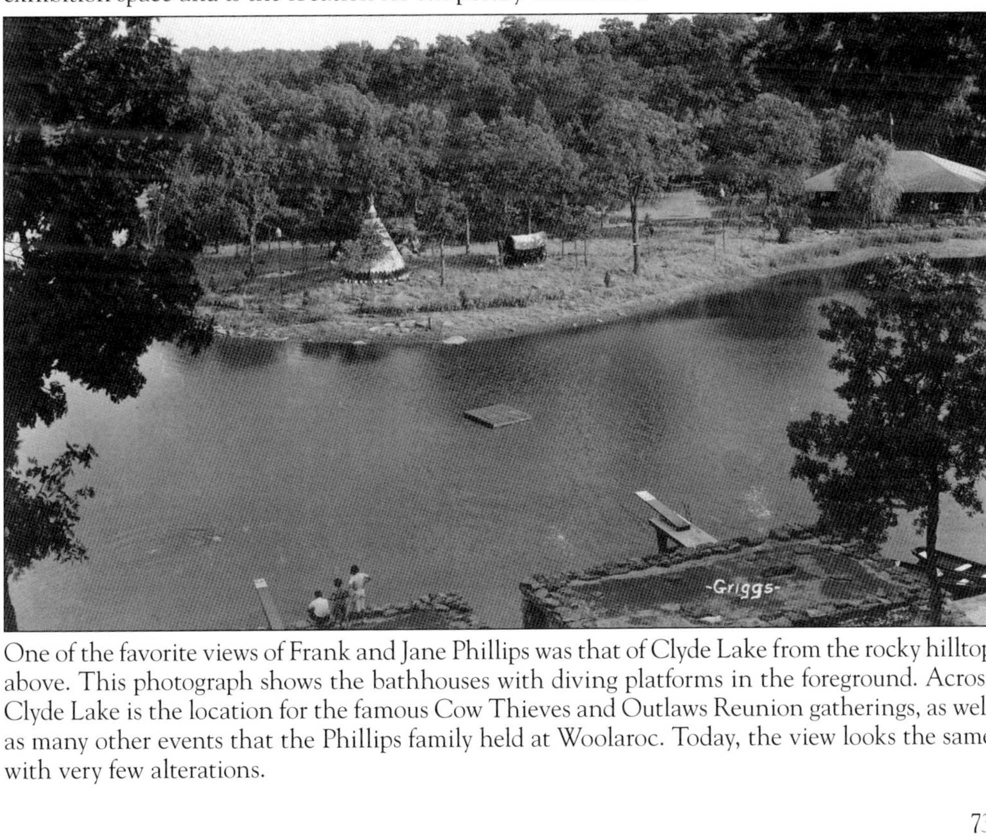

One of the favorite views of Frank and Jane Phillips was that of Clyde Lake from the rocky hilltop above. This photograph shows the bathhouses with diving platforms in the foreground. Across Clyde Lake is the location for the famous Cow Thieves and Outlaws Reunion gatherings, as well as many other events that the Phillips family held at Woolaroc. Today, the view looks the same with very few alterations.

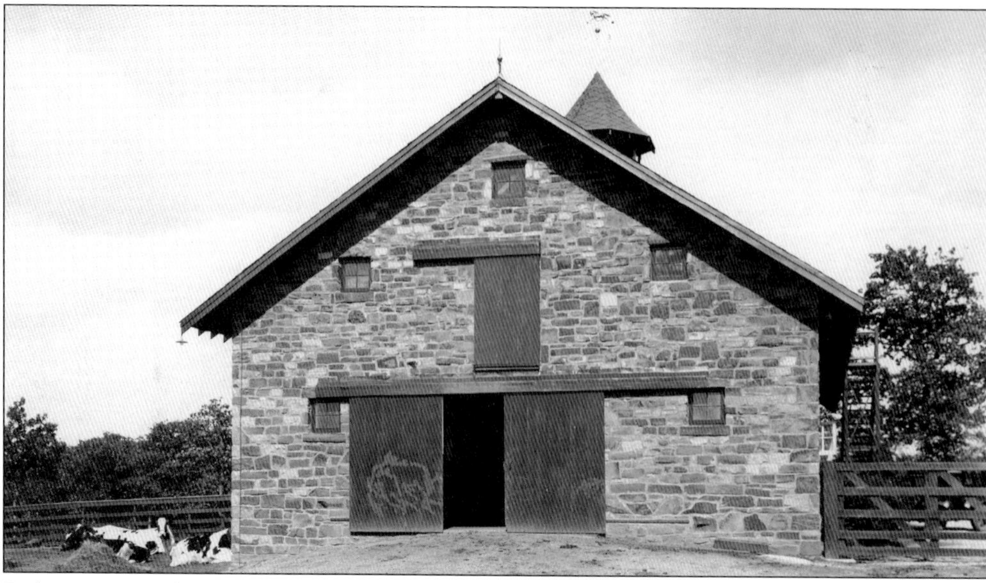

Perhaps in a nod to his Nebraska and Iowa farming roots, Frank Phillips kept a herd of prized Holstein cows. Pictured here, the Holsteins are resting comfortably outside the horse barns. The barns, outbuildings, fences, and other facilities at the ranch were a source of immense pride for Phillips. He enjoyed playing the role of gentleman farmer and wanted to share that part of Old West history with his visitors.

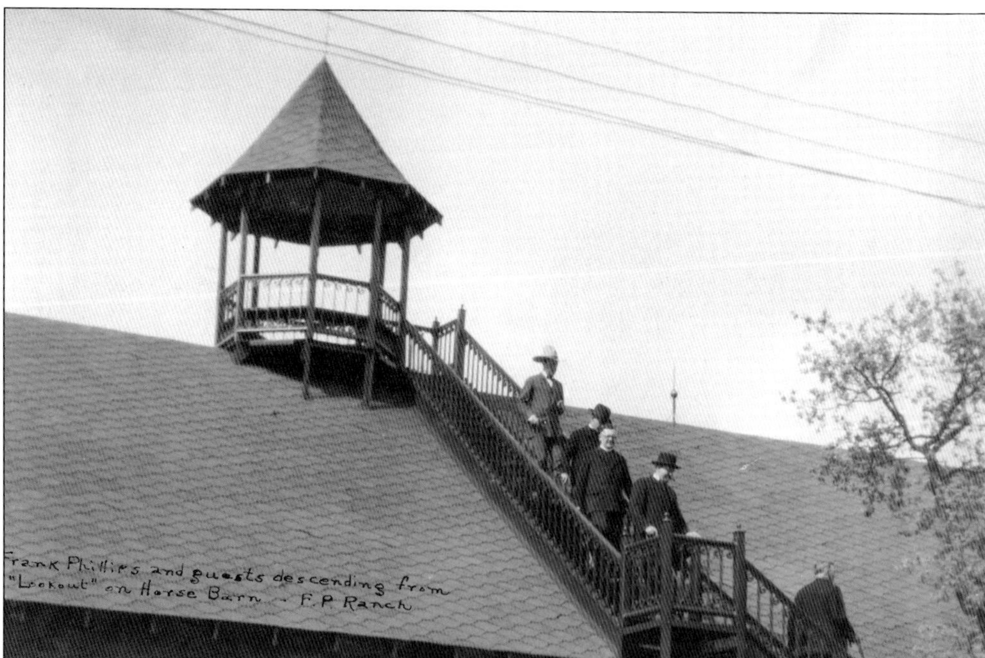

To take full advantage of the amazing vistas of his ranch, Phillips had a staircase and special observation tower installed on the roof of the horse barn. From this high point, Frank could take his guests up top for an amazing view of his ranch. Pictured here Phillips (wearing his trademark cowboy hat at the rear of the line) trails a group of visitors down from the lookout. Visitors can still ascend the steps to the tower today and take in the views.

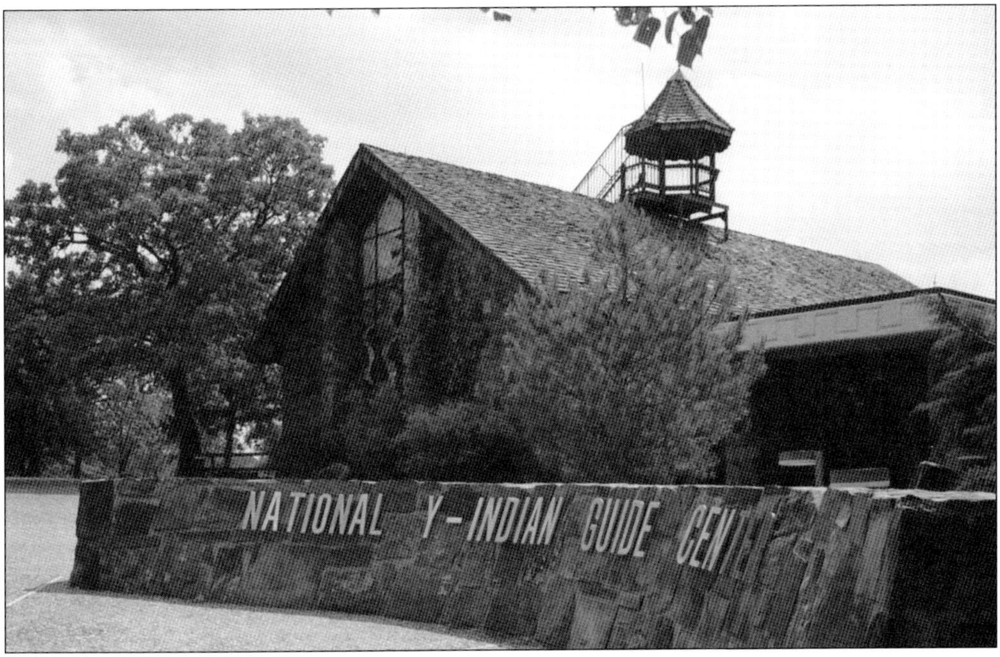

Using the horse barn as its core, the National Y-Indian Guide Center was established at Woolaroc in 1972. With the addition of a special domed theater room, the facility was cutting edge upon its completion. The Y-Indian Guide program was developed in 1925 to develop and foster stronger family bonds among American Indian families and tribes. The center at Woolaroc featured a multimedia display that used 60 feet of multiple screens and a domed ceiling area to project *Arrows Skyward*, a film about American Indian life and culture. Currently, the building is home to exhibit space and the welcome center. There, visitors can cool off, eat lunch, and watch video presentations about the history of Woolaroc.

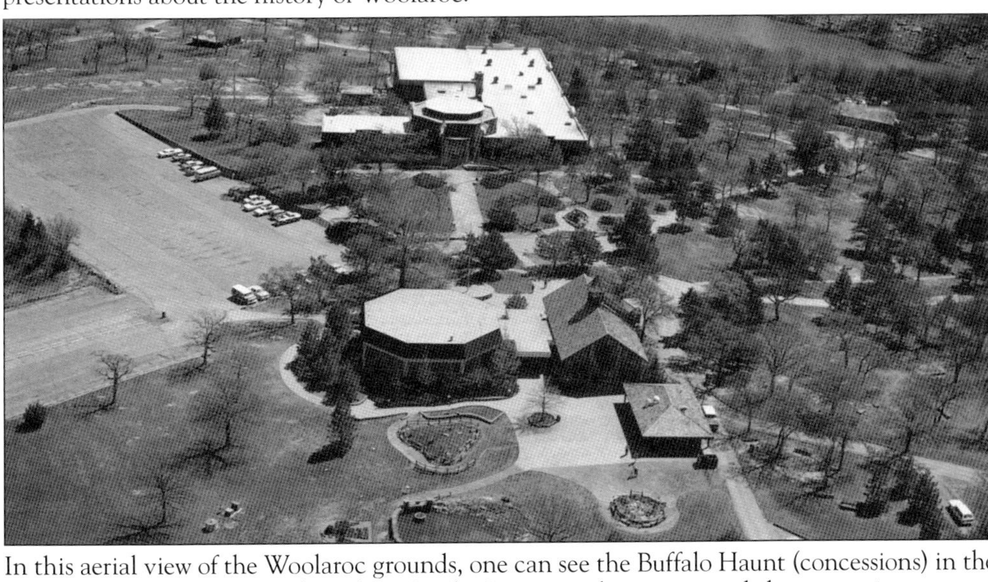

In this aerial view of the Woolaroc grounds, one can see the Buffalo Haunt (concessions) in the foreground, the Horse Barn/Y-Indian Guide Center in the center, and the expansive museum complex to the top of the frame. With a world-class museum, the Phillips retreat home, and a host of additional facilities, Woolaroc became a focal point for travelers.

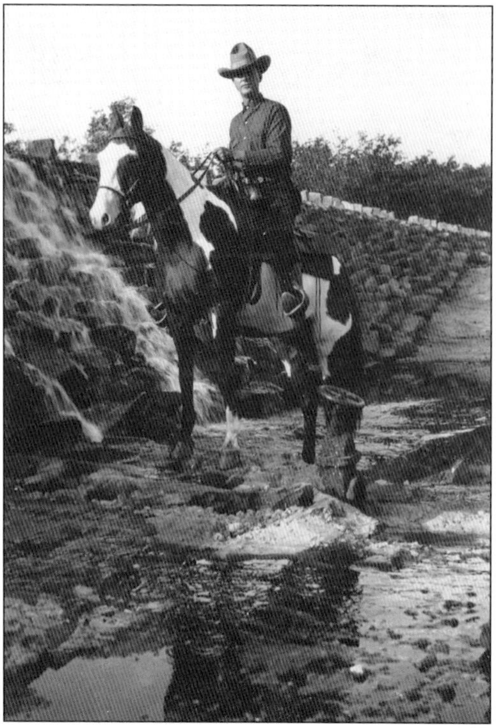

Grif Graham was most comfortable on the back of a trusty horse. Here, Grif rides the ranch inspecting animals, roadways, and dams. Graham was one of the original employees at the ranch.

Frank Phillips takes a moment to pose for a photograph on the shore of Clyde Lake next to the pavilion. The Clyde Lake location figures prominently in the history of Woolaroc, especially the Cow Thieves and Outlaws Reunions held from 1926 to 1930.

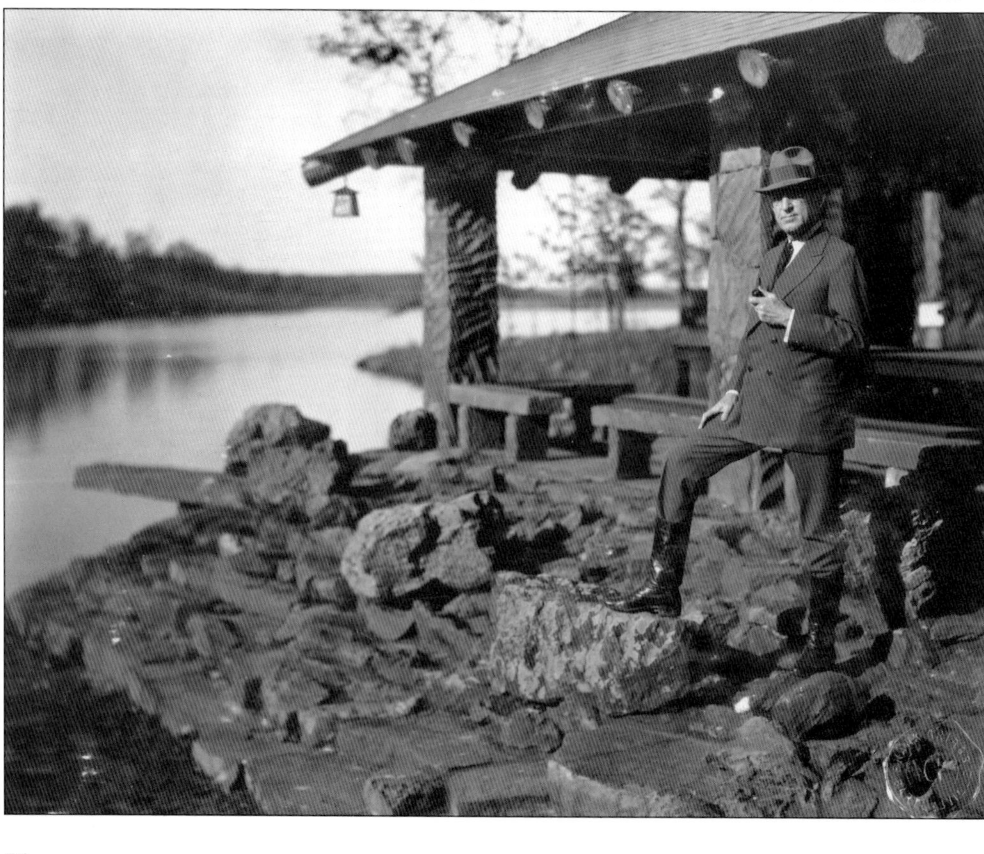

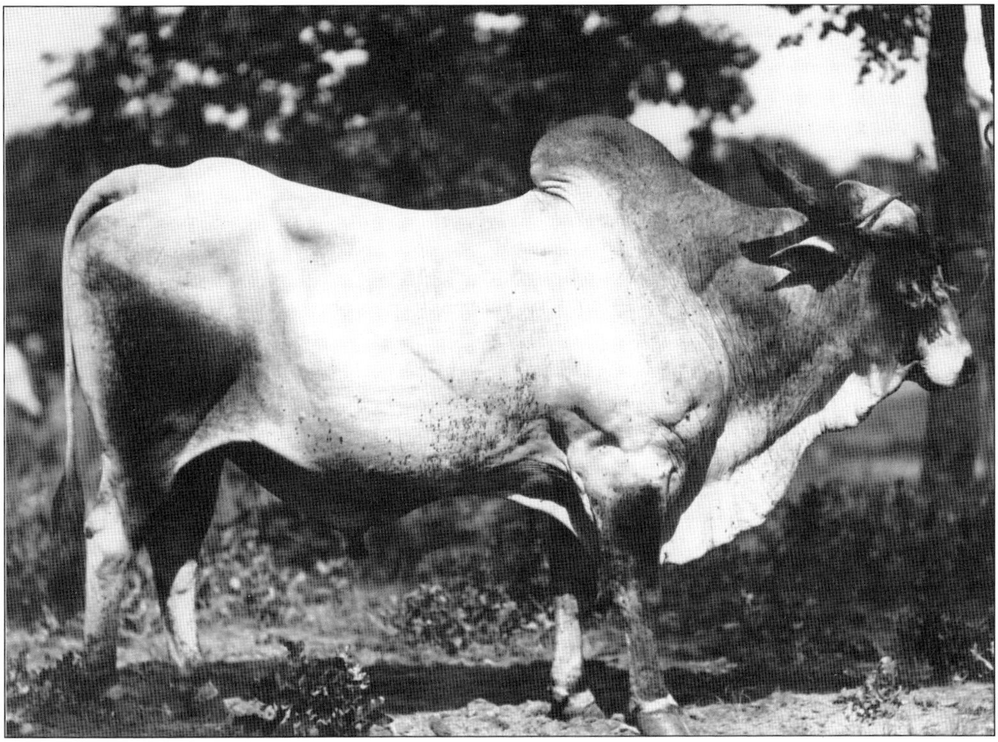

Frank Phillips set out almost at once to assemble a large and diverse collection of animals for his ranch. He was particularly fond of various breeds of cattle. This fine specimen of Brahma cattle was just one of several found on the ranch.

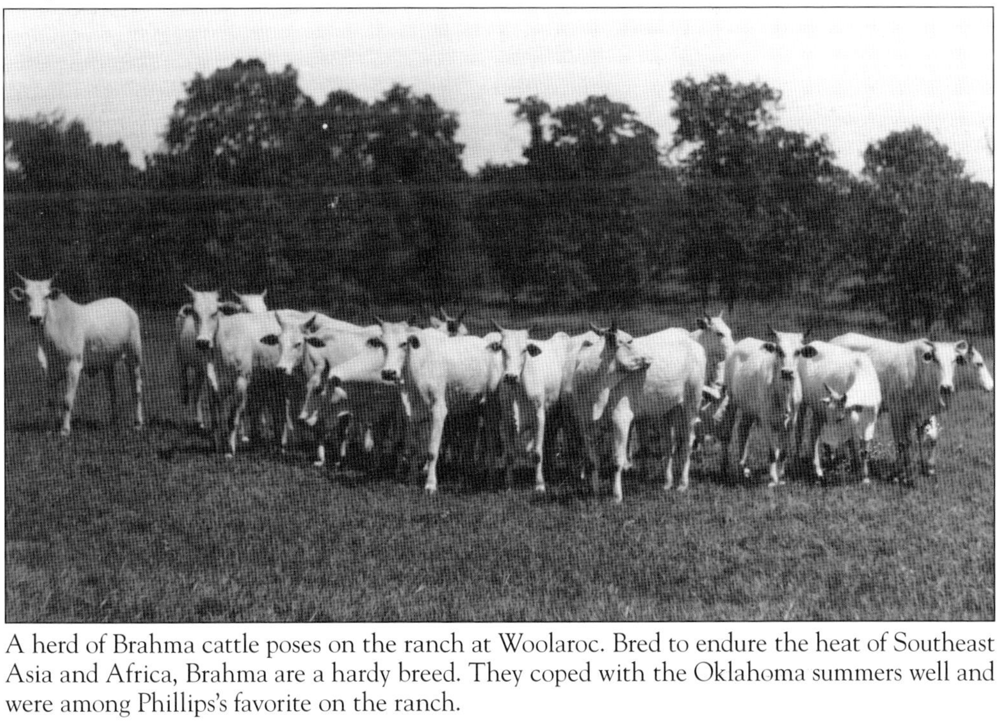

A herd of Brahma cattle poses on the ranch at Woolaroc. Bred to endure the heat of Southeast Asia and Africa, Brahma are a hardy breed. They coped with the Oklahoma summers well and were among Phillips's favorite on the ranch.

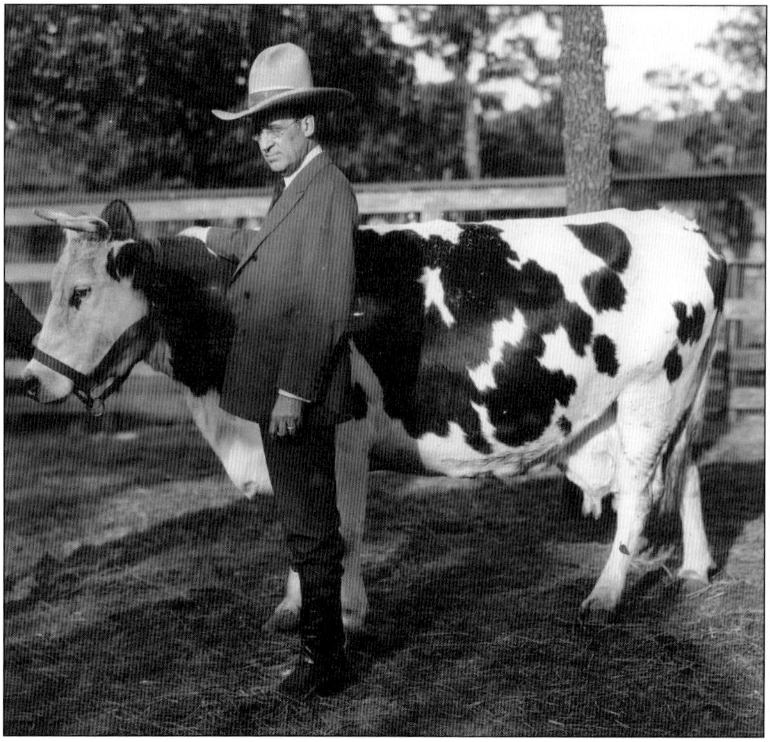

Some of Frank Phillips's most beloved cattle were his herd of fine Holsteins. His cattle were entered in livestock shows and county fairs. Here, Phillips poses with one of his prizewinning Holsteins. He was intensely proud to be a farmer and rancher. Woolaroc gave Phillips the outlet to indulge in his interest in animal husbandry.

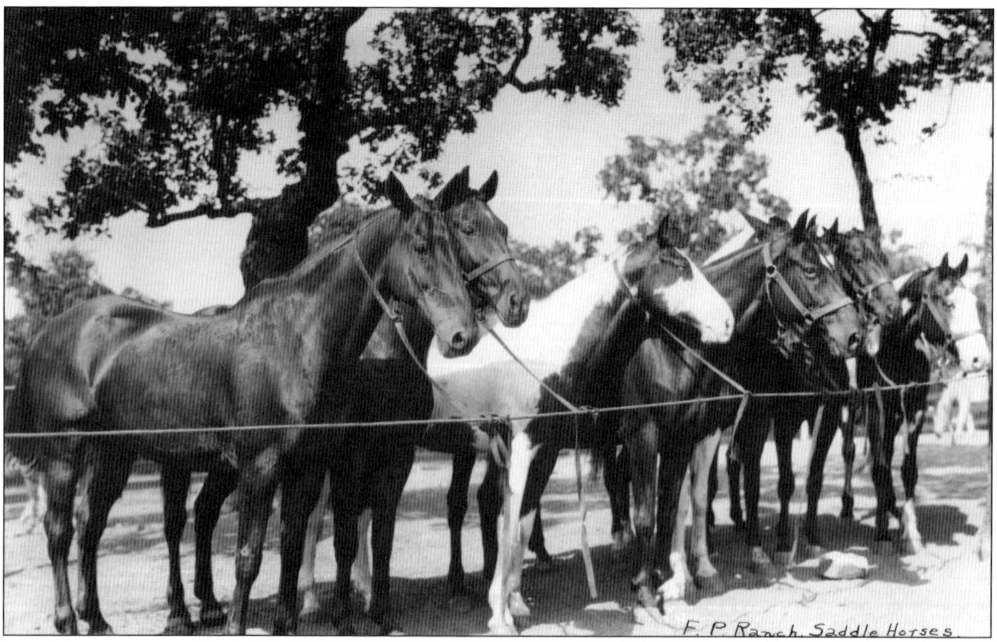

In addition to a fondness for cattle, Phillips also loved horses. He kept many finely trained horses in the stables at Woolaroc and enjoyed riding the grounds as often as possible. The horses kept at Woolaroc were always the highest quality, and Phillips enjoyed taking tenderfoot visitors from the East out for a day in the saddle.

Many "exotic" breeds of animal found their way to Woolaroc. The more interesting or unique the animals, the more Frank Phillips wanted to have them at the ranch. A kangaroo with its joey tucked away in the pouch could be found at the ranch.

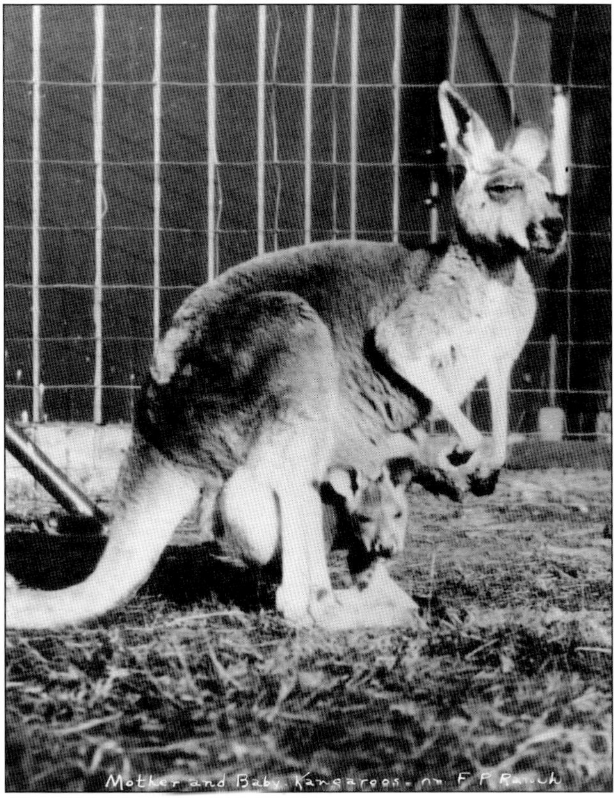

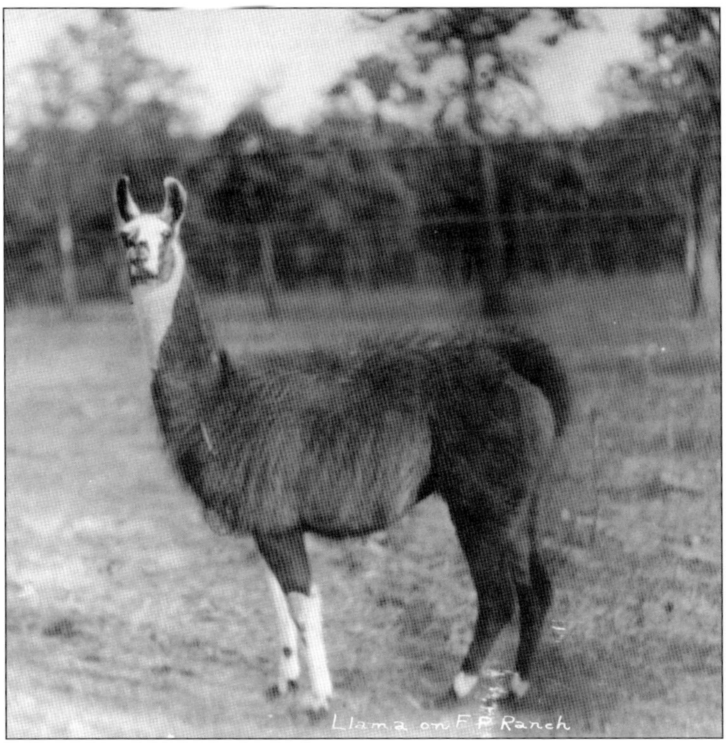

Llamas from South America were also brought to the ranch. Llamas were prized for their fur, which could be shorn like sheep and made into yarn. Woolaroc legend holds that Phillips found it amusing when a llama would "spit" on visitors from the East, horrifying them. Today, visitors crossing the bridge over Stone Lake on their way to the museum are greeted by the llamas.

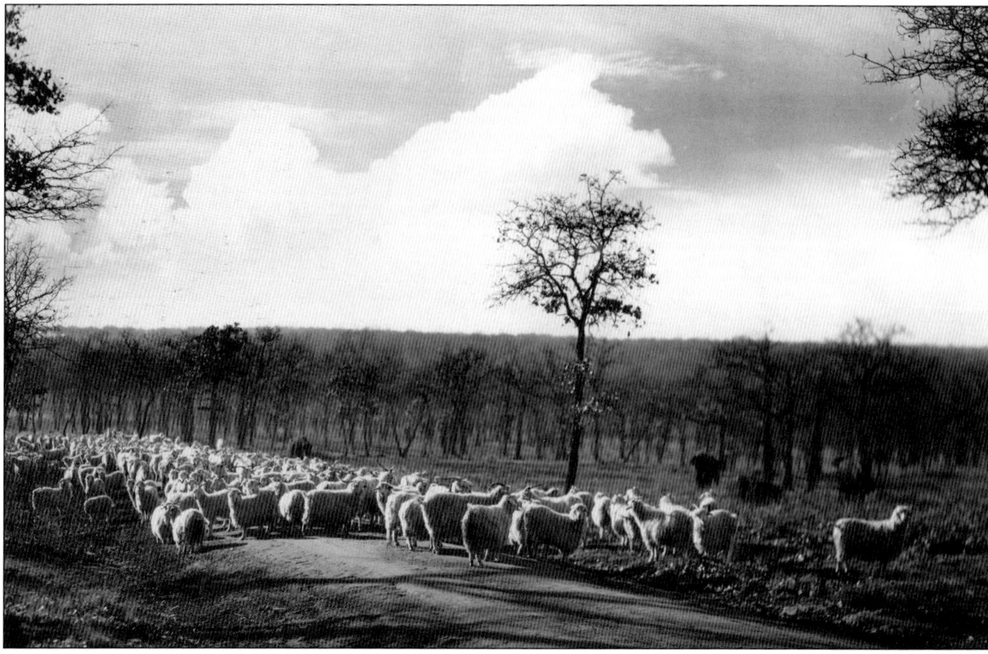

Sheep were also found on the ranch in abundance. They also could be shorn, and their wool was used for yarn and weaving. Here, the entire herd blocks one of the roads through the ranch. One of the interesting facets of the ranch is that most of the animals were not housed in enclosures and were free-ranging. This practice is continued today.

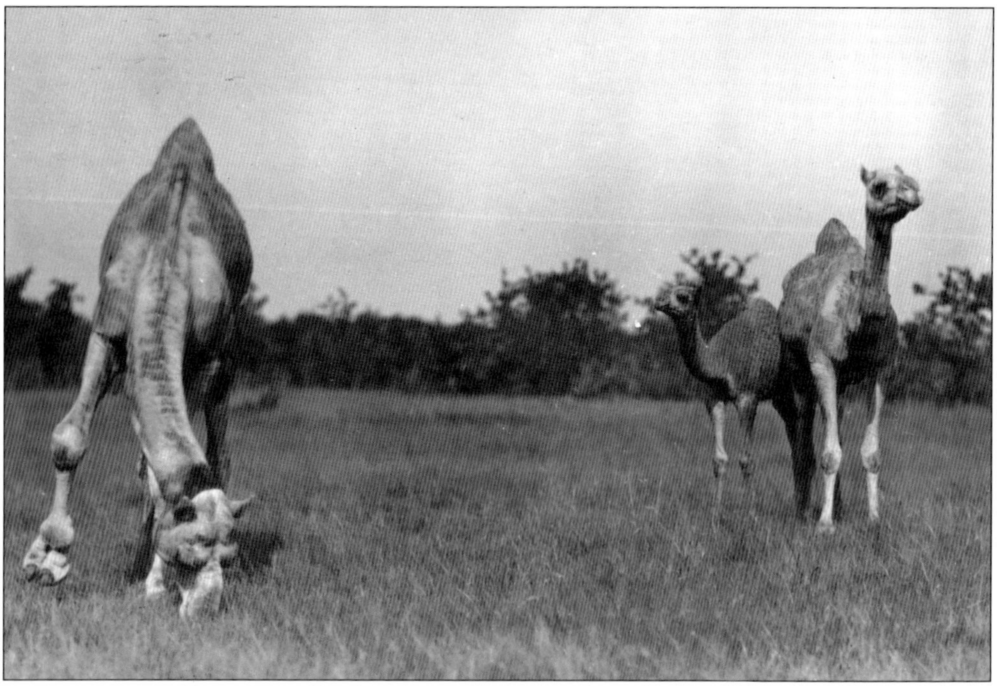

Next to the two ill-fated giraffes that did not survive the Oklahoma climate long, perhaps the most exotic animals to call Woolaroc home were these camels. Grazing on lush Oklahoma grasses all day and sauntering around the grounds made for a relaxing life.

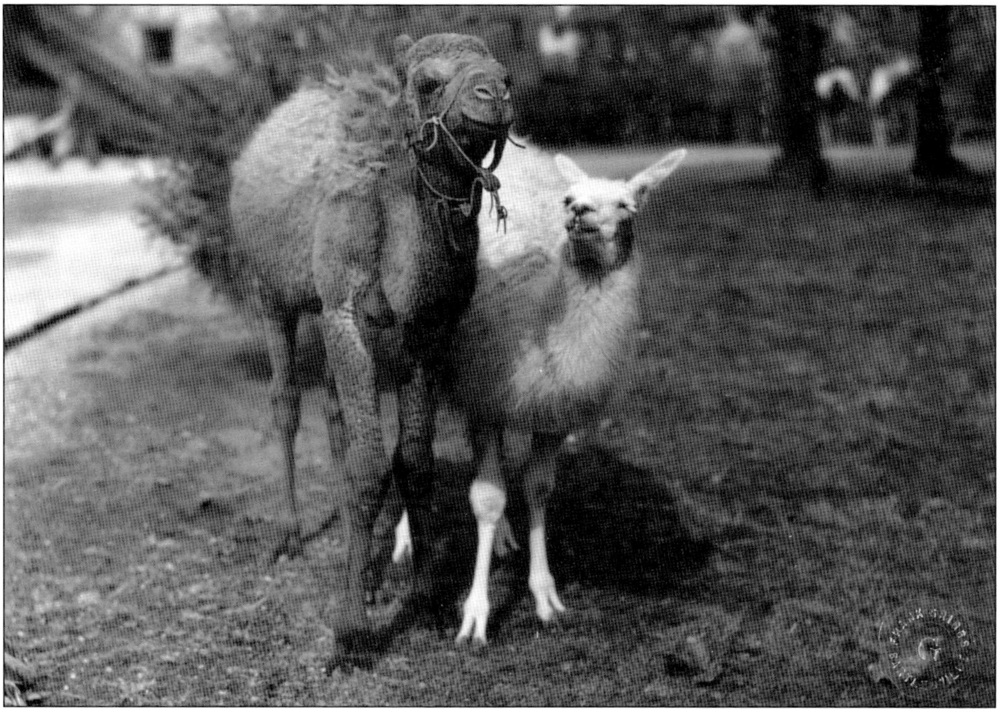

A juvenile camel and llama pose for a photograph on the ranch. To entertain his guests, Phillips would at times have the ranch hands saddle and bring the camels to events. Visitors could, with great assistance, climb atop a camel and take a ride.

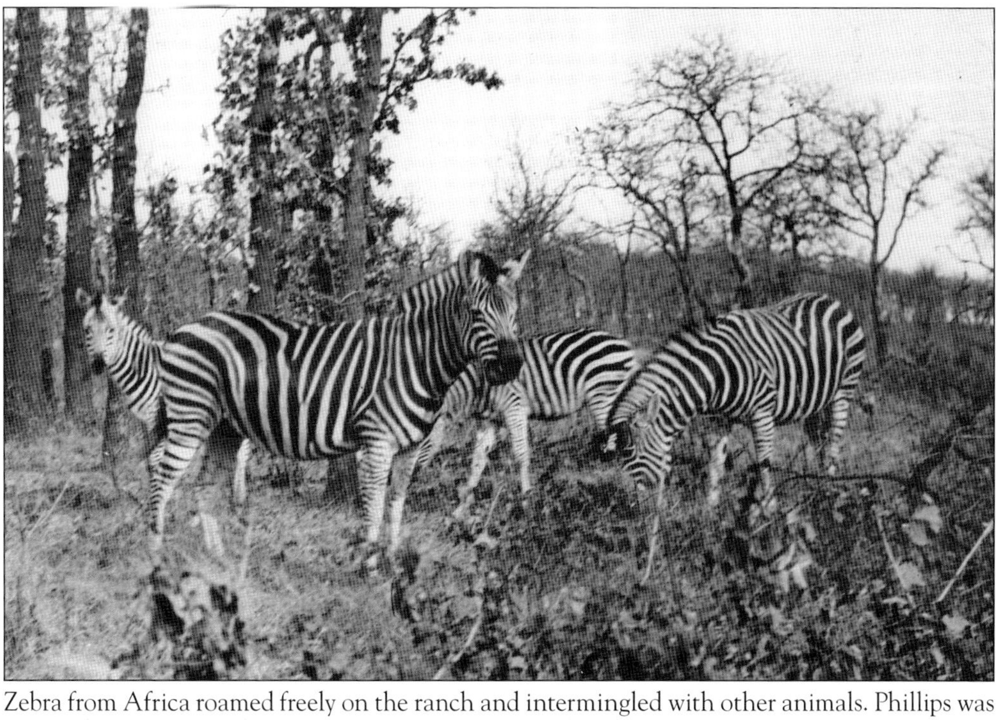

Zebra from Africa roamed freely on the ranch and intermingled with other animals. Phillips was accumulating a veritable Noah's ark of animal life in the Osage Hills.

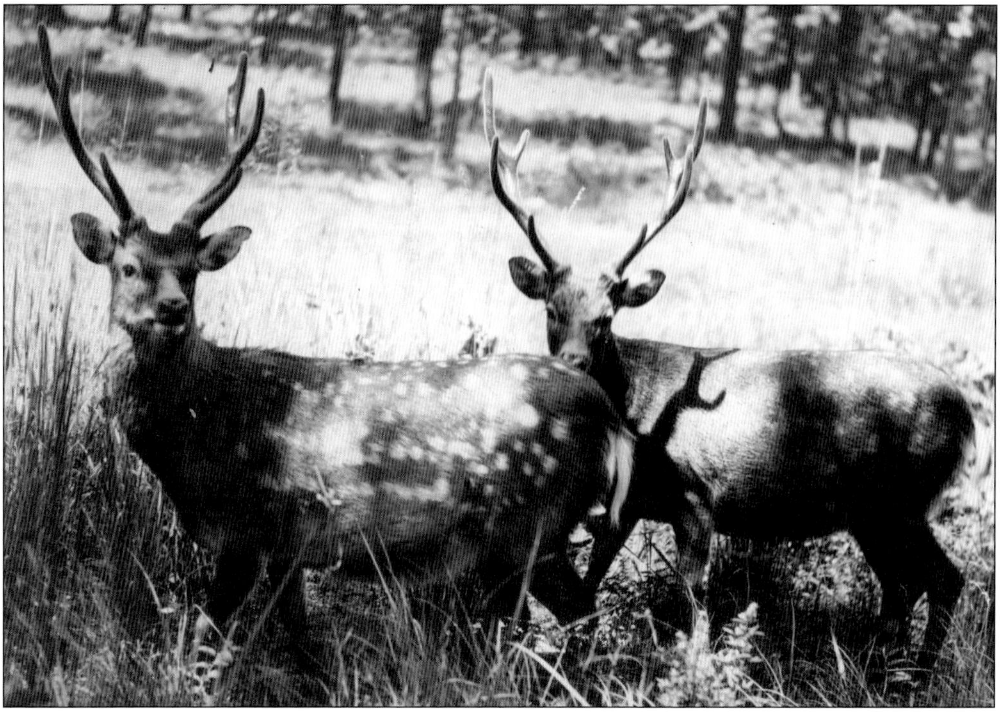

The ranch was already home to various native species of deer. Other unique breeds, like Sika deer from Japan, were brought to the ranch to supplement the herds already present.

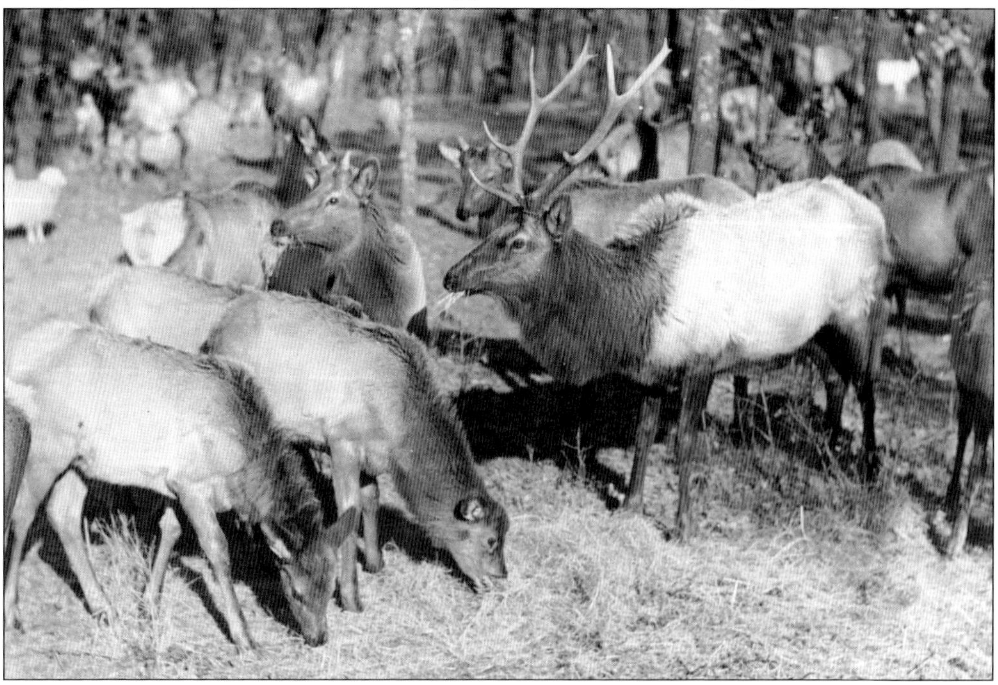

Another large herding and ranging animal that was found on the ranch in abundance was elk. Here, groups of elk are seen grazing with sheep in the background. Like the other animals on the ranch, they roamed freely.

This young elk is photographed while out roaming the ranch grounds. The diversity of animal life on the ranch was a source of immense pride for Phillips.

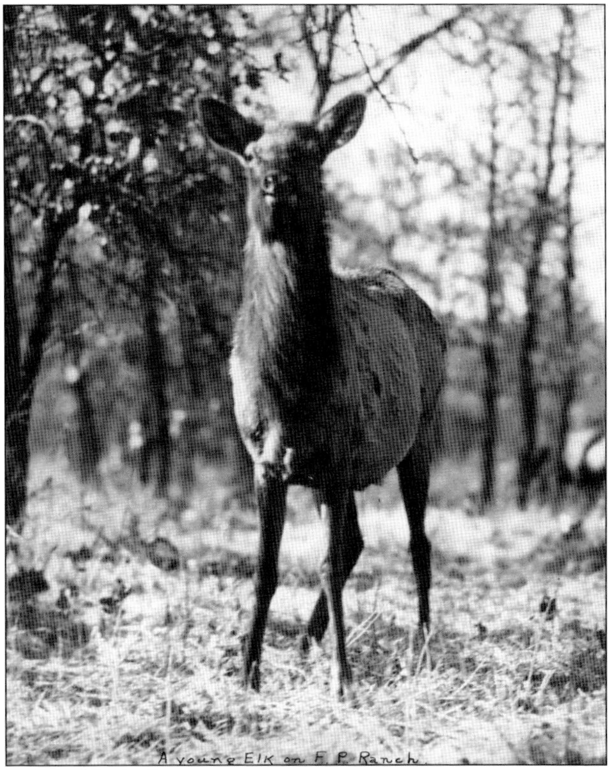

Two water buffalo cool off in one of the many lakes on the ranch grounds. The water buffalo proved to also be hardy and able to adapt to the Oklahoma climate.

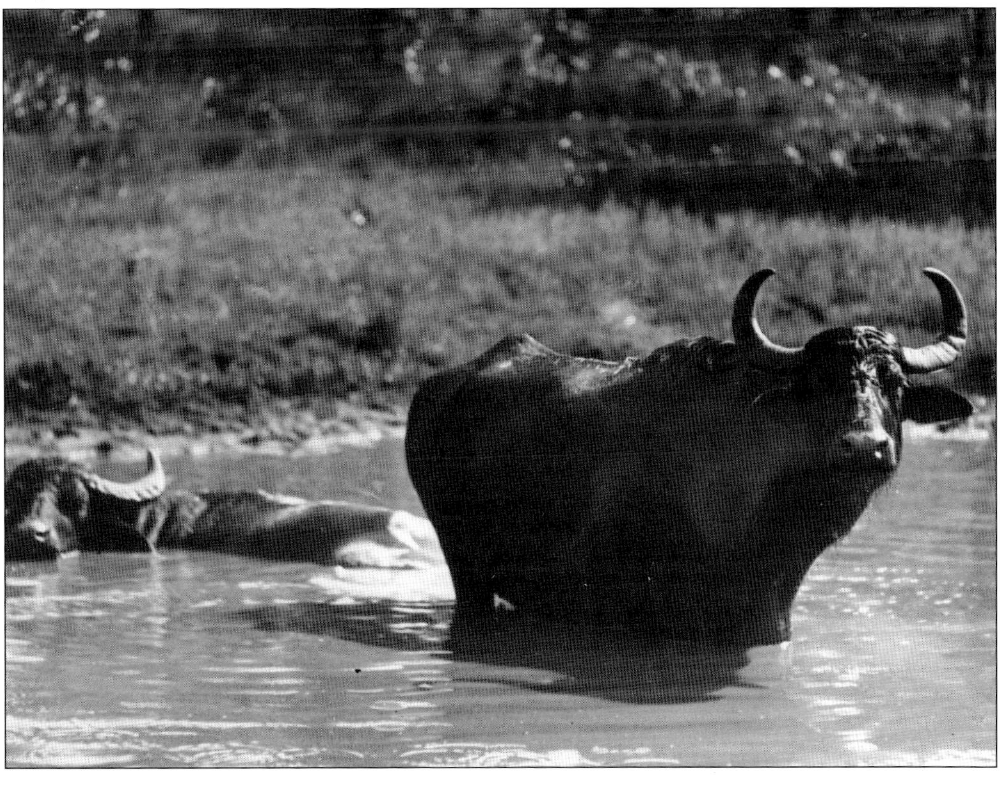

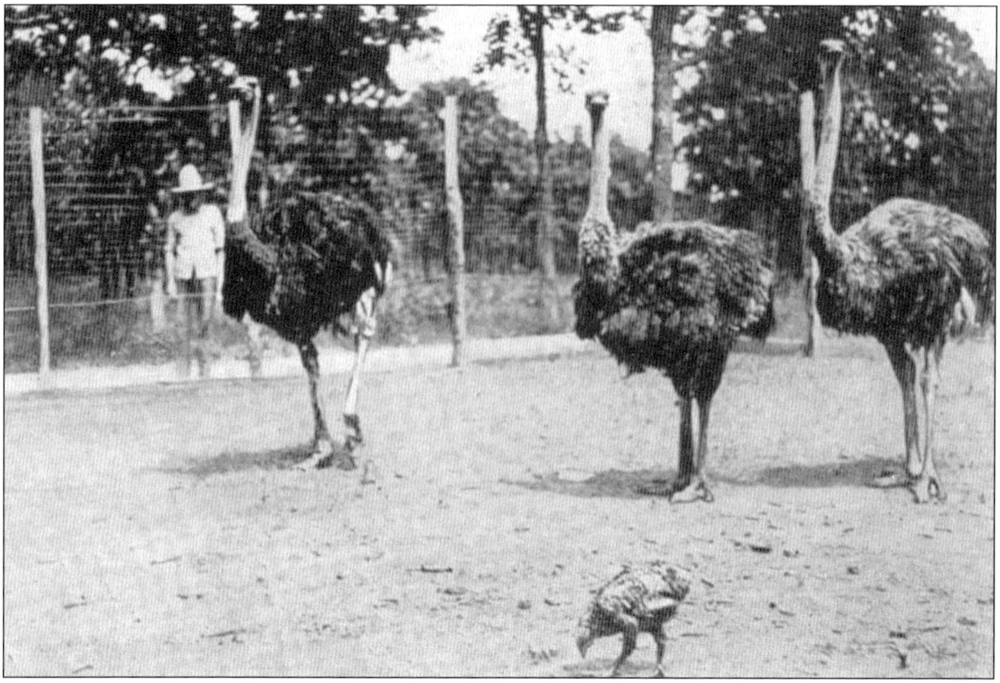

Another unusual animal found on the ranch, these ostriches were kept in enclosed spaces due to their very poor eyesight. They are pictured here with a chicken in the foreground. Today, there are several ostriches that make the ranch their home, much to the delight of visitors.

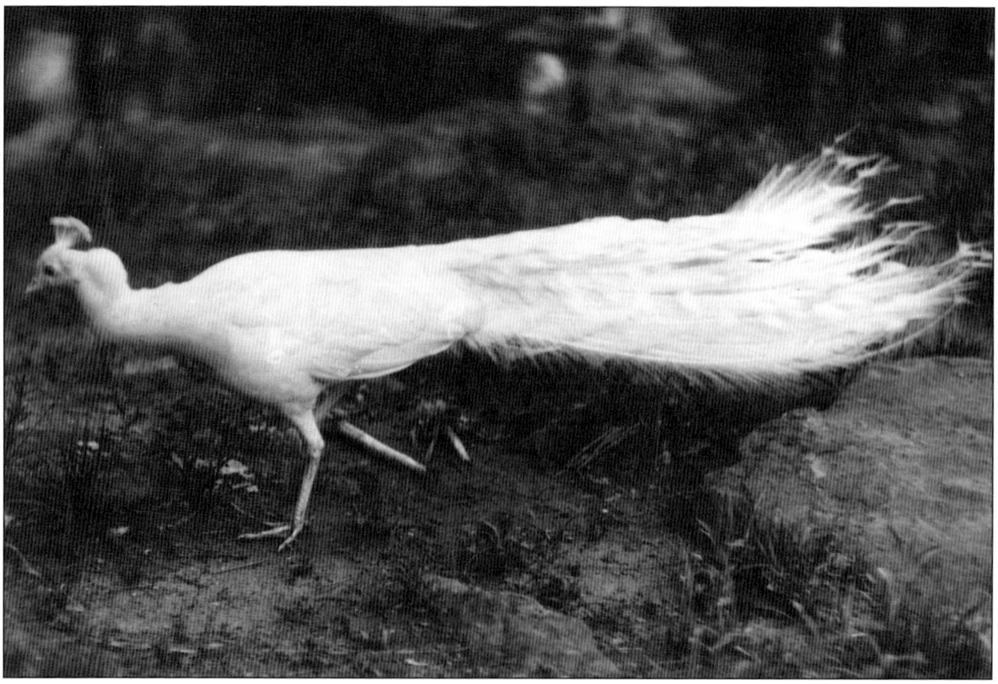

Peacocks and other exotic birds could also be found at Woolaroc. Here, an albino peacock strolls the grounds in search of food. At any given time, peacock feathers could be found on the grounds, and the birds' shrill calls echoed through the grounds.

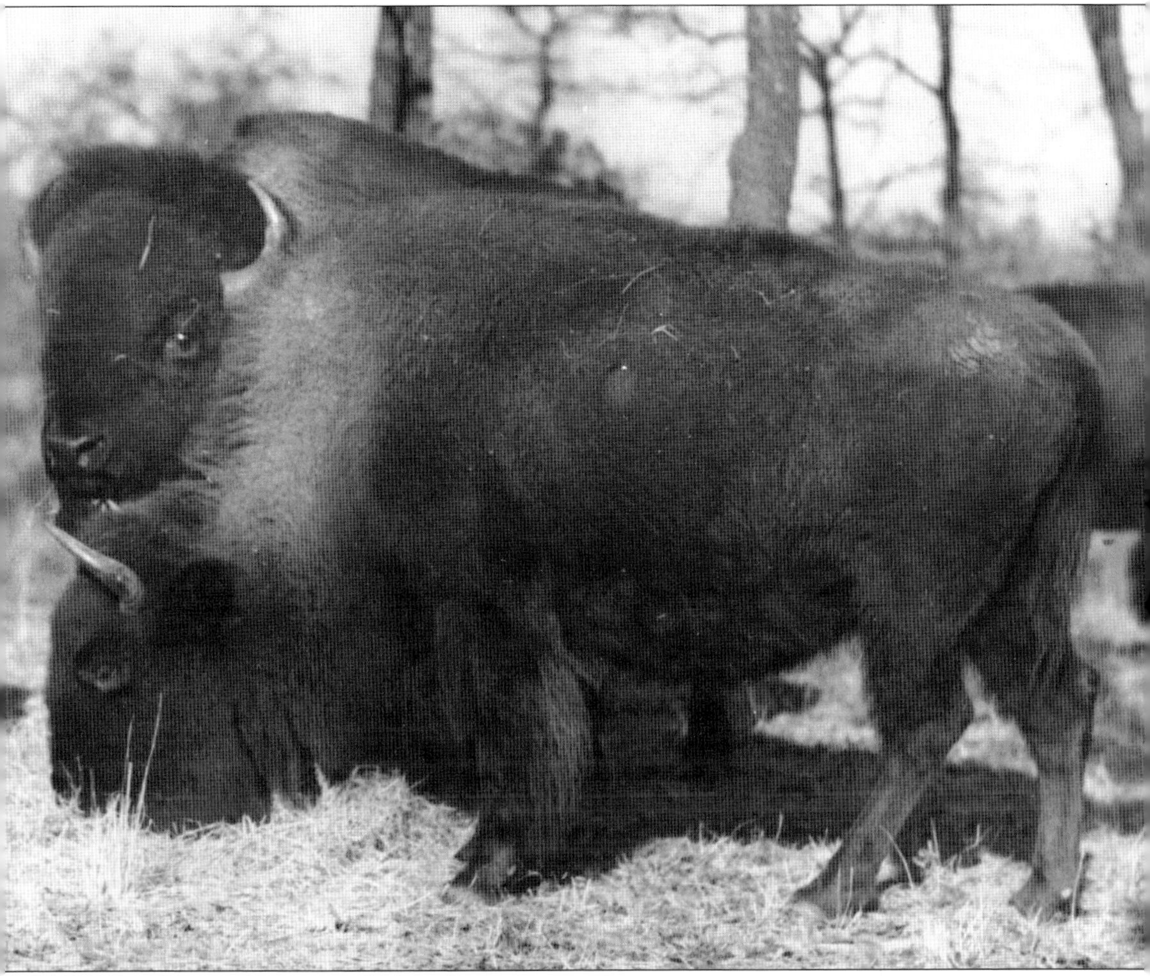

The sound must have been deafening as the herd of bison was released on the ranch in 1926. A herd of buffalo were purchased and brought to Woolaroc from Pierre, South Dakota. Some of the most amazing home movie footage in the collection at Woolaroc shows the herd making their way out into the Oklahoma prairie.

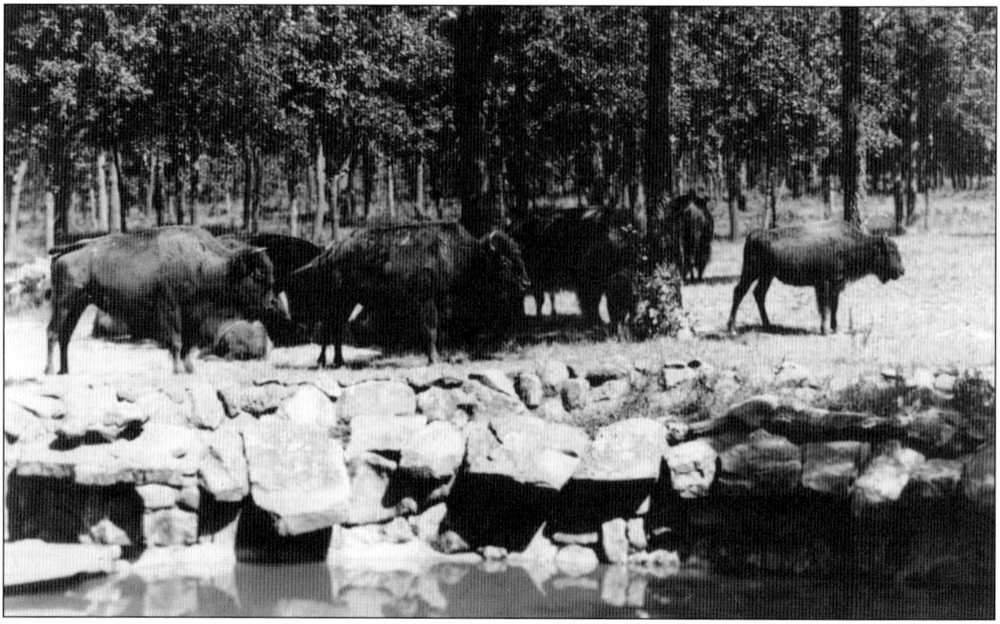

Always free-ranging, the bison were emblematic of the Old West that Frank Phillips wished to preserve and share with future generations. Before the arrival of the bison, it was evident that Phillips planned on having the hard-to-contain animals on the ranch, as the fencing that was built included barbed wire on the top to provide added protection against their wily ability to escape.

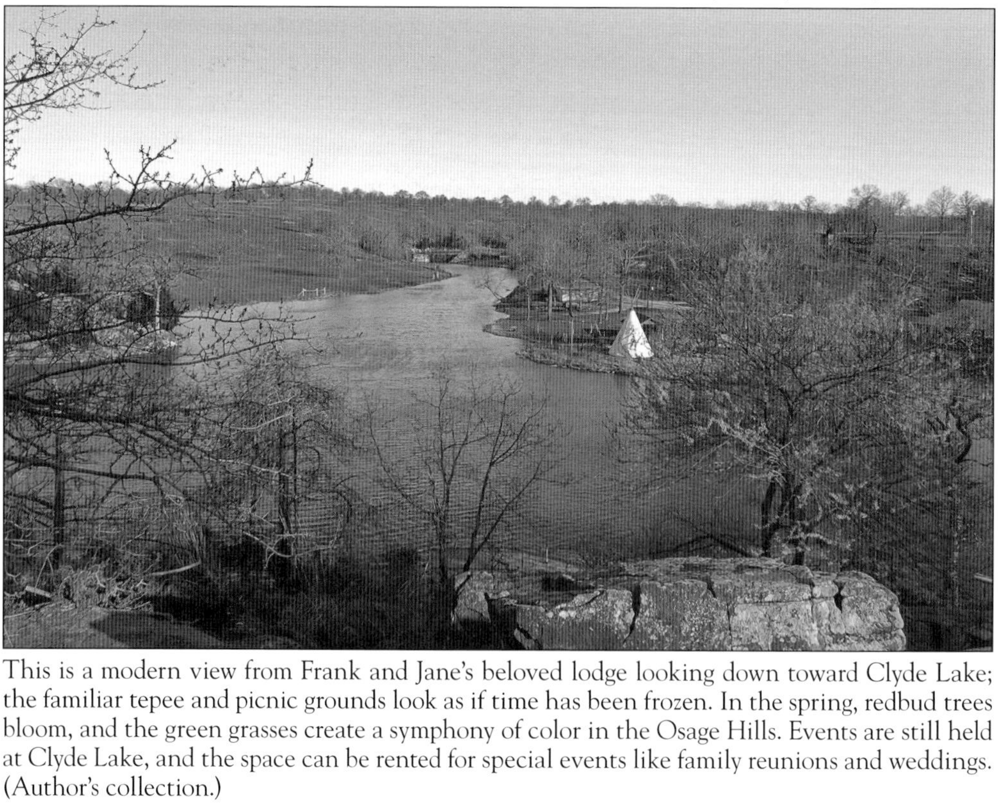

This is a modern view from Frank and Jane's beloved lodge looking down toward Clyde Lake; the familiar tepee and picnic grounds look as if time has been frozen. In the spring, redbud trees bloom, and the green grasses create a symphony of color in the Osage Hills. Events are still held at Clyde Lake, and the space can be rented for special events like family reunions and weddings. (Author's collection.)

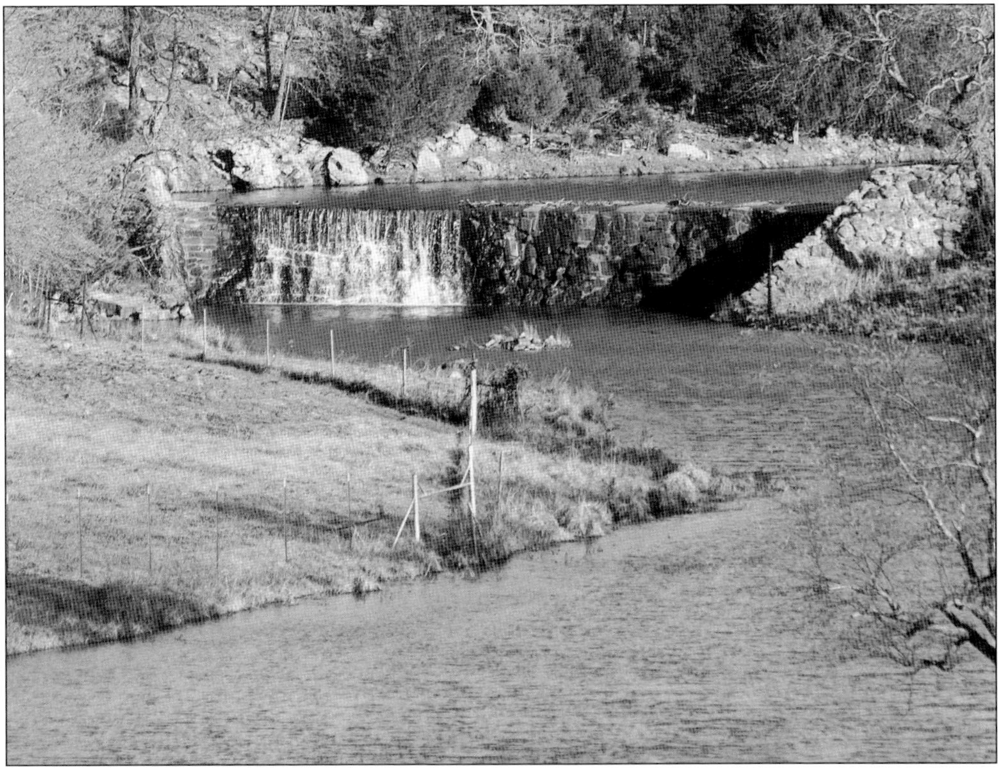

One of the original waterfalls on the grounds can be seen from the lodge. (Author's collection.)

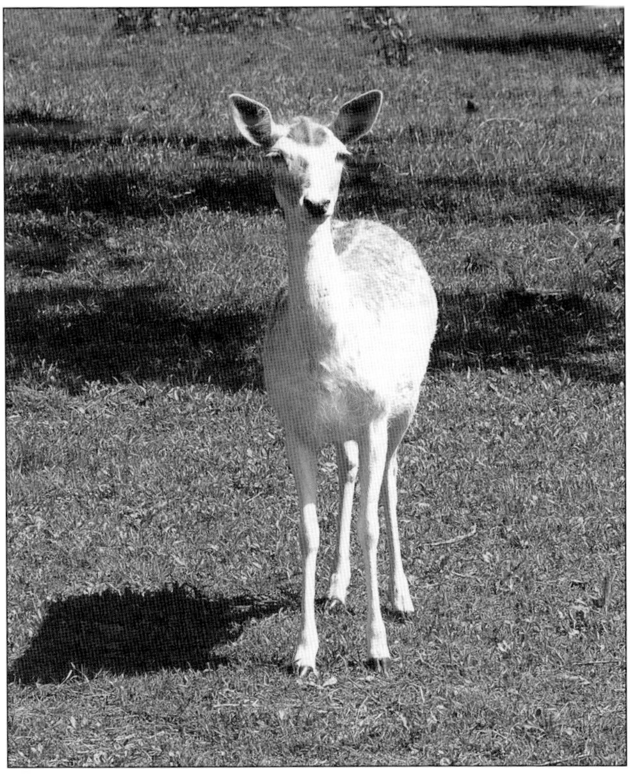

Deer are just one of the many animals that can be found roaming the grounds of Woolaroc today. For Frank Phillips, preserving not only the historical heritage of the west was important but also the animal life that was a part of that history. The fallow deer can frequently be seen grazing and lounging in pastures alongside the bison. (Author's collection.)

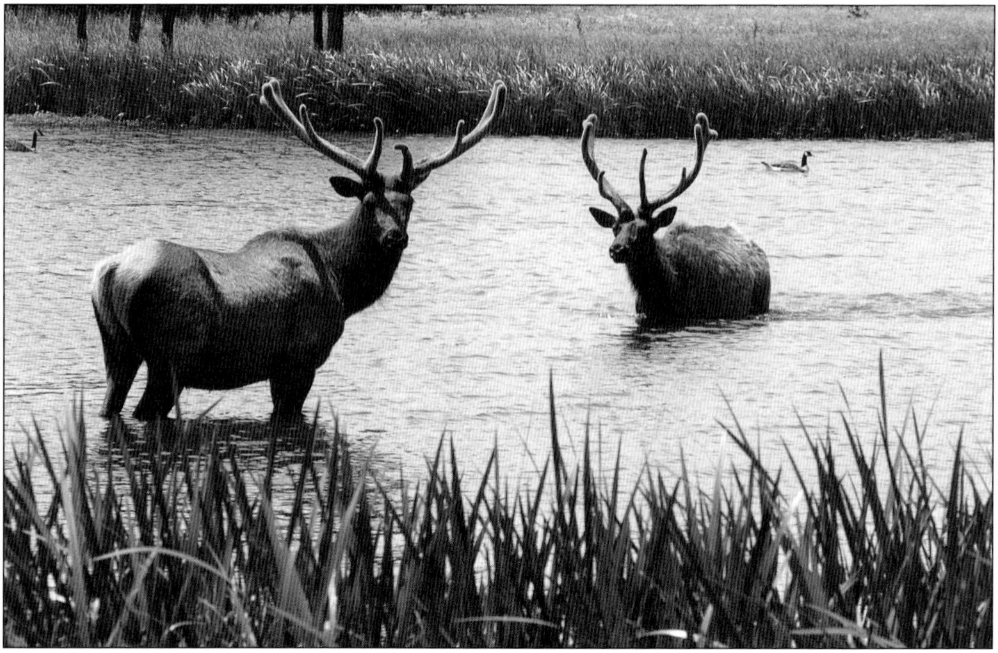

Two adult elk take a summer swim in Crystal Lake near the Woolaroc Mountain Man Encampment. The elk can be seen alongside the two-mile roadway leading from the gate to the museum. Their imposing size and impressive horns make them a favorite of Woolaroc visitors, and they are much photographed. (Author's collection.)

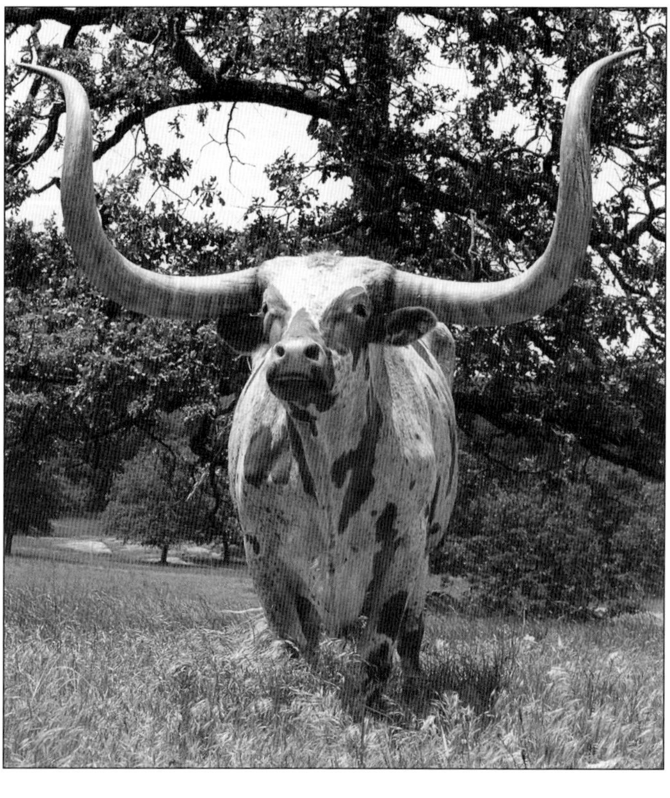

Affectionately called Tex by the Woolaroc ranch hands, this Texas longhorn was named by Woolaroc visitors. A special competition was held to name the longhorn. Called Goal Post by visitors, he grazed lazily on the Woolaroc pastures until his passing. Upon his passing, he joined many of the other animals that lived their lives at Woolaroc; he is preserved through the art of taxidermy and graces the museum walls today. (Author's collection.)

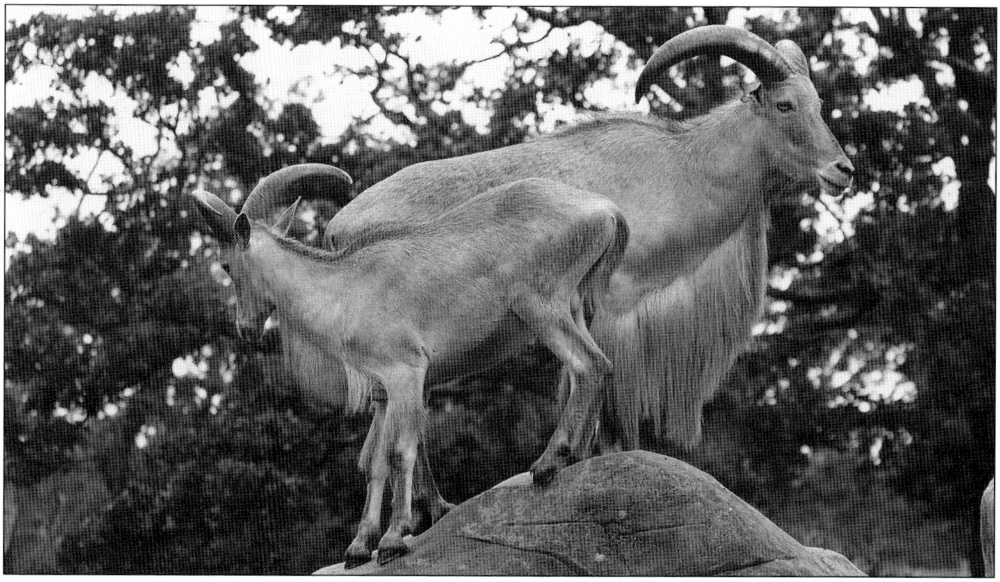

Perched high atop their enclosed habitat, these aoudads survey the landscape as visitors drive by on their way to the museum. These hardy, nimble climbers live across from the Woolaroc Museum near the Petting Barn and with other animals that soak up the attention visitors give them. (Author's collection.)

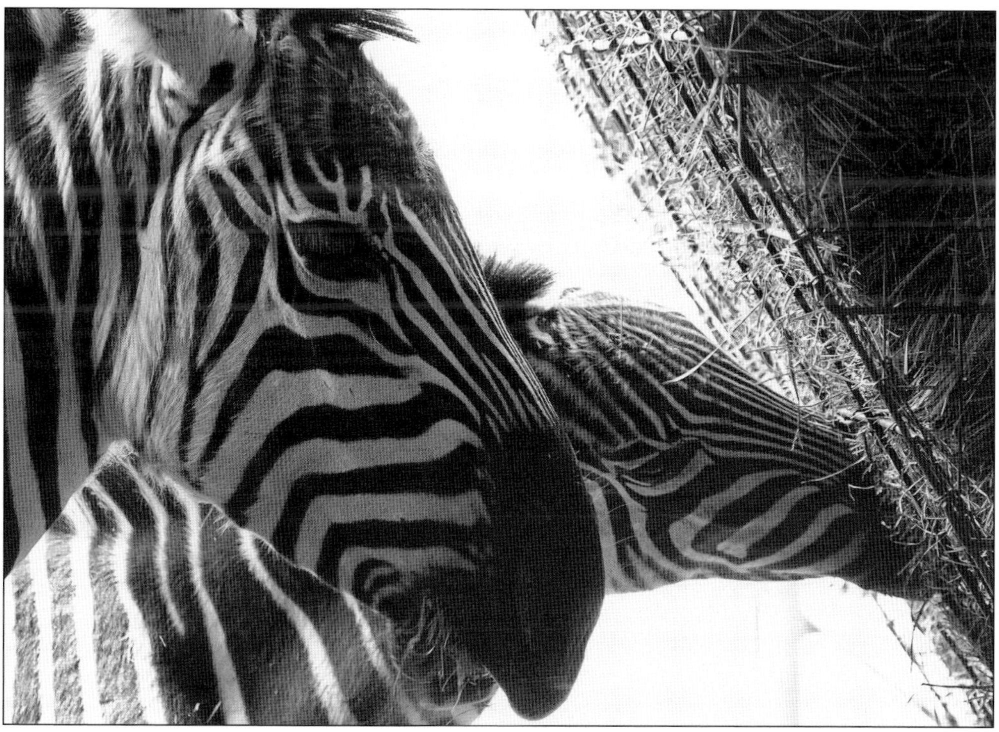

After an absence on the ranch, zebra have made a comeback through the generosity of Marcus Low, the grandson-in-law of Frank and Jane Phillips. Low purchased a pair of zebra and gave them to Woolaroc so a new generation of visitors could enjoy them as he did as a young child. (Author's collection.)

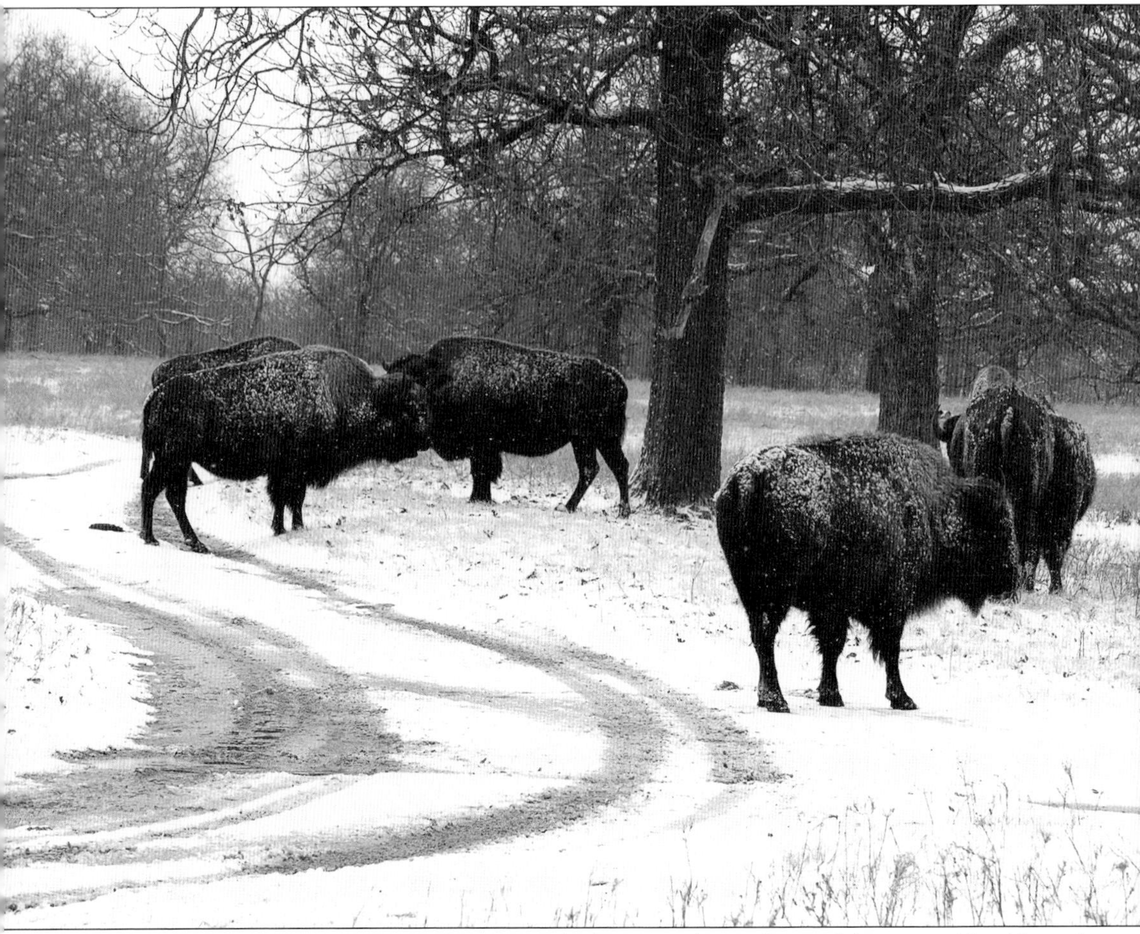

Seen here along the tour road in the winter, the bison are descendants of the original herd brought in from South Dakota in 1926. These robust animals are spectacular when on the run. They have been known to cause traffic to slow to a crawl on the tour road through Woolaroc when they refuse to move off the roadway. (Author's collection.)

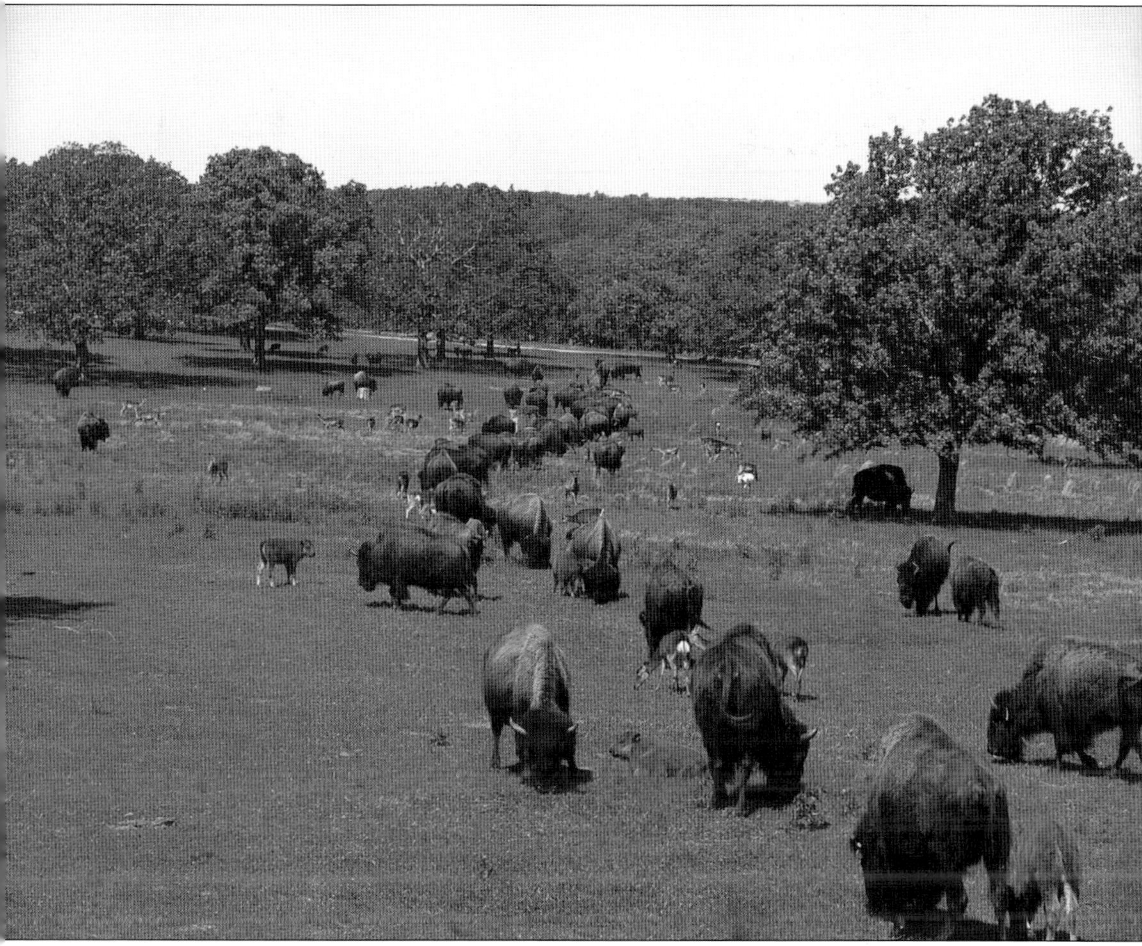

In the spring, the ranch teems with new life. Nearly every species sees the birth of young in the spring, and the bison are no exception. Here, the herd grazes on fresh spring grasses with calves close by under the watchful supervision of nervous mothers. (Author's collection.)

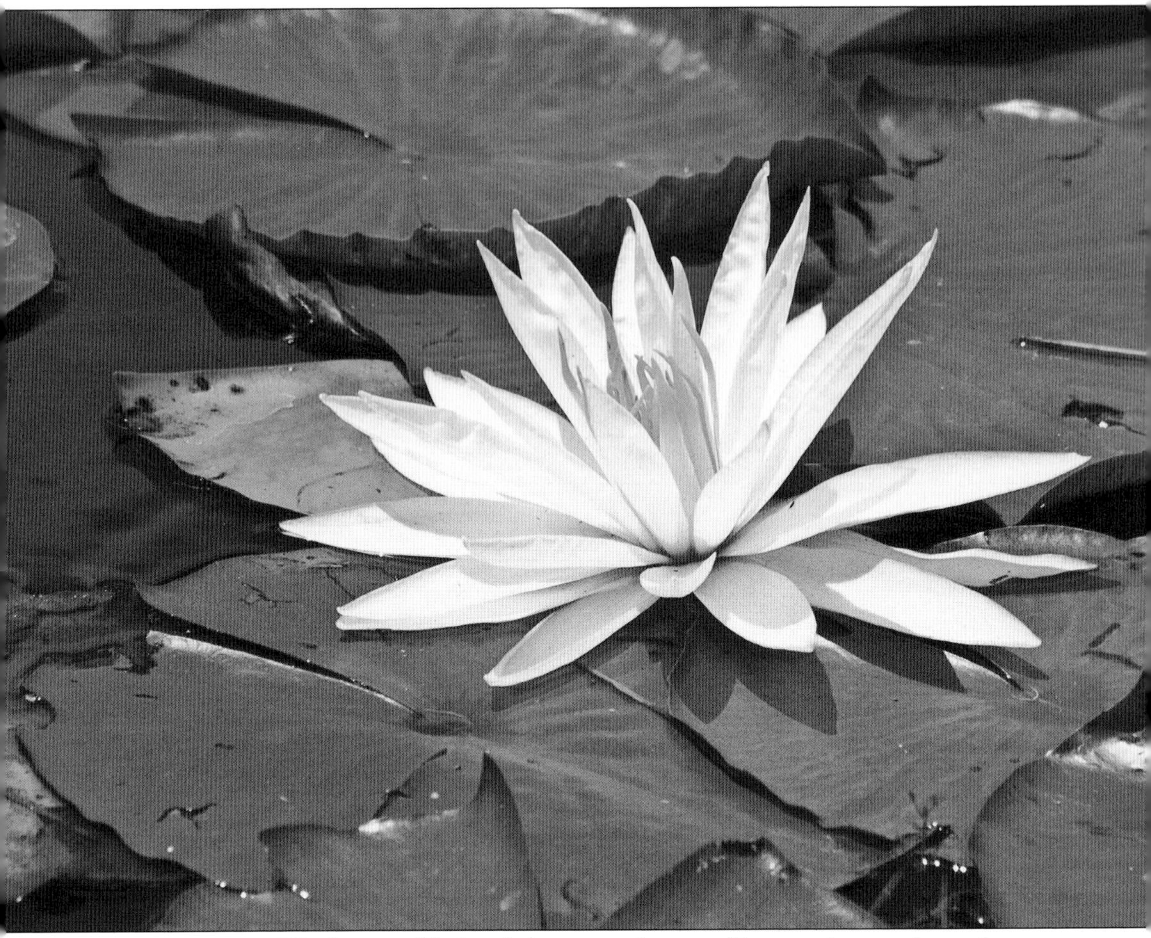

Every season at Woolaroc is filled with beauty and magic. Two ponds near the main entrance are a popular location for families to stop and pose for photographs before entering the grounds. Water lilies on the pond create wonderful photo opportunities. The natural beauty of the woods, lakes, and rocks drew Frank Phillips to the Osage Hills and it continues to call to people today. (Author's collection.)

Five
Entertaining Phillips Style

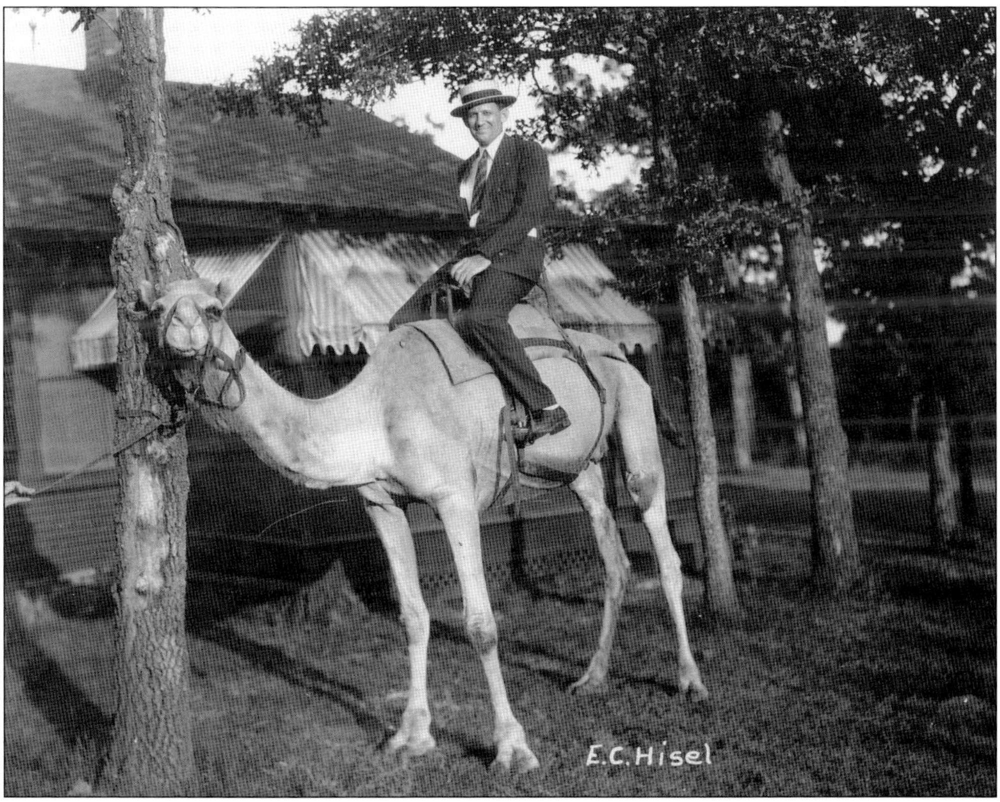

An invitation to visit Frank and Jane Phillips at the lodge at Woolaroc was seldom turned down. For young Phillips Petroleum executives, it was a mark of favor. Business associates from the East Coast found their visits to be exotic and fascinating. Riding on a camel, milking buffalo, shooting, water skiing, boating, swimming, and joining in sing-alongs were just a few of the activities enjoyed at the lodge. E.C. Hisel's visit to Woolaroc, captured in this photograph, included a camel ride. Entertaining Phillips style meant all would have a good time.

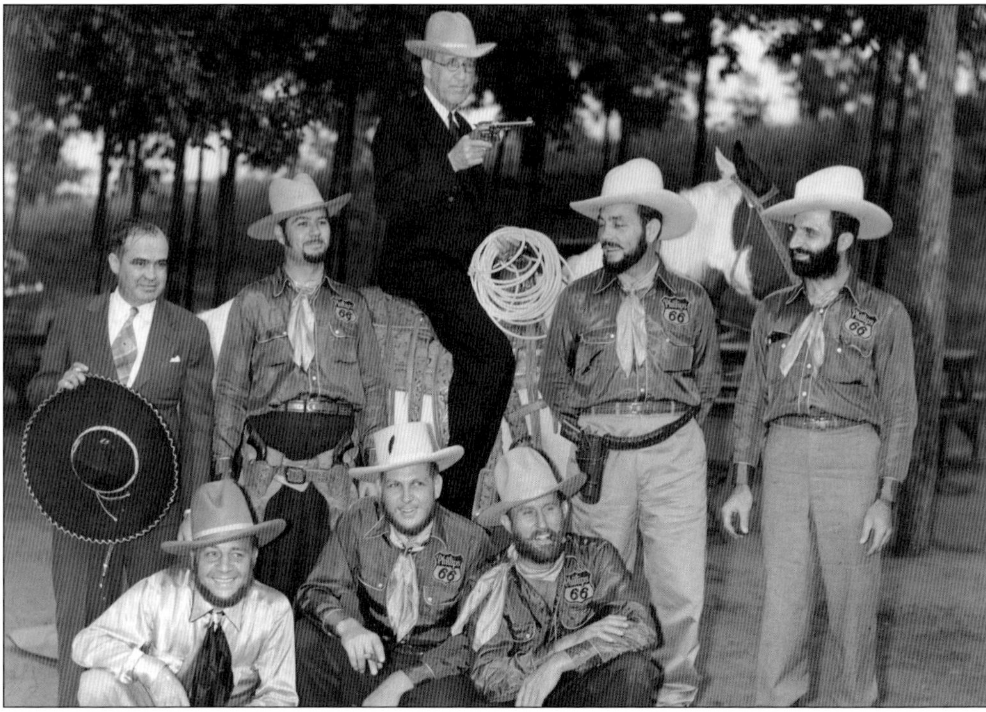

Frank Phillips loved the American West and its varied and colorful history. He embraced the spirit of the West when he entertained at Woolaroc. Pictured here on horseback, Frank draws a six-shooter while his guests, dressed in cowboy-inspired garb, take in the sights at Woolaroc. For Phillips, the lodge, ranch, and (later) museum were useful business tools. Woolaroc proved to be the perfect place to take business associates, employees, and executives for meetings away from the confined atmosphere of the boardroom.

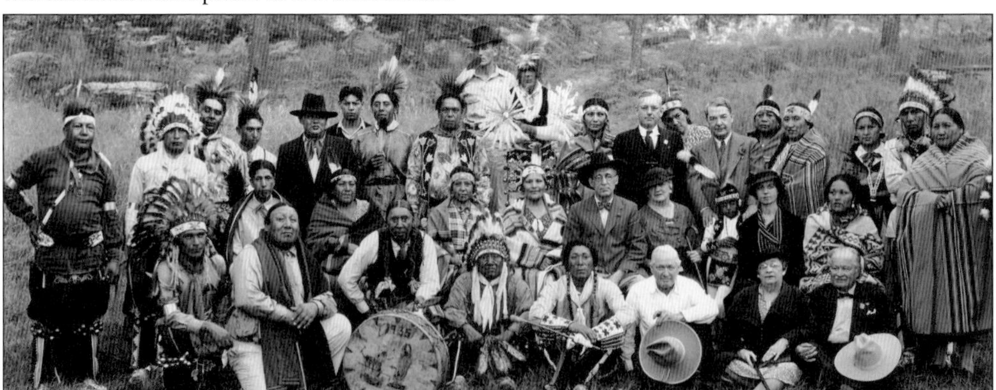

Politicians were frequent visitors to Woolaroc at the invitation of Frank and Jane Phillips. Governors, senators, congressmen, and local officials visited Woolaroc, and photo ops were plentiful. Posing with a group of Pawnee and Sioux American Indians brought to the ranch by Wild West Show impresario Pawnee Bill (first row, far right), Oklahoma governor E.W. Marland and his young wife, Lydie, pose for a photograph. Frank (in his dark cowboy hat) and Jane (in her fashionable hat with a bow) are flanked by American Indians to their left and, to the right, Lydie Marland (in a black ensemble with a striped scarf). Governor Marland (standing above his wife) rests his hand on the shoulder of one of the American Indian children.

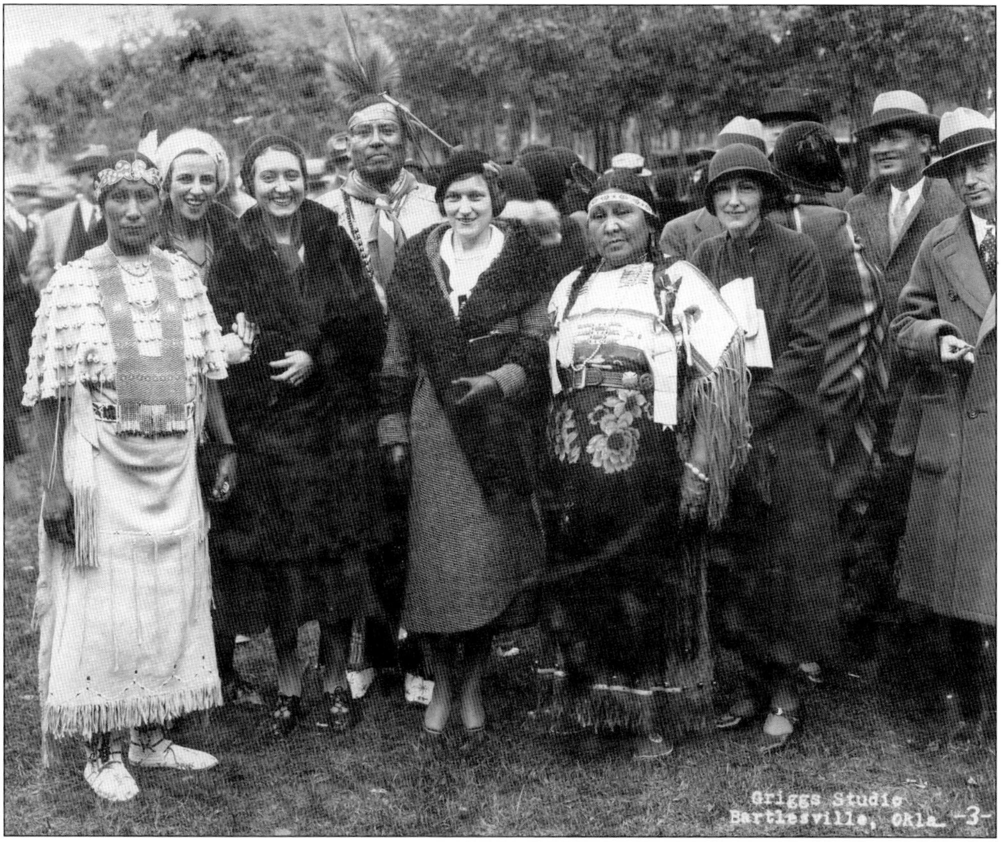

Various organizations began to seek out Clyde Lake and Woolaroc as a place to hold gatherings. Frank and Jane Phillips were only too happy to host events at the ranch. Phillips believed that he had been blessed with much and had an obligation to give back to the community. Members of the Traffic Clubs of America post for a photograph with American Indian tribal members brought to entertain guests with their traditional songs and dances.

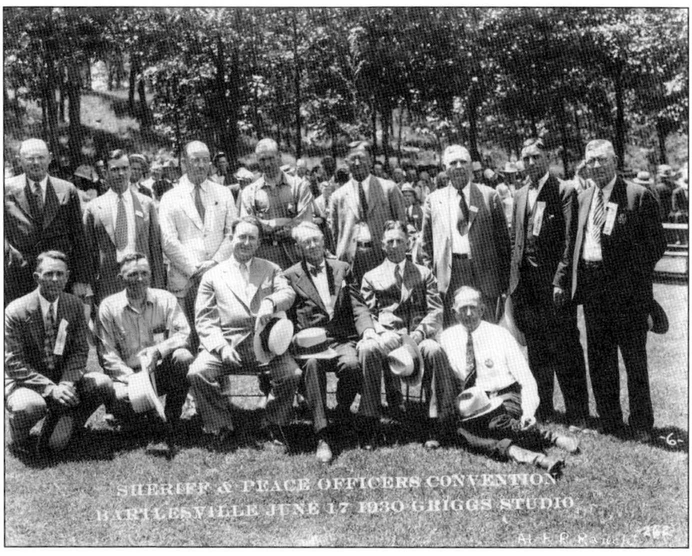

During the territorial period, Oklahoma was wild and untamed. Outlaws found safe haven in the gulleys, ravines, and rolling hills of what would become Osage County. Woolaroc was the perfect locale for the Sheriff & Peace Officers Convention in June 1930. Delegates to the conference take time to enjoy the grounds at Clyde Lake.

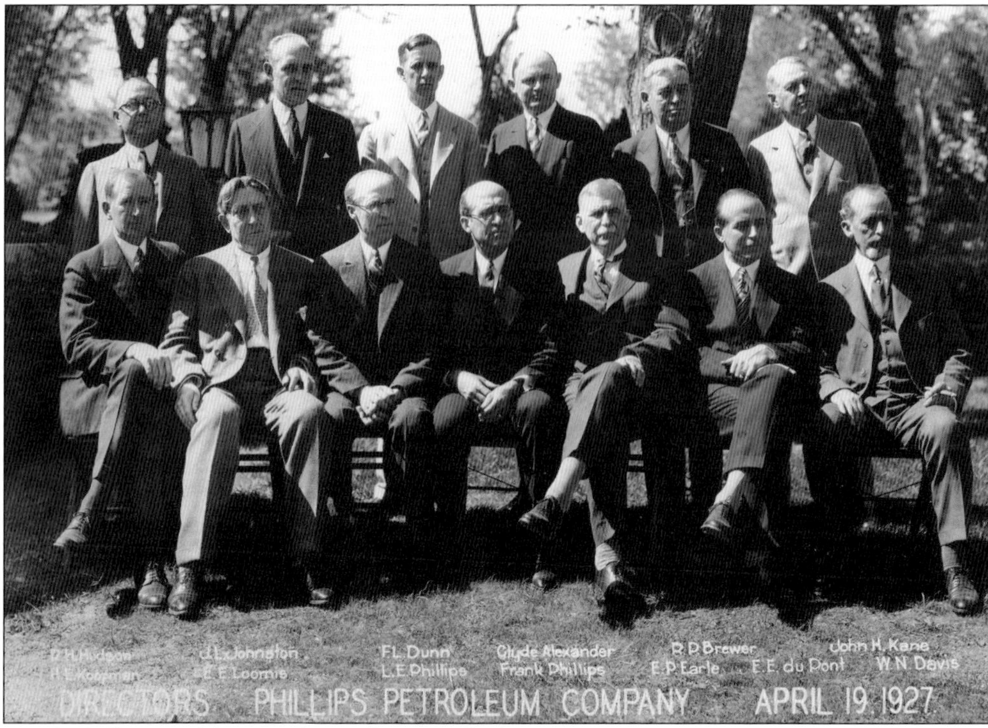

Frank Phillips used his ranch as a location for his executives from Phillips Petroleum to meet outside the confines of their offices in downtown Bartlesville. Notables in attendance include John H. Kane (second row, far right), a local attorney; L.E. and Frank Phillips (first row, center); and E.E. du Pont (Eugene E. du Pont Jr.), the son of E.E. du Pont of du Pont chemical.

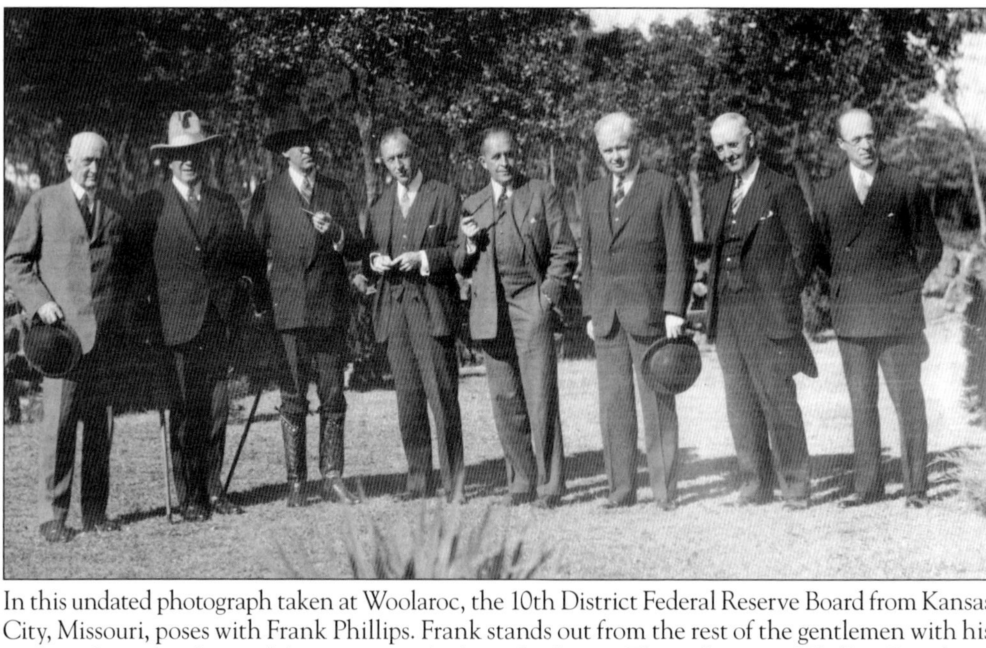

In this undated photograph taken at Woolaroc, the 10th District Federal Reserve Board from Kansas City, Missouri, poses with Frank Phillips. Frank stands out from the rest of the gentlemen with his trademark cowboy hat and dress pants tucked into his boots. The influence of Phillips Petroleum was evident in the visitors that came to the ranch to meet, discuss business, and socialize.

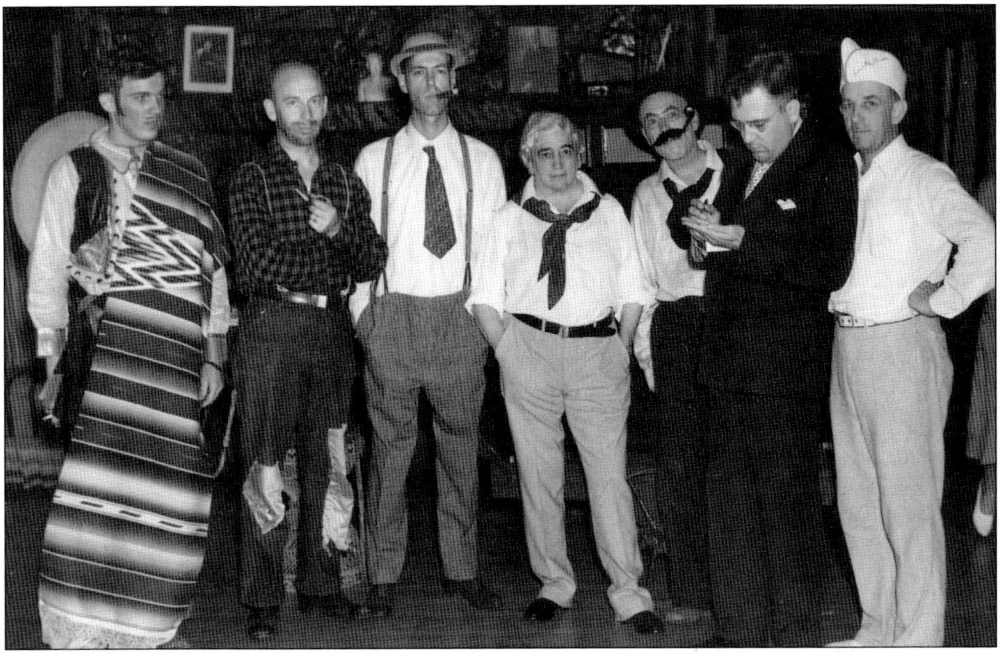

To lighten the mood and steer thoughts away from business and financial matters, the Phillips family loved to throw parties. Costume parties at the lodge were a particular favorite of the family, especially for Jane. She figures prominently in this photograph at a costume party dressed as a man with a dark neck scarf, pictured fourth from the left. Jane's sense of humor was boundless.

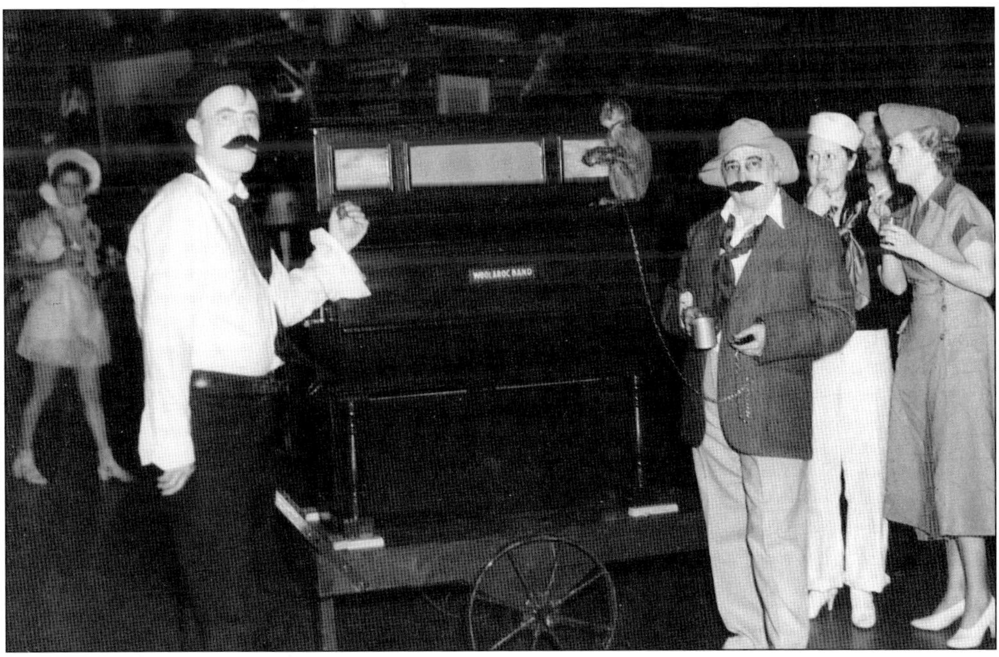

In a scene from the same costume party, Jane, now donning a moustache and hat, takes hold of a monkey on a leash and plays the role of an organ grinder. Flanked by other partygoers, Jane was the life of the party. Today, the organ and the monkey (now preserved via taxidermy) can be seen in the lodge.

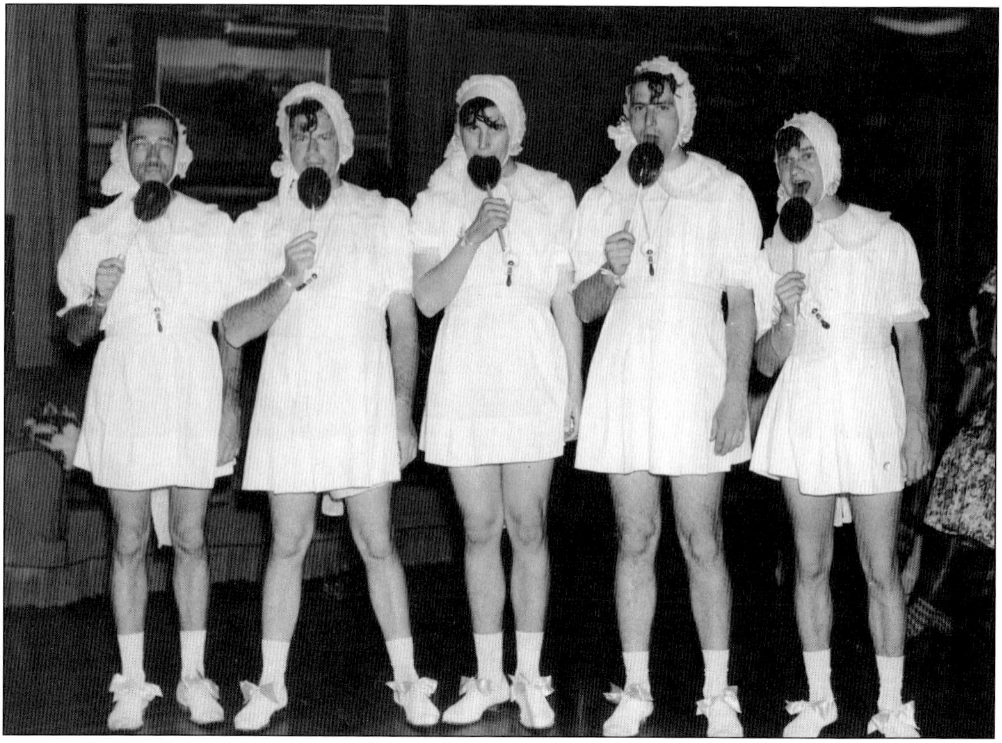

No one was safe at one of the Phillips costume parties. From left to right, C. Granville, Dean Low, Marcus Low, Max Minning, and Walter Granville all take part in one of the costume parties dressed as babies. Many of these parties were held on weekends when they were not entertaining business associates or large groups. The family's private parties were held for the enjoyment of the younger members of the family and gave Frank and Jane great pleasure.

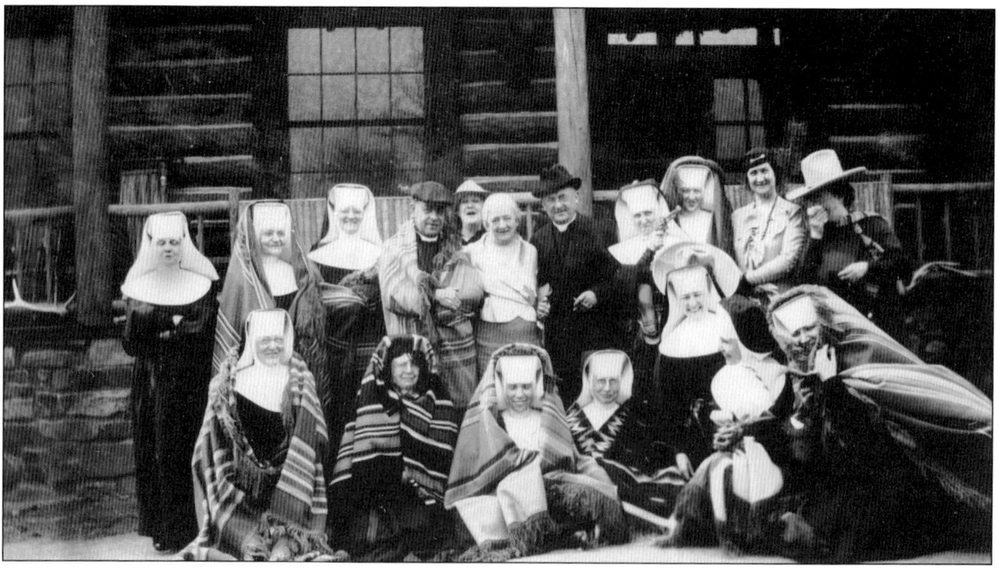

Frank and Jane also opened the doors of Woolaroc to members of the religious clergy. On one visit, a group of Ursuline nuns embraced the spirit of Woolaroc and posed outside the lodge wrapped in Indian blankets. Their time at the lodge was a dramatic change of pace from their convent.

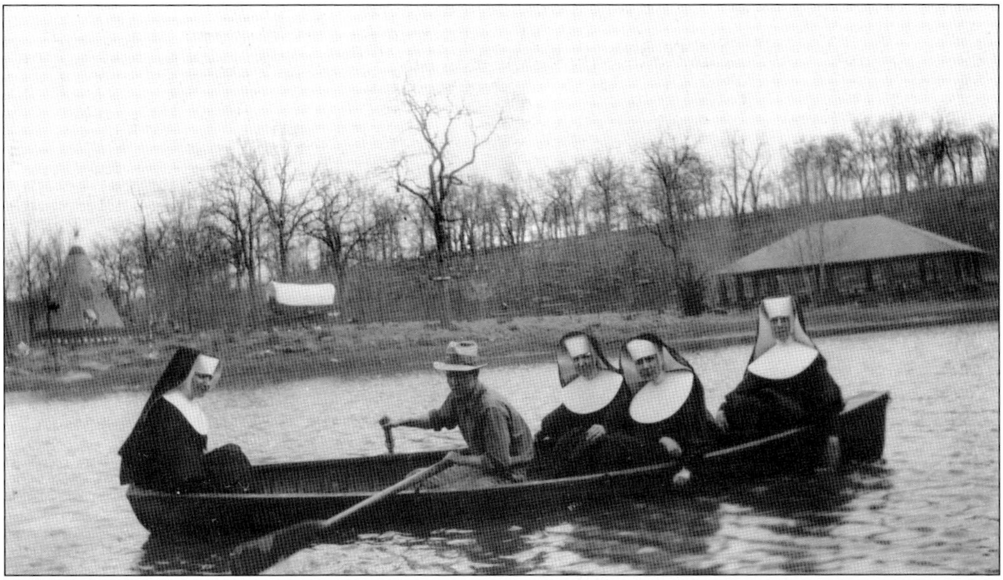

With the assistance of ranch manger Grif Graham, some of the nuns take to the waters of Clyde Lake and enjoy and afternoon of boating. Boating was a favorite pastime at Woolaroc, which was enjoyed by the family and their guests at events.

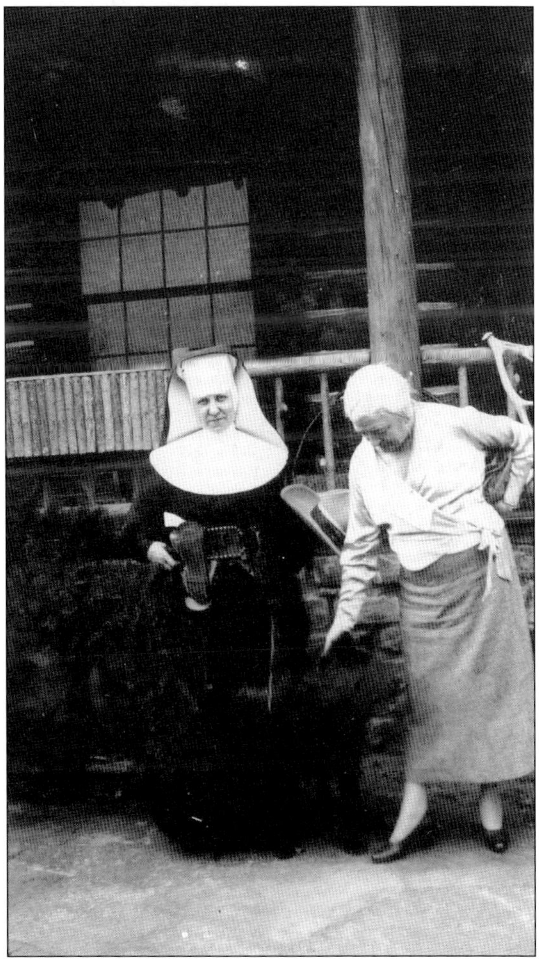

Under the watchful supervision of Jane Phillips, this unidentified nun straps on a gun belt and takes hold of a six-shooter. Even nuns were not immune to the lure of the Old West that Woolaroc embraced.

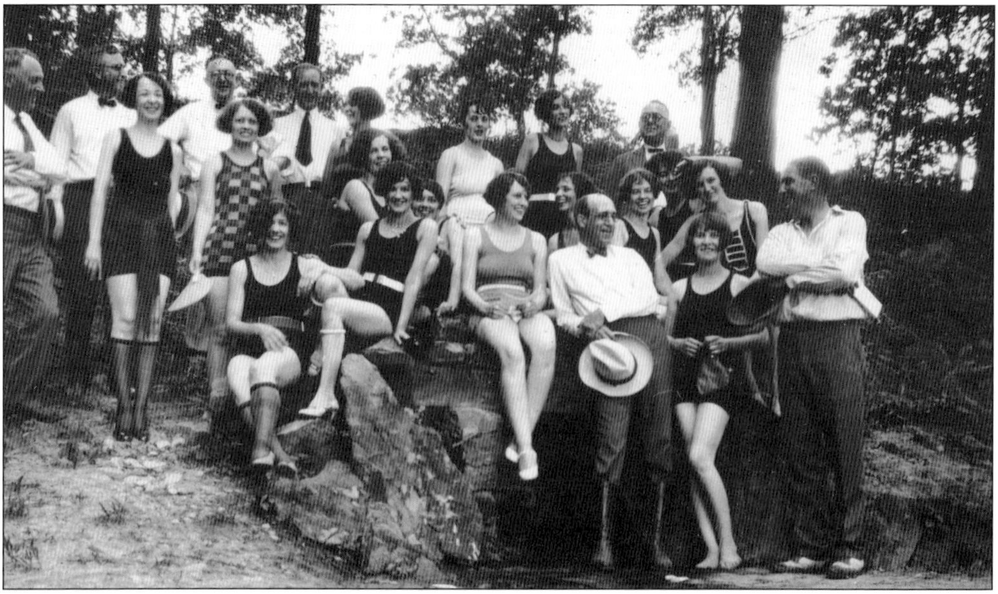

One of Frank Phillips's more pleasant duties as host at Woolaroc came in July 1926 when he was asked to assist in the judging of a beauty pageant held at Woolaroc. The pageant was part of the festivities connected with the Phillips Picnic for company employees. Here, Phillips, hat in hand and leaning against the rocks, poses with pageant contestants. By today's standards, the bathing suits seem tame, and the fact some of the ladies are wearing knee stockings seems out of place with swimwear.

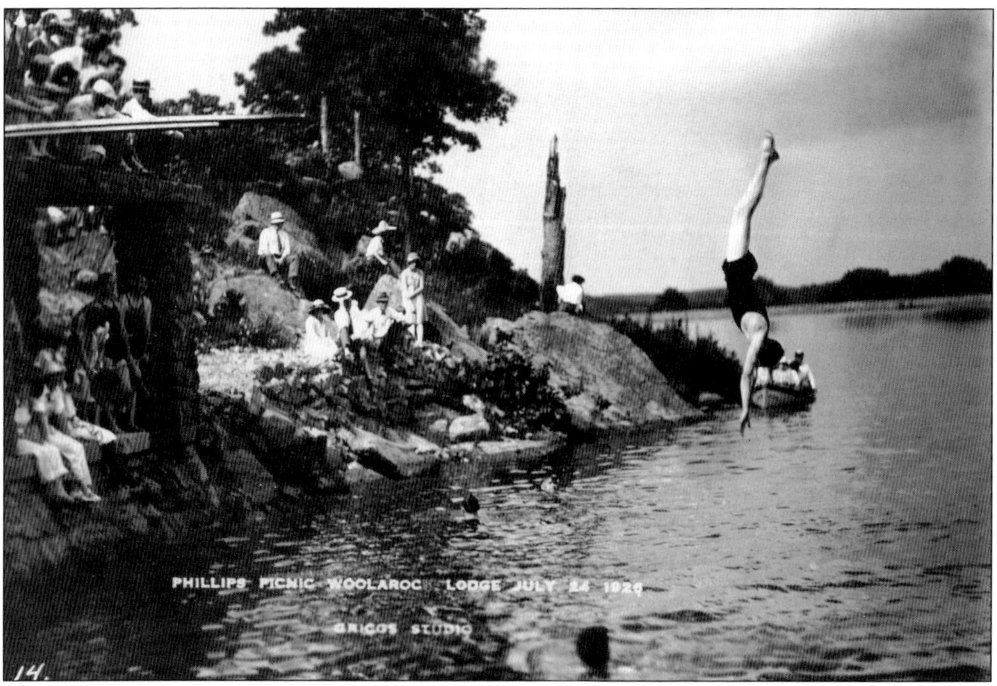

July 24, 1926, marked the first time Frank and Jane Phillips threw the gates of Woolaroc open to the employees of Phillips Petroleum and held the annual company picnic at their weekend retreat. Here, divers take the plunge from the diving boards at the bathhouses at Clyde Lake.

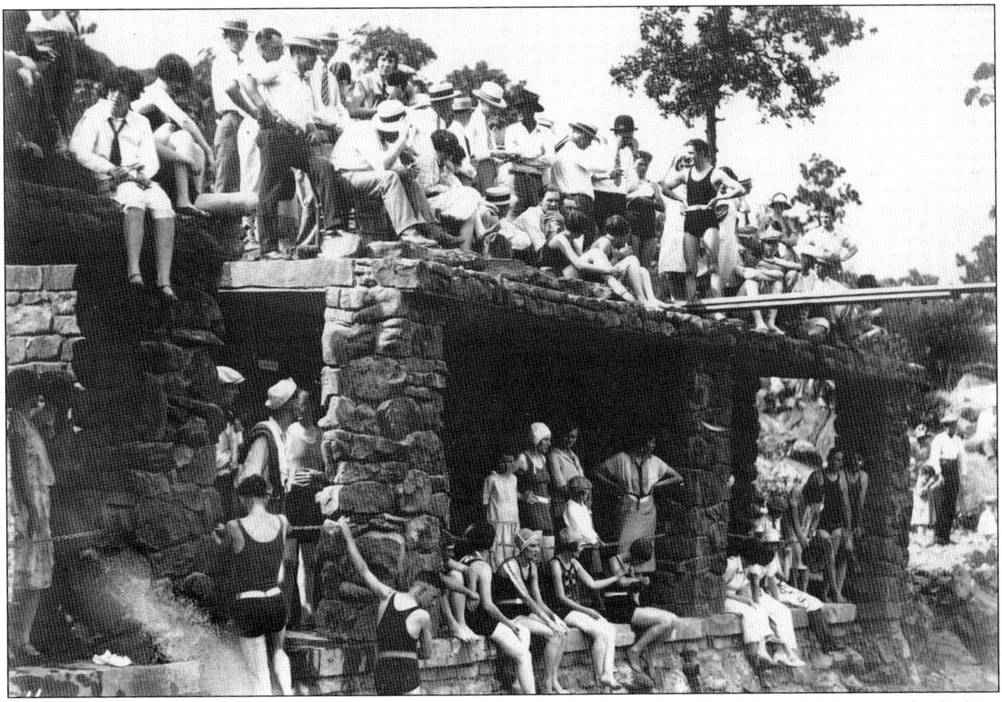

Bathers and non-bathers gather at the bathhouses located on the shoreline of Clyde Lake below the lodge at Woolaroc for the Phillips Company Picnic in July 1926. For men, the fashion of the day called for white shirts and flat straw hats. This would be the first of many events for Phillips employees at Woolaroc.

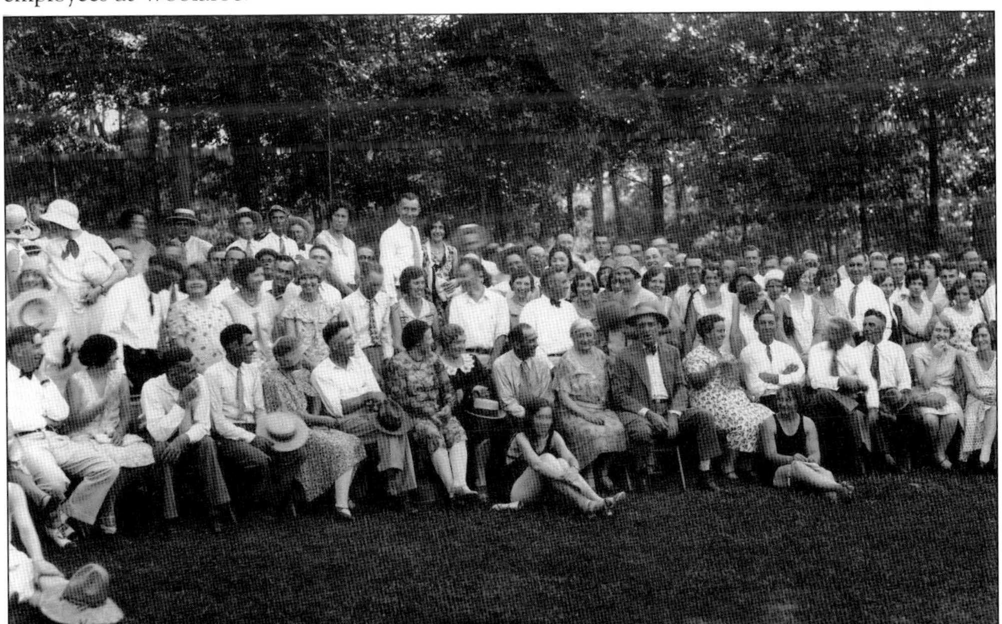

Another large Phillips Petroleum gathering at Woolaroc produces yet another group photograph. Frank and Jane as always are seated in the front row near the center; Frank is donning one of his many distinctive hats.

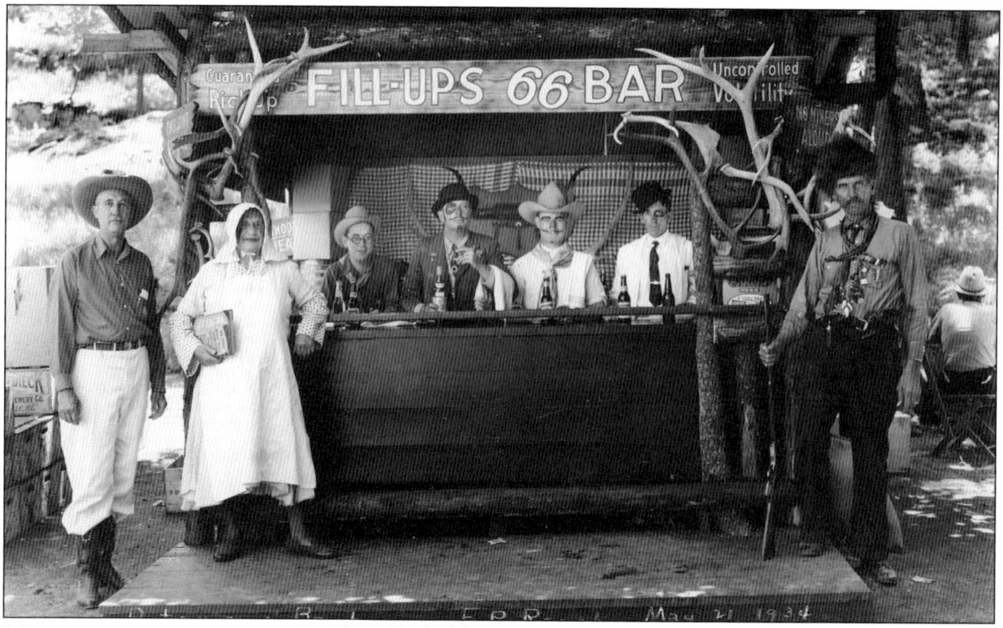

Many civic organizations in Bartlesville held events at Woolaroc or were invited for outings by the Phillips family. In 1934, the Rotary Club Barbecue was held at Clyde Lake. The Fill-Ups 66 Bar was a common backdrop for group photographs. Embracing the spirit of the West, many partygoers dressed the part. A cast of Western characters is seen here bellying up to the bar.

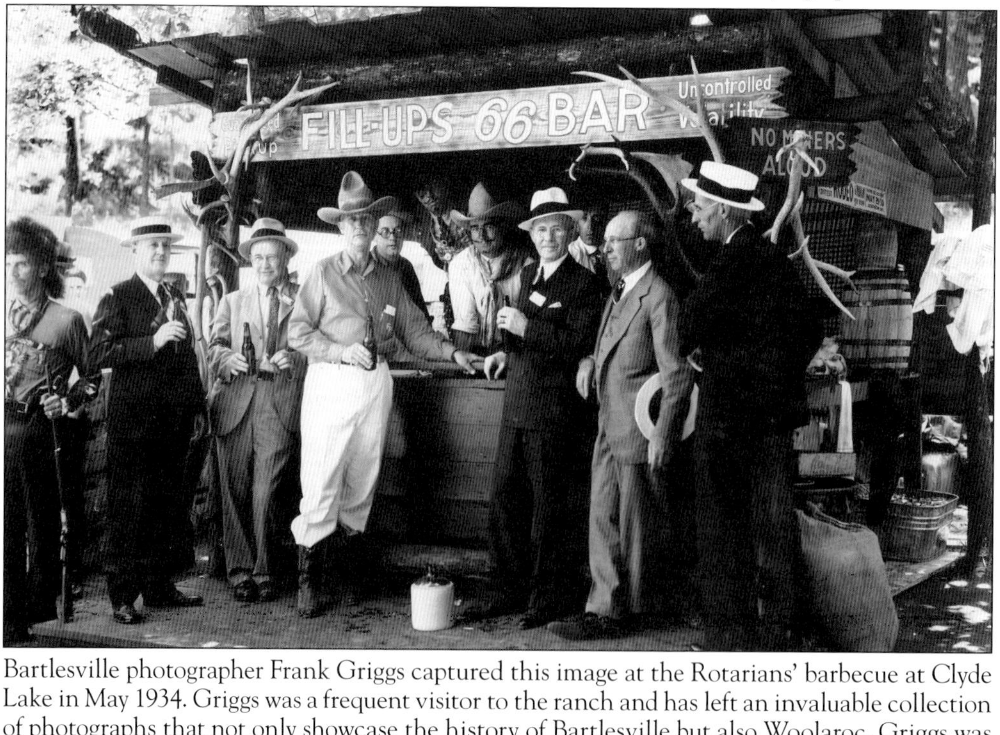

Bartlesville photographer Frank Griggs captured this image at the Rotarians' barbecue at Clyde Lake in May 1934. Griggs was a frequent visitor to the ranch and has left an invaluable collection of photographs that not only showcase the history of Bartlesville but also Woolaroc. Griggs was invited by the Phillips family to capture many of the public and private moments, like this one, for posterity.

In another image by Frank Griggs, two Native Americans are shown at Clyde Lake guarding the cases of beer during Prohibition. Lone Chief Matlock (Pawnee) and Lone Wolf (Pawnee) were brought to the ranch by the Wild West Show promoter Pawnee Bill. Native Americans of many tribal affiliations were present at the ranch when Frank and Jane Phillips entertained.

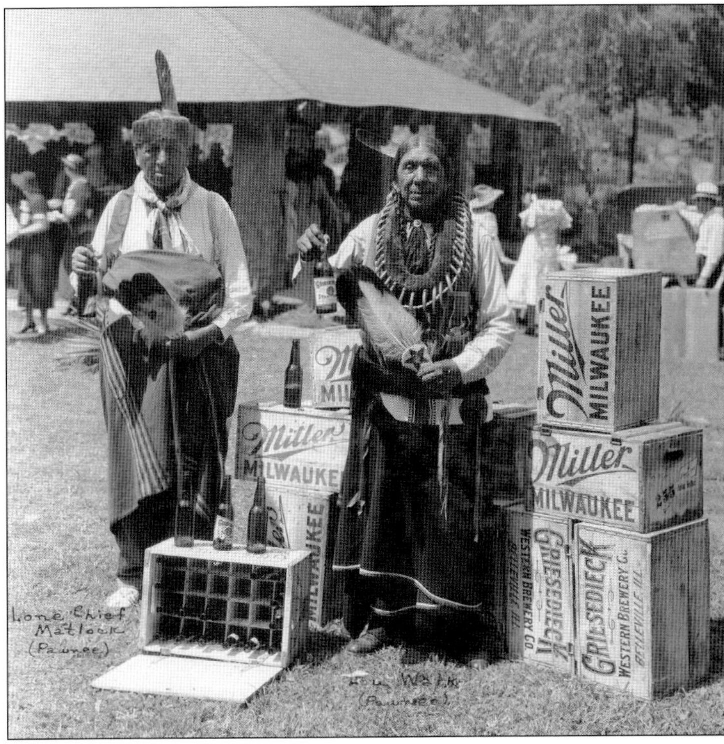

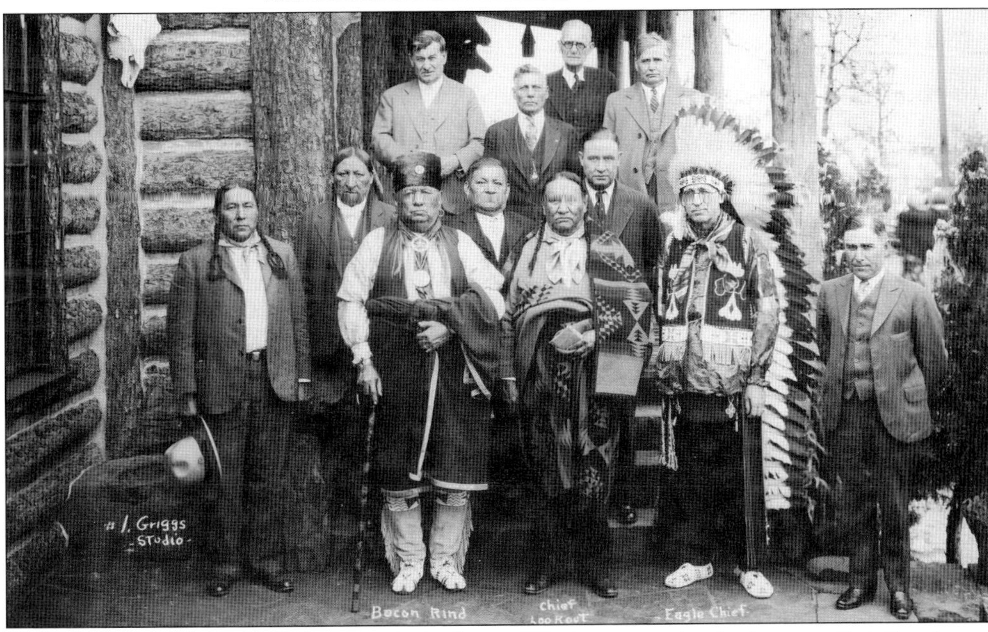

One of the proudest moments for Frank Phillips at Woolaroc was the day he was officially adopted into the Osage tribe. In March 1931, the dining room of the lodge was filled with over 100 people gathered to wish Frank well. Again, Frank Griggs captured the event for posterity and left a visual record. On the steps of the lodge, Frank Phillips (Eagle Chief) is pictured with Osage Chiefs Bacon Rind and Fred Lookout; they are posing for Griggs's camera. From time to time, Osage tribal leaders would hold meetings at Woolaroc with their Eagle Chief playing the role of host.

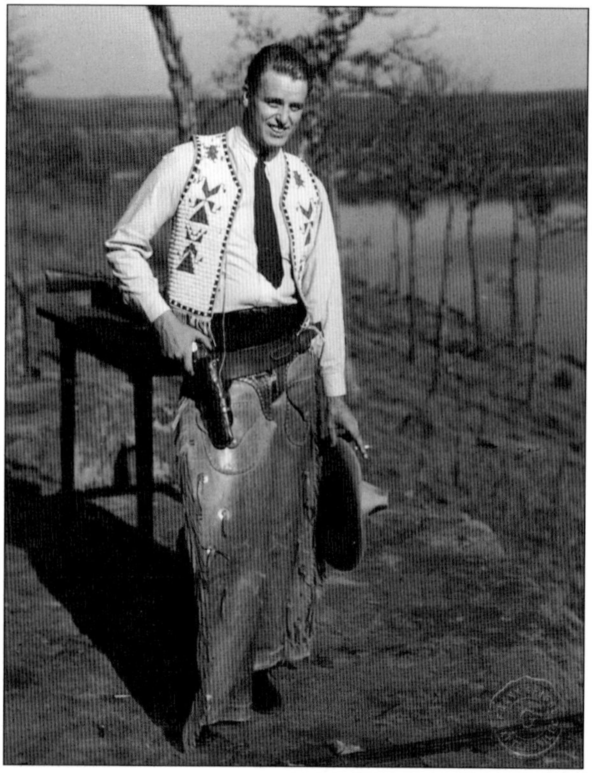

Everyone who visited Woolaroc could not help but embrace the spirit of the West. Elliott Roosevelt, the son of Pres. Franklin D. Roosevelt and First Lady Eleanor Roosevelt, visited the ranch. Despite the fact that Frank Phillips was a staunch Republican, the son of the Democratic president was welcomed warmly.

Woolaroc lore holds that, on his initial hunt, young Roosevelt was given a gun that did not fire properly or was outfitted with blanks. After a frustrating day of hunting buffalo, ranch manger Grif Graham was said to have taken Roosevelt's gun and felled a buffalo with one shot. On another day of hunting and with a proper rifle, Roosevelt showed that he was a plainsman and shot this buffalo that weighed 1,300 pounds.

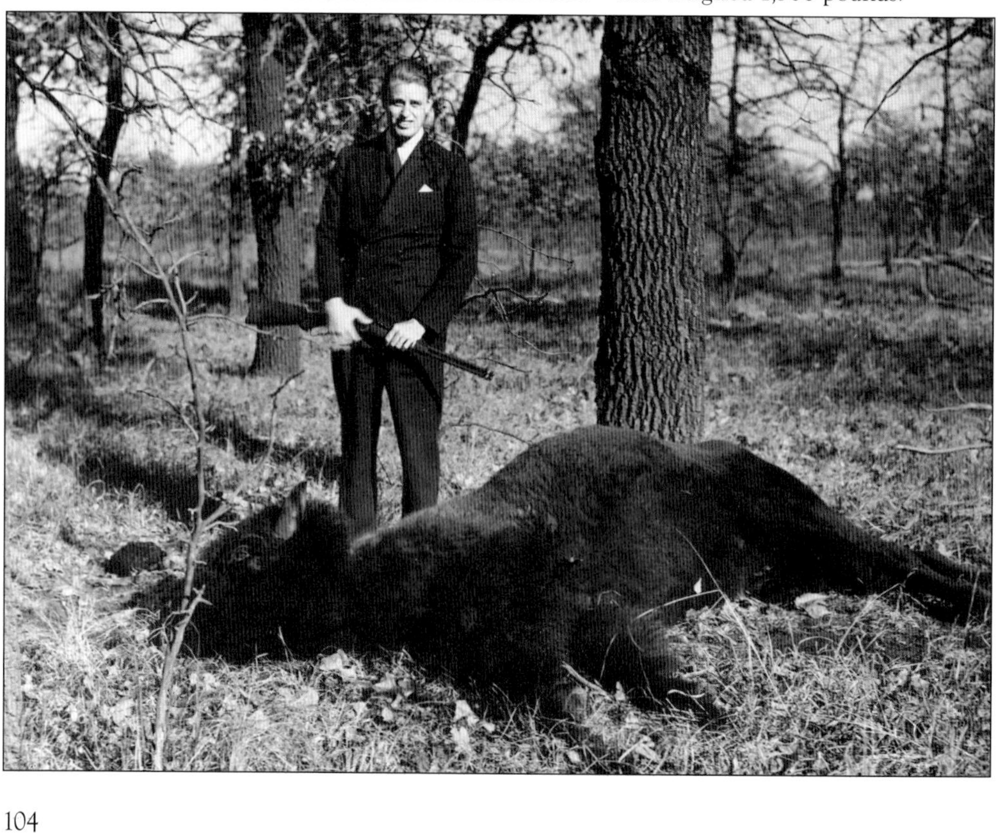

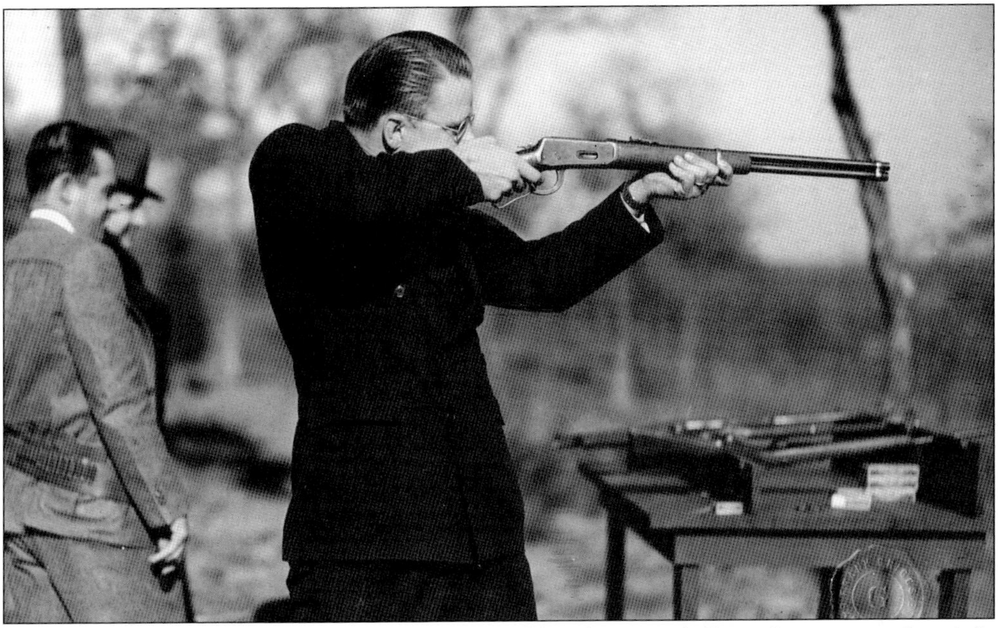

With onlookers behind, Elliott Roosevelt shows off his shooting skills, with a proper rifle, while visiting at Woolaroc. Shooting, riding, fishing, and hunting were favorite pastimes enjoyed at the ranch by family, friends, and guests.

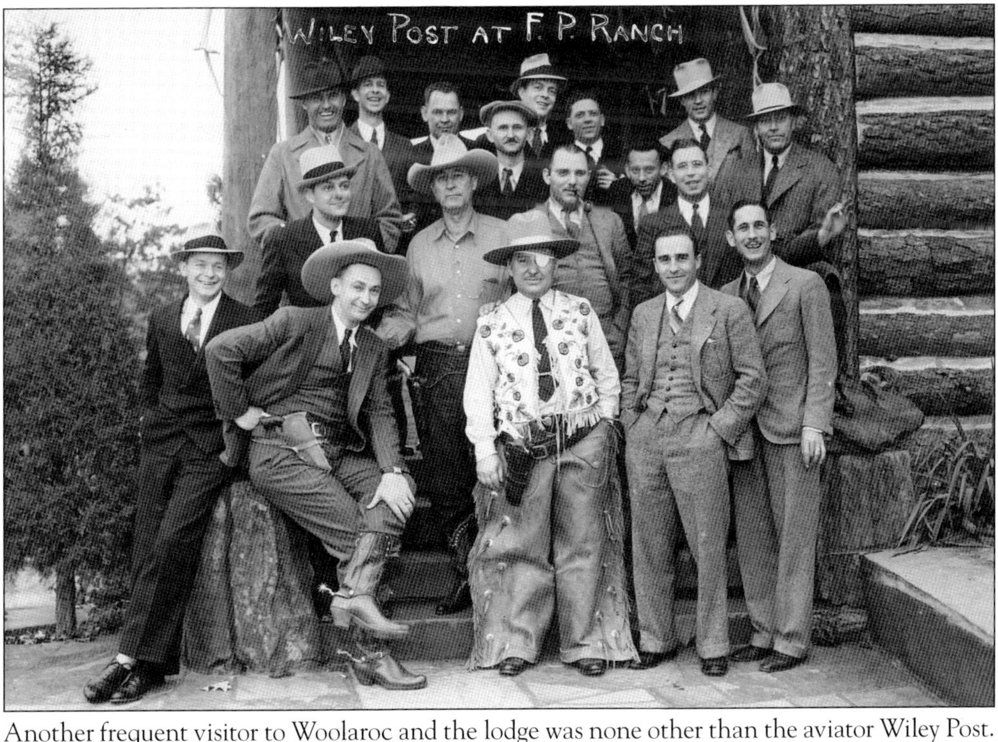

Another frequent visitor to Woolaroc and the lodge was none other than the aviator Wiley Post. Today, one can see Post's signature in the guest book in the lodge alongside that of pilot Arthur Goebel. Here, other visitors to the lodge flank Post dressed in chaps, a large cowboy hat, and decorated vest.

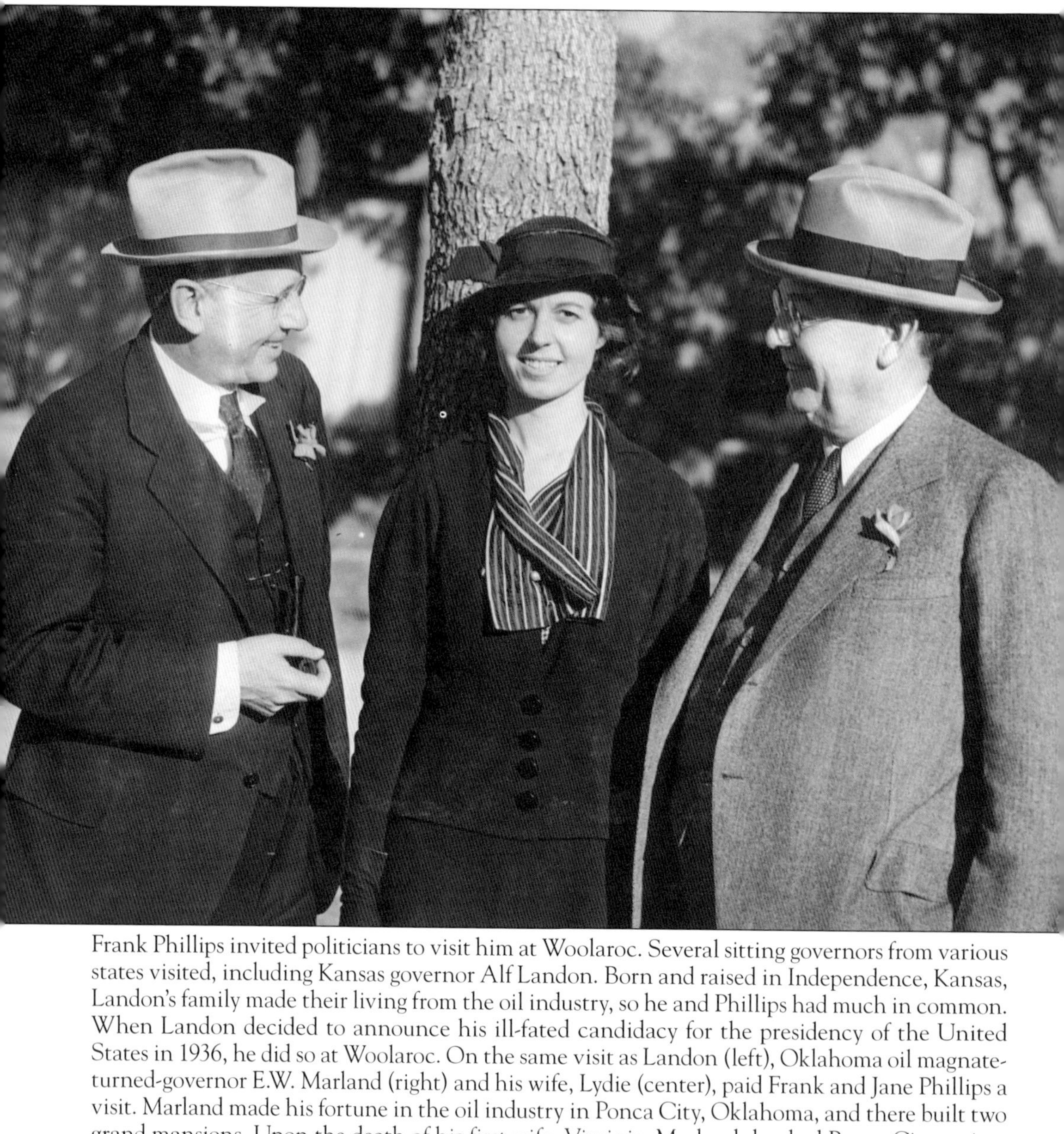

Frank Phillips invited politicians to visit him at Woolaroc. Several sitting governors from various states visited, including Kansas governor Alf Landon. Born and raised in Independence, Kansas, Landon's family made their living from the oil industry, so he and Phillips had much in common. When Landon decided to announce his ill-fated candidacy for the presidency of the United States in 1936, he did so at Woolaroc. On the same visit as Landon (left), Oklahoma oil magnate-turned-governor E.W. Marland (right) and his wife, Lydie (center), paid Frank and Jane Phillips a visit. Marland made his fortune in the oil industry in Ponca City, Oklahoma, and there built two grand mansions. Upon the death of his first wife, Virginia, Marland shocked Ponca City society by un-adopting his adopted daughter and marrying her.

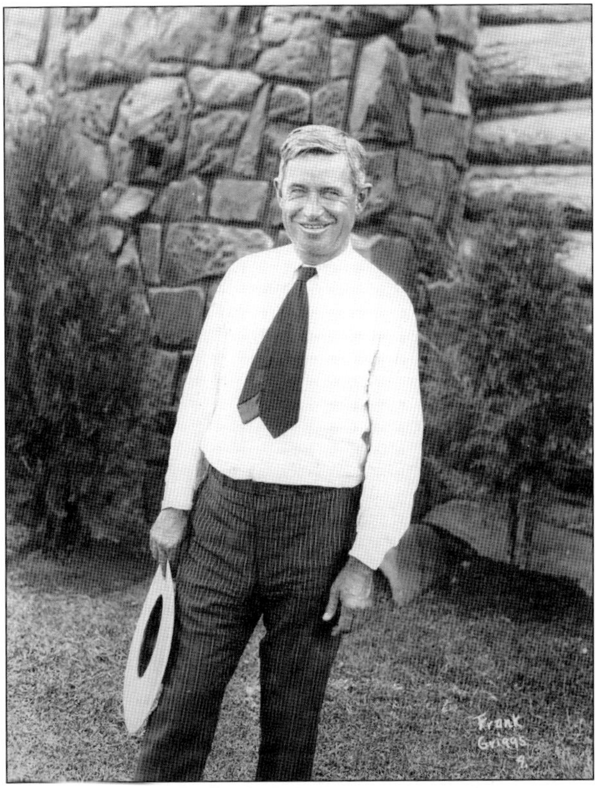

One of the most famous Americans to visit Woolaroc was, without doubt, Will Rogers. Known as the "Cherokee Kid," Rogers was born and raised in Oologah, Oklahoma. A cowboy, comedian, vaudeville performer, writer, and political humorist, Rogers was a friend of pilot Wiley Post. Frank Phillips sponsored post's development of his stratospheric flight suit, and the connection between the three men was the emerging field of aviation. Phillips was fascinated with aviation, as was Rogers.

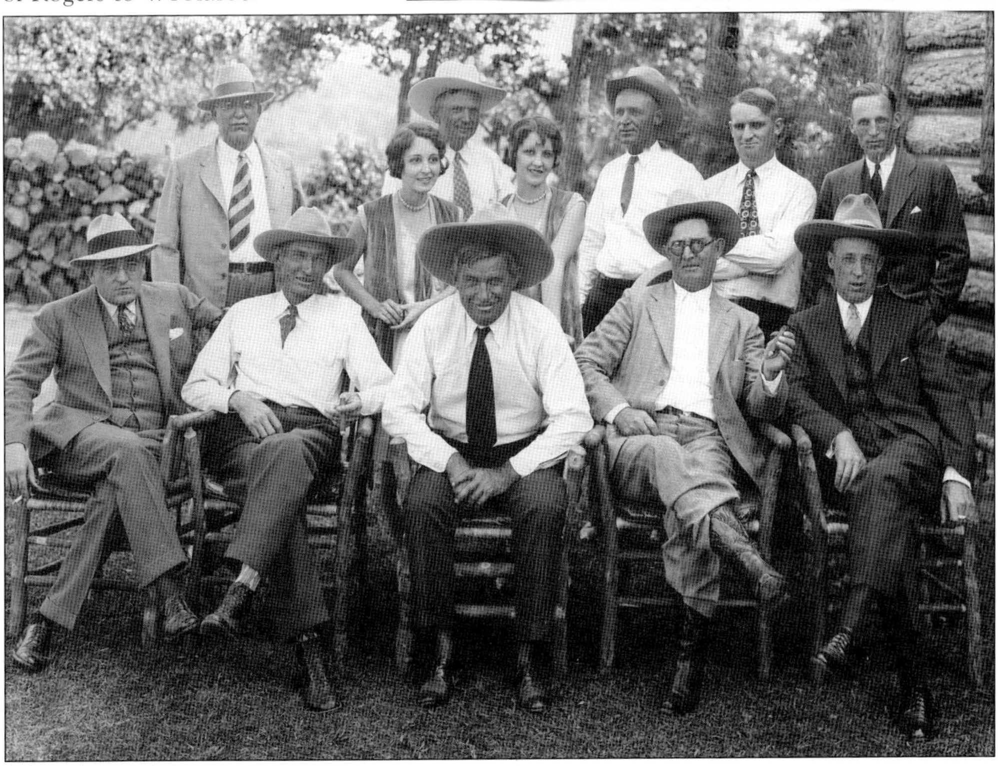

Seated in the center with his cowboy hat tipped back and his dark tie straight, Rogers poses for a photograph on the lawn near the lodge. This is the only documented trip of Rogers to Woolaroc.

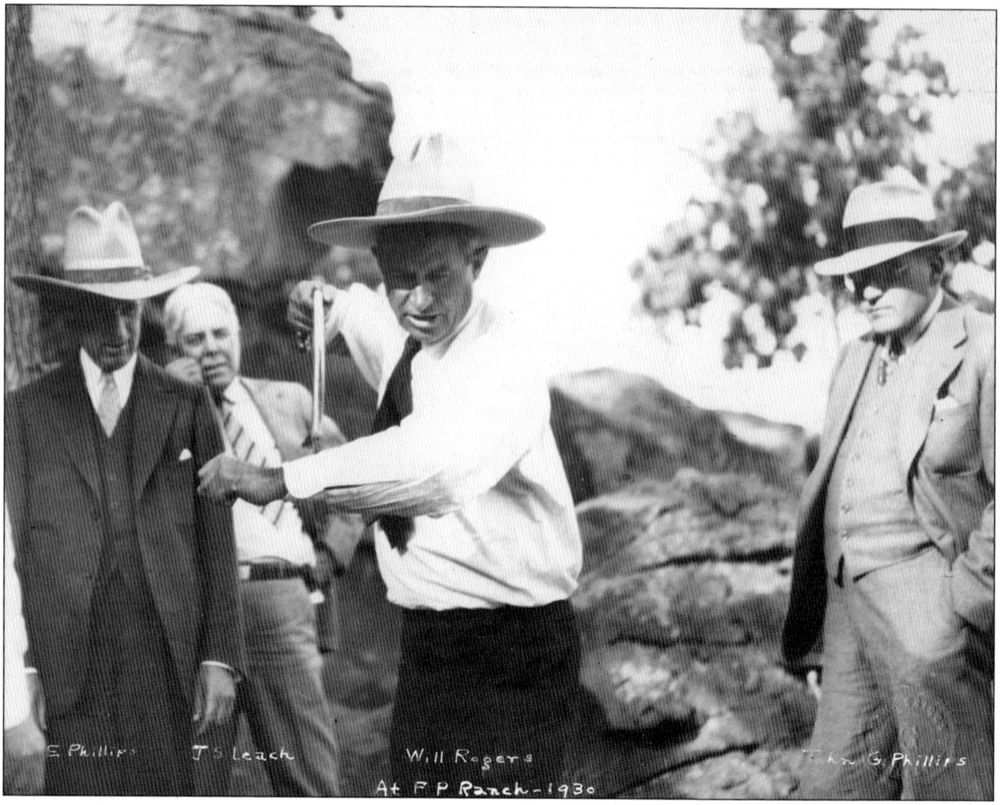

Rogers shows visitors to Woolaroc many of his rope tricks that gained him fame on the vaudeville stage early in his career and in the movies. L.E. Phillips (left), J.S. Leach (rear), and John Gibson Phillips, Frank, and Jane's son John (right) watch in awe at Rogers's prowess with the lariat.

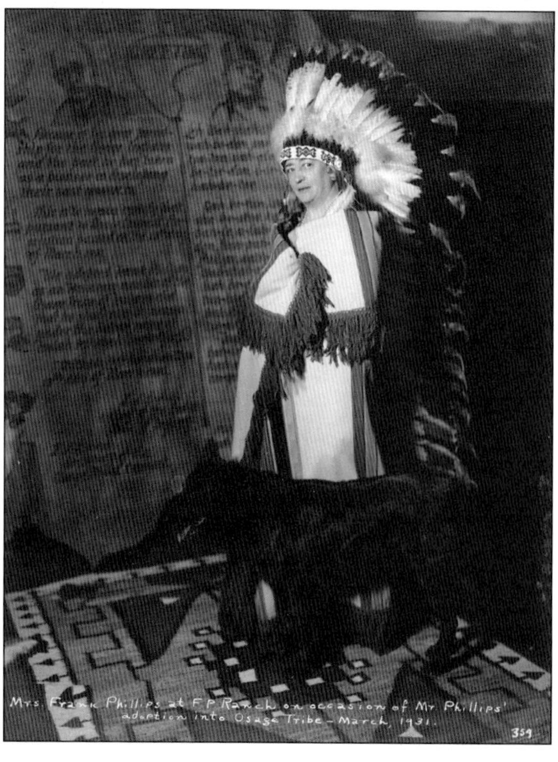

Jane Phillips was also highly respected by members of the Osage tribe. Here, Jane is pictured on the day of Frank's adoption into the tribe. She would also later be adopted into the tribe and presented with gifts, as was the Osage custom. The family passed many happy memories at Woolaroc, and it figured prominently in their business and social lives.

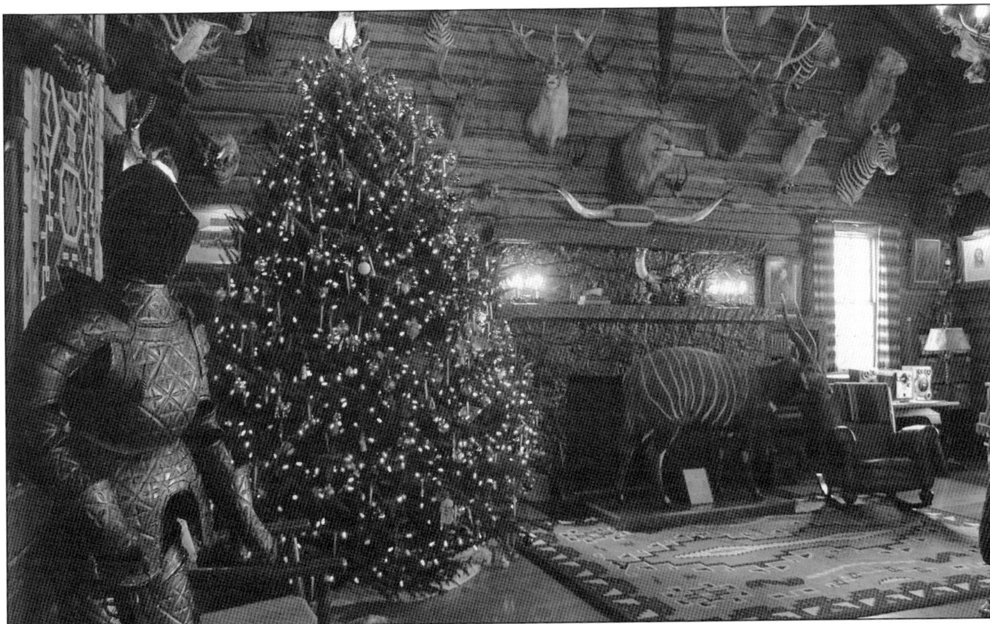

Frank and Jane's beloved lodge hosts several events during the year. One such event is Woolaroc Wonderland of Lights, held each year from Thanksgiving weekend through mid-December. On Friday through Sunday evenings, Woolaroc's gates are open late and visitors can see the ranch lit with over 500,000 holiday lights. Visitors to the lodge can see the enormous Christmas trees and sample hot chocolate and cookies in the dining room. (Author's collection.)

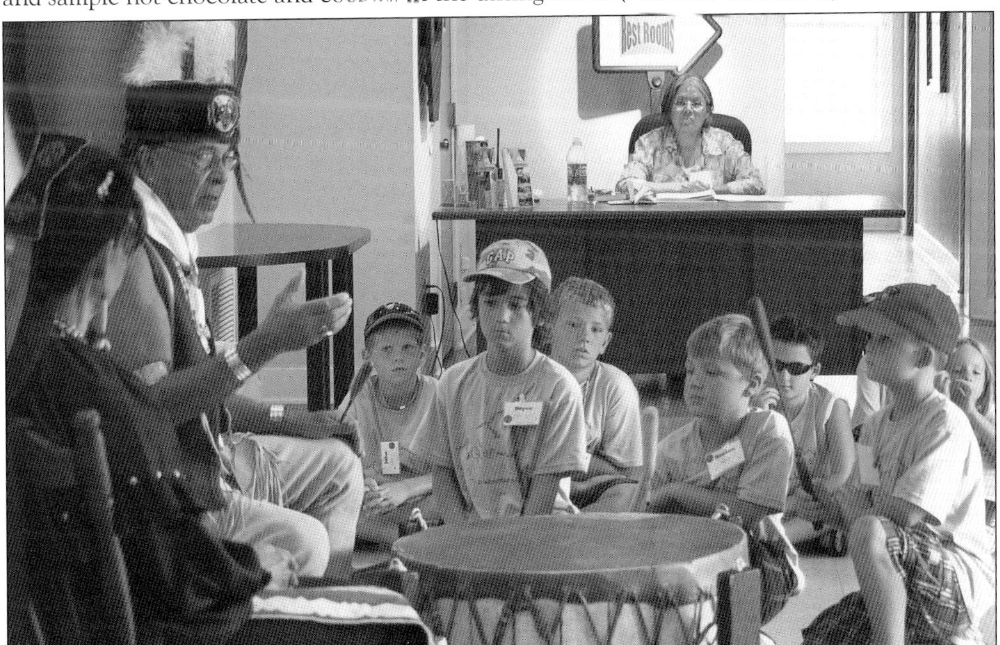

Each summer, Woolaroc is overrun with eager youngsters for two weeks in July when Camp Woolaroc is in session. Youngsters learn about the ranch, animals, nature, history, and the museum and its incredible collections. Here, campers learn about traditional Delaware songs and dances with Dee and Annette Ketchum in the Bunkhouse. (Author's collection.)

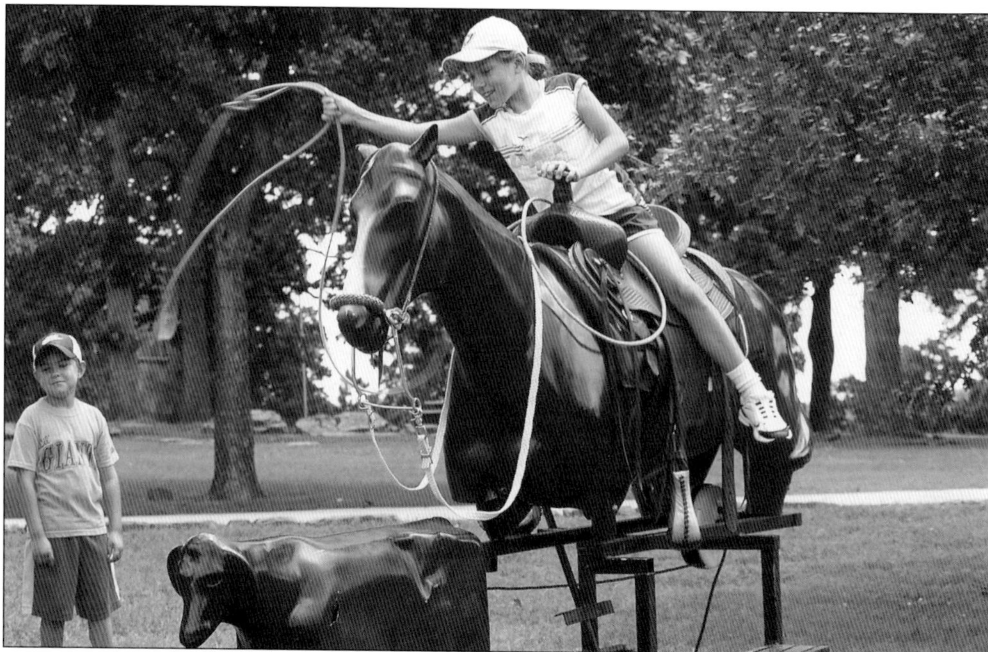

Each June, the grounds of Woolaroc are alive with the sounds of laughter and family fun when Kidsfest rolls into town. With games, activities, entertainment, and food, Kidsfest is a great opportunity for families to share the magic of Woolaroc together. (Author's collection.)

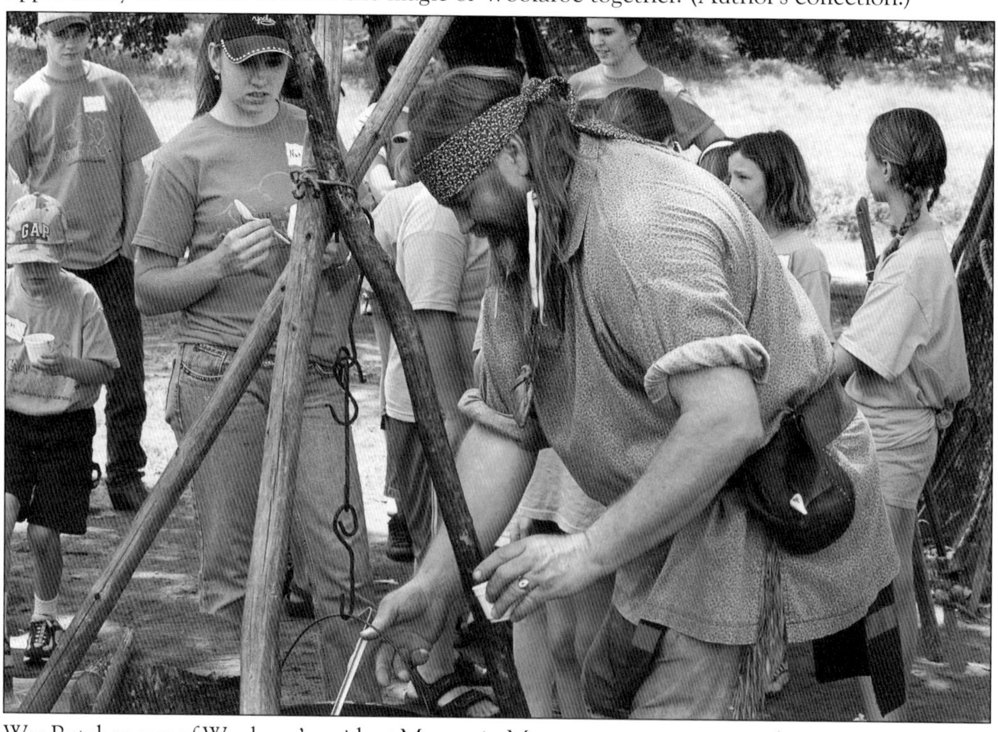

Wes Butcher, one of Woolaroc's resident Mountain Men, serves up some campfire stew to campers at Camp Woolaroc. The Mountain Man Encampment is a favorite attraction for Woolaroc visitors. There, Wes and his brother Roger bring the era of the fur trade to life for visitors. (Author's collection.)

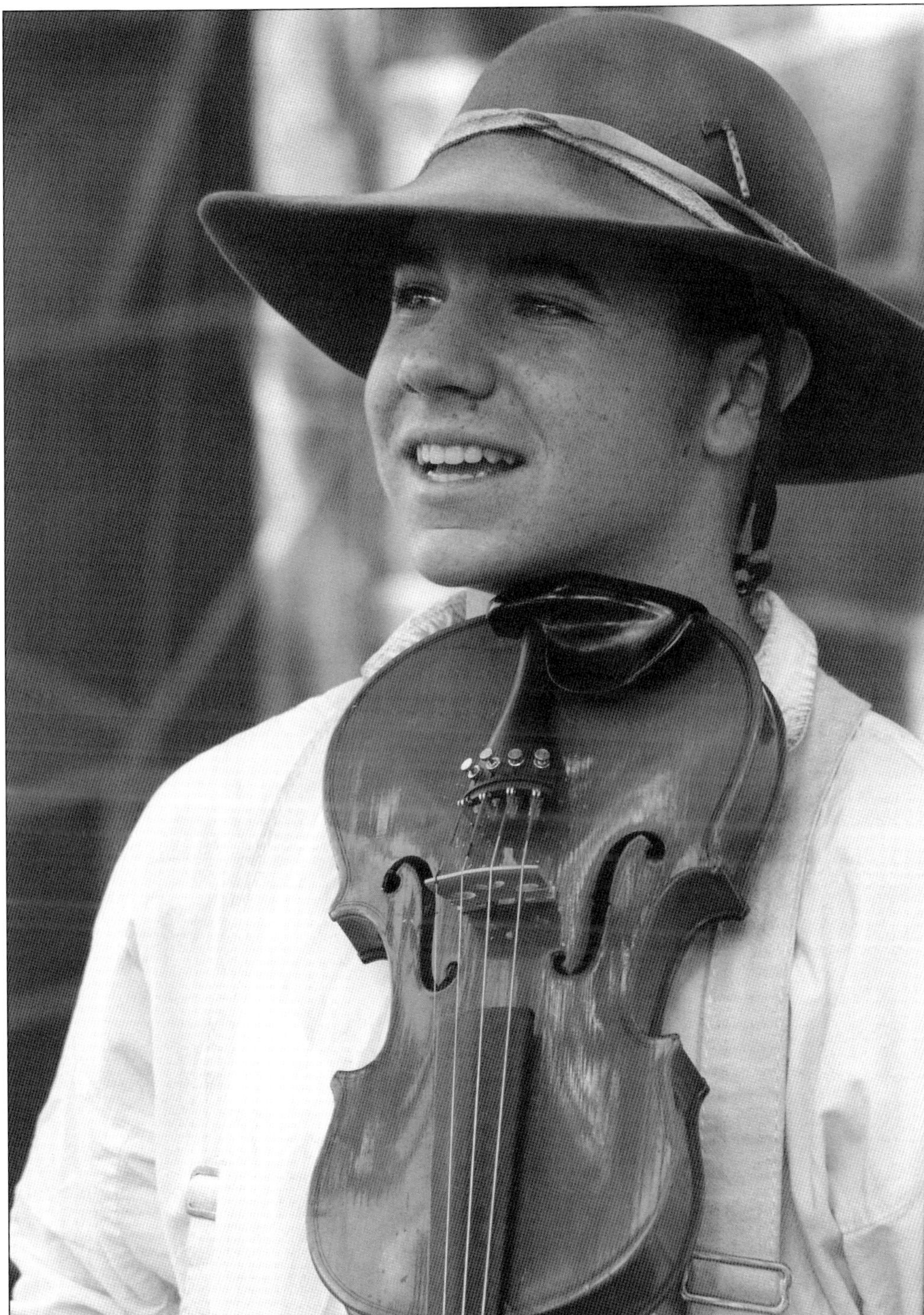

Woolaroc relies upon the support of staff and volunteers to bring history to life for visitors. Tyler Sydebotham plays the fiddle and shares 19th-century music with visitors. Tyler is the fourth generation of his family to volunteer or work at Woolaroc and help preserve Frank and Jane's legacy for future generations. (Author's collection.)

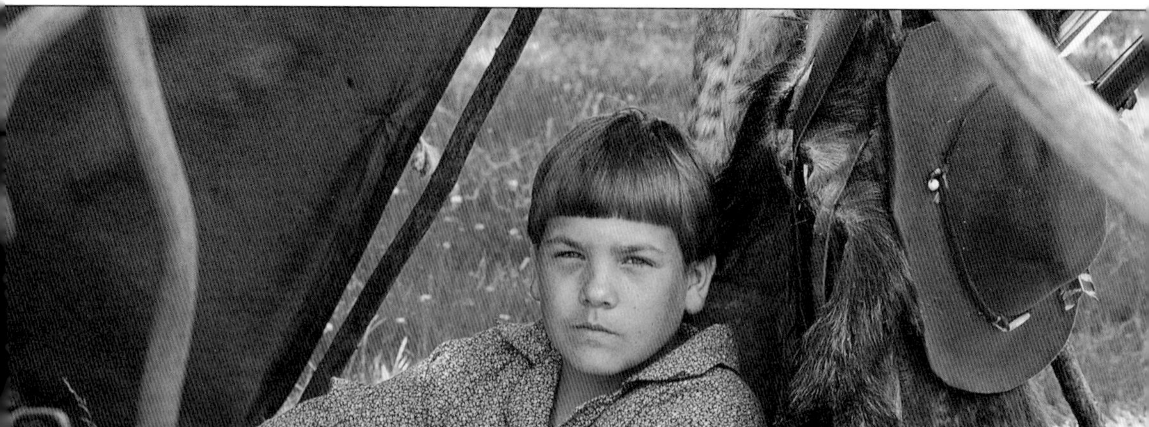

Alex Butcher, affectionately known in the Mountain Man Encampment as Stick-Tight, relaxes on a sunny afternoon. The Mountain Man Encampment provides visitors to Woolaroc a unique glimpse into the lives of European fur traders and trappers that lived in the Osage Hills before organized communities developed in the 19th century. (Author's collection.)

Six

A Reunion Like No Other

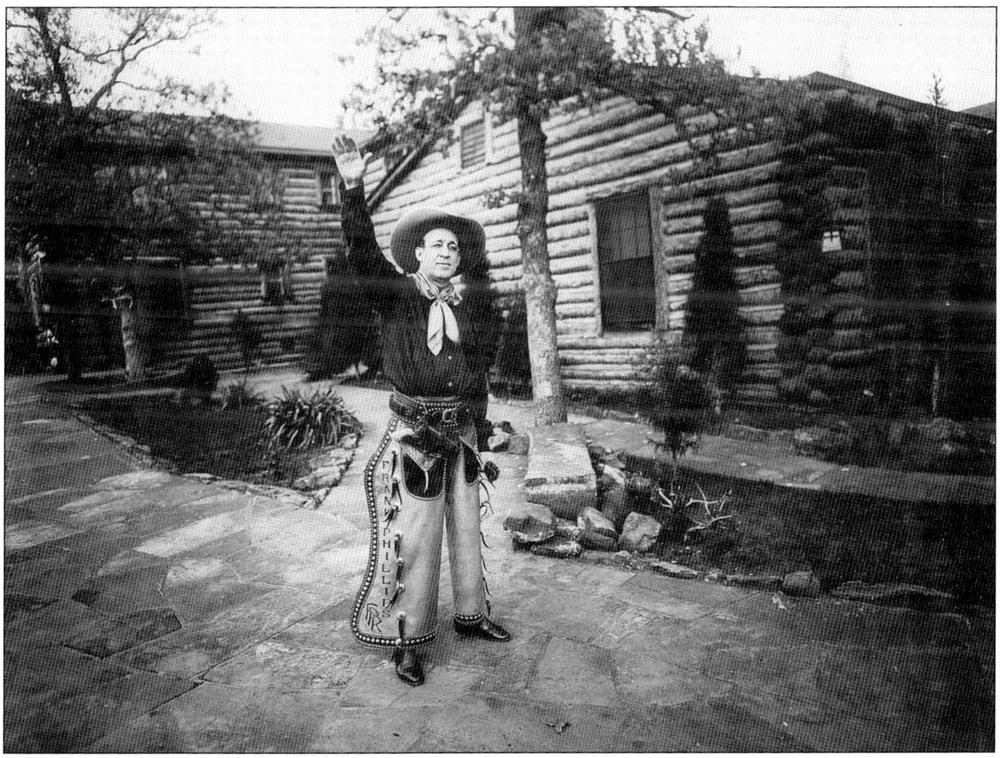

Cattle rustlers, thieves, outlaws, and bandits all found refuge in the rolling Osage Hills that would become Woolaroc. A student of history, Frank Phillips embraced the romance of the Old West and its storied past. To celebrate this history, Phillips threw open the gates of Woolaroc and threw a party the likes of which none had experienced. Dressed in a fine set of leather, hand-tooled chaps presented to him by the Cow Thieves and Outlaws Committee in 1928, Frank Phillips waves to visitors at the lodge. In 1926 with the Wild West Show, in 1927 Early Day Cowboy Picnic, and later the Cow Thieves and Outlaws Reunion, Phillips started a tradition that endures to this day.

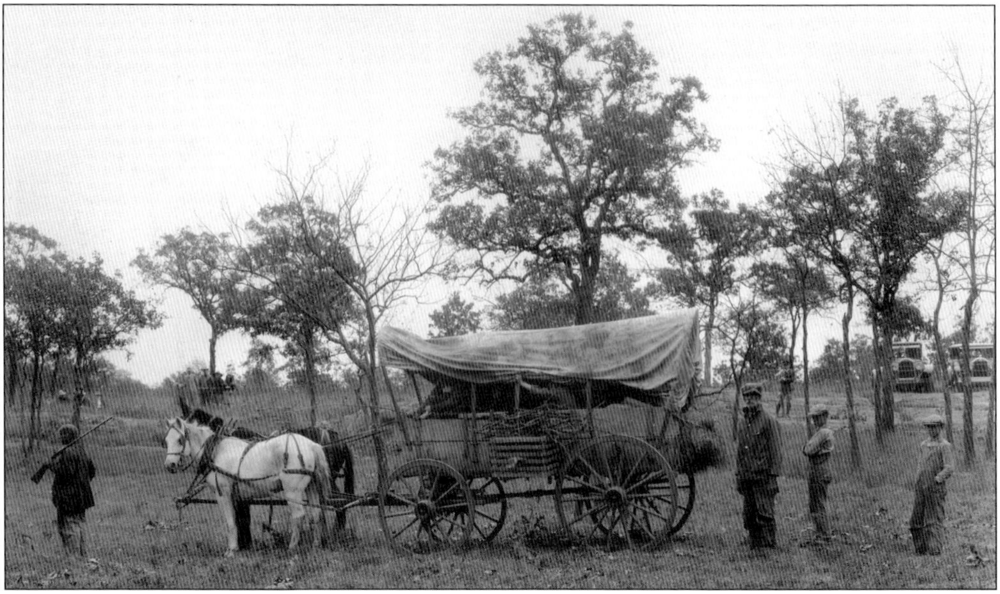

One of the most celebrated figures in American Western history is, without doubt, the cowboy. Moving cattle from Texas to Kansas along the dusty Chisholm Trail, young cowboys created iconic images that are known the world over today. At the Early Day Cowboy Picnic in 1927, Frank and Jane Phillips brought together all the elements of the West—the cowboy, the chuck wagon, the outlaw, and the lawman—for one day at Woolaroc. This would evolve into the famed Cow Thieves and Outlaws Reunion.

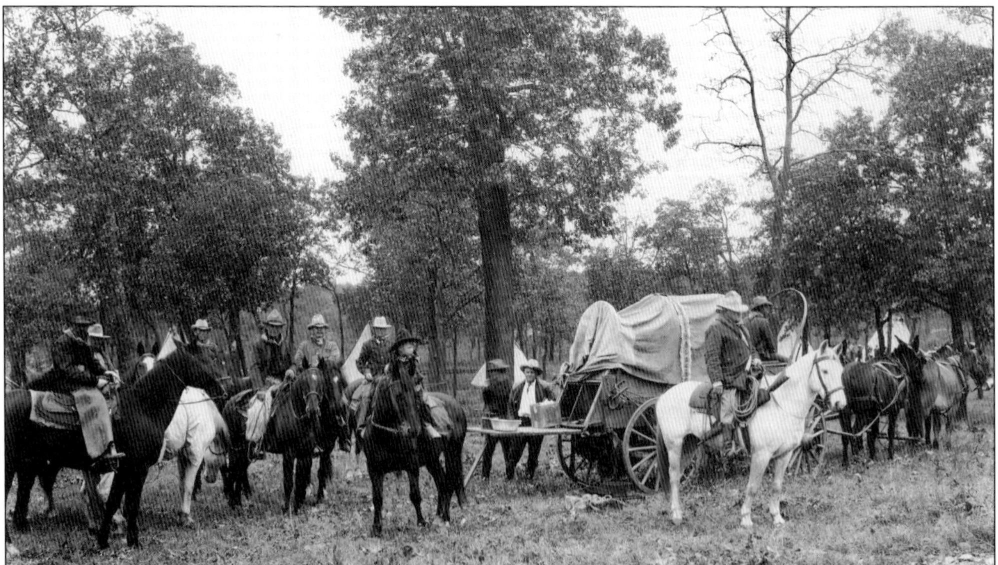

Cowboys move horses and wagons into position to greet and amaze visitors at the first Cow Thieves and Outlaws event in 1929. Held at the Clyde Lake picnic grounds, the event was a huge success for Phillips. An invitation to the Cow Thieves and Outlaws Reunion was highly coveted. True to its name, the event did actually include real-live outlaws, cow thieves, and lawmen who were sworn to leave their shooting irons at the gate in a show of amnesty for one day. A chuck wagon was presented to Frank by local rancher Mort Keefer in honor of the occasion.

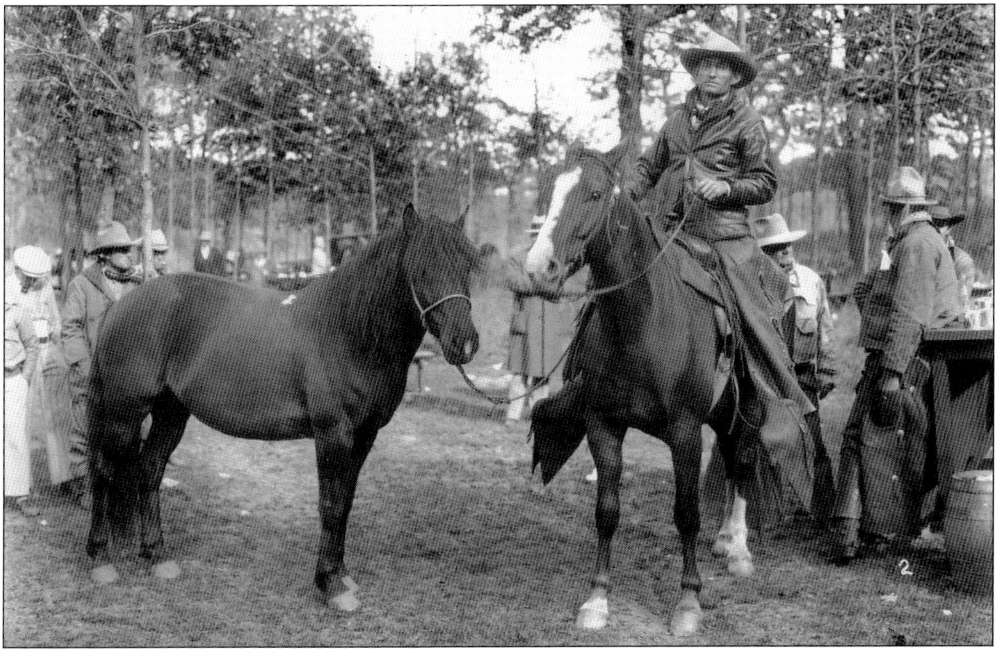

Jimmy Ryder, a local cowboy, poses for a photograph with a horse in tow at the Cow Thieves and Outlaws Reunion. Frank and Jane Phillips both appreciated fine horses and horsemanship. The men that helped entertain partygoers at the event were some of the best horseman in the country.

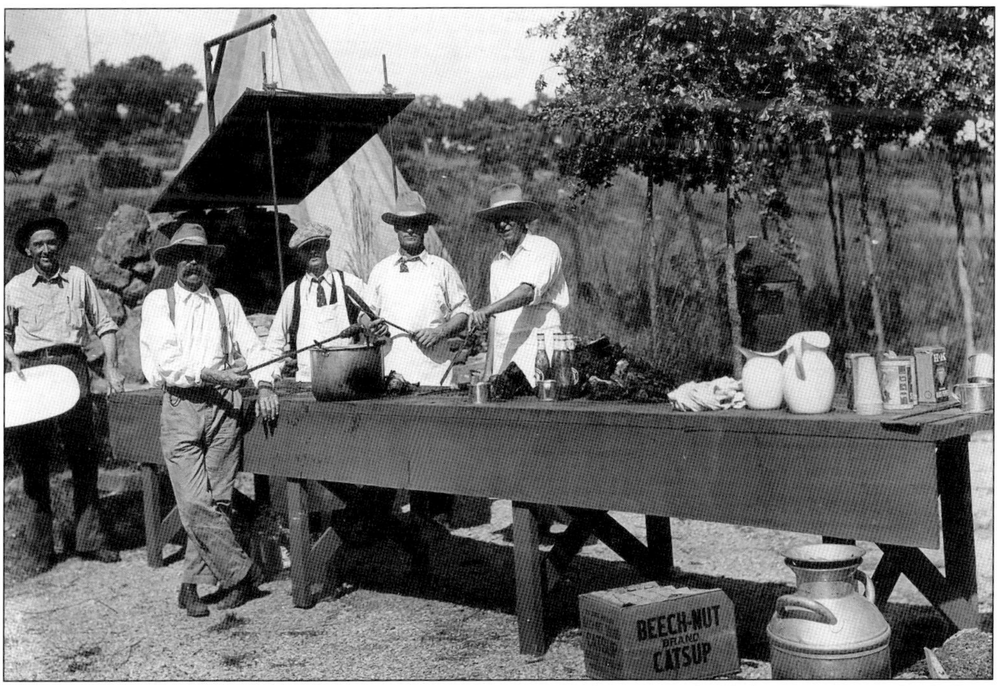

In order to feed everyone, cooks diligently prepared barbecue and all the requisite side dishes. Here, the cook crew, known as the Barbecue Boys, poses before their day's work begins and they ring the dinner gong and feed partygoers.

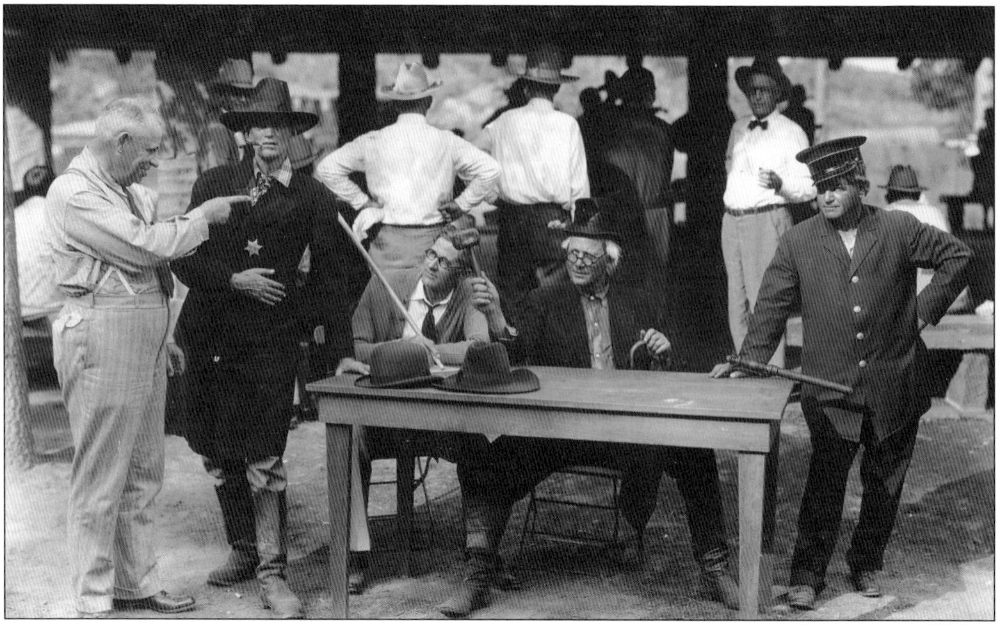

Another aspect of the Cow Thieves and Outlaws Reunion was the entertainment provided for guests. The Kangaroo Court was a crowd favorite. Here, dressed in comical costumes, the court in session decided the fate of guests and performed comedy skits. The court also collected money for their comedic antics and, then in 1927, presented Frank Phillips with a cowboy hat as a token of their esteem.

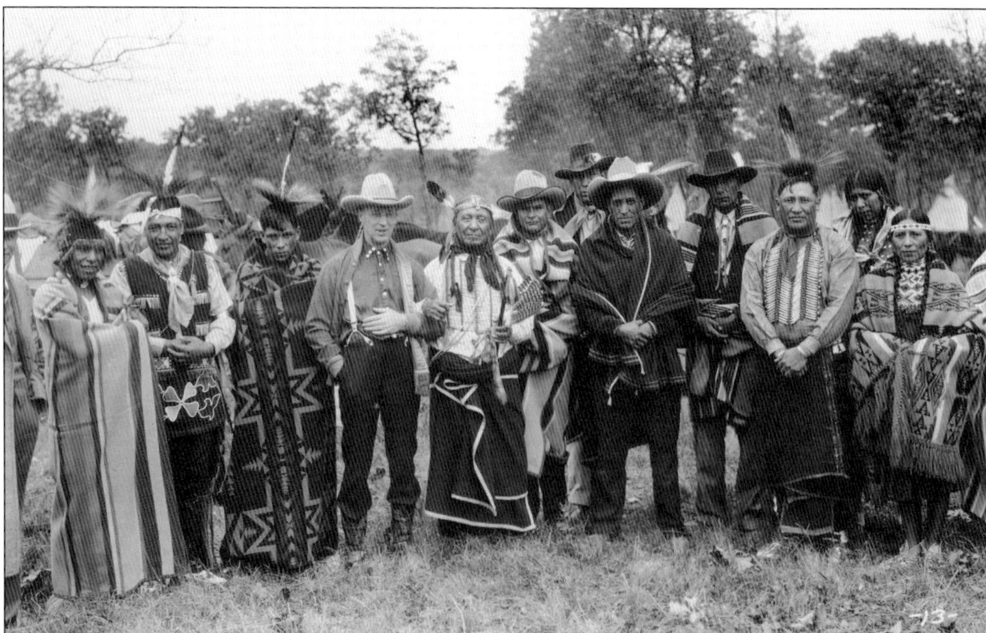

American Indian performers from two famous Wild West shows were a regular feature at Cow Thieves and Outlaws. Pawnee Bill (Col. G.W. Lillie) and the famous Miller Brothers of the 101 Ranch and Wild West Show brought performers from their shows to Woolaroc. Dancing, singing, drumming, trick riding, and roping were some of the skills they displayed for guests.

Cow Thieves and Outlaws guests were encouraged to dress the part of the Old West, and many took the directive to heart. Sporting Western costumes, these participants look as if they stepped out of the pages of history. The event was a way for Phillips and his friends to celebrate the history of the West, kick back, relax, and blow off some steam.

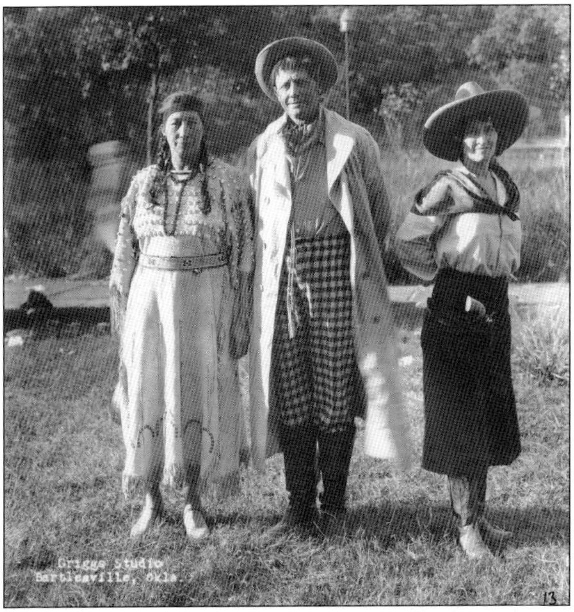

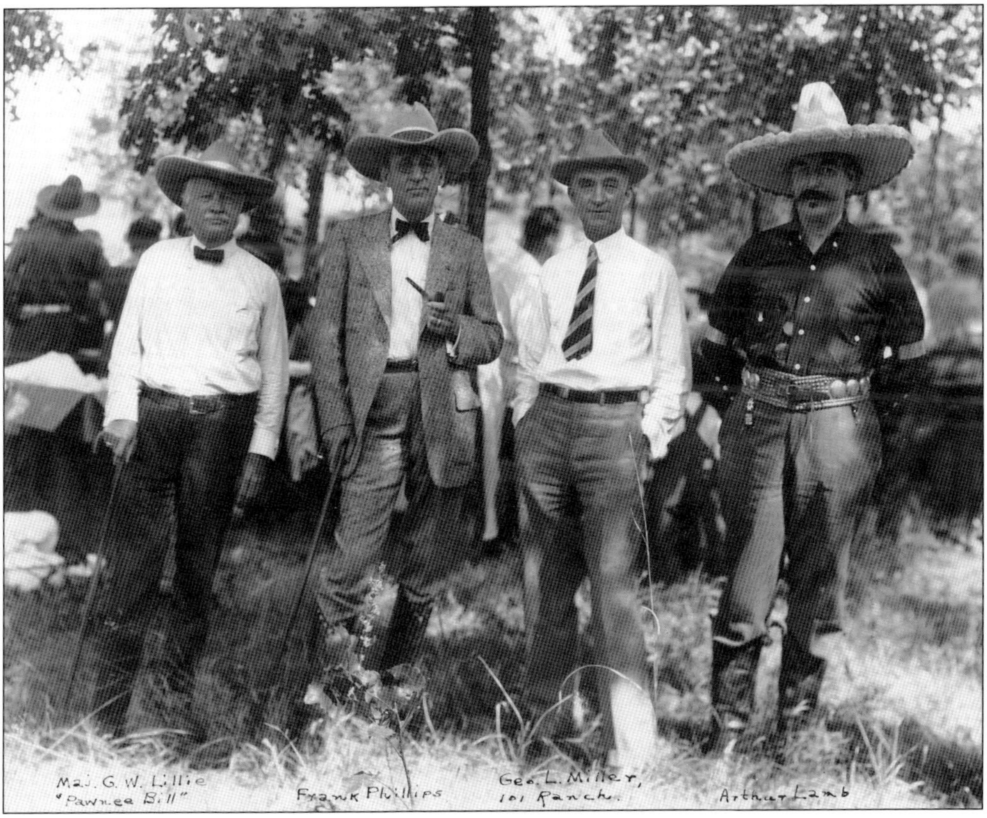

In this Cow Thieves and Outlaws photograph, G.W. Lillie (Pawnee Bill), Frank Phillips, George Miller (101 Ranch and Wild West Show), and Arthur Lamb pose for the camera. Arthur Lamb, the Sage of the Osages, collected the folk tales, legends, and stories of northeast Oklahoma and was a renowned storyteller. He was a frequent visitor to the ranch along with Lillie and Miller.

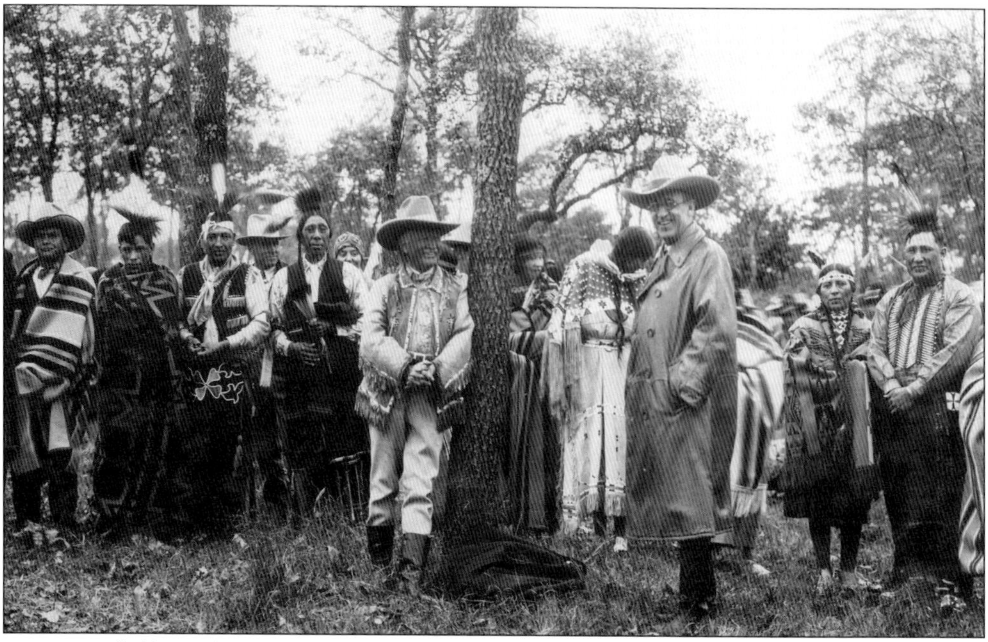

Pawnee Bill (dressed in his showman's attire and leaning against the tree) and Frank Phillips (donning his trademark hat) pose with the American Indian performers from Pawnee Bill's Wild West Show. Born in Illinois in 1860, Lillie was always fascinated with the West. After his family moved to Wellington, Kansas, he made his way to Indian Territory (now Oklahoma), lived among the Pawnee, and made friends in the tribe. He gained the name Pawnee Bill because of his close relationship with the Pawnee in Kansas and Indian Territory.

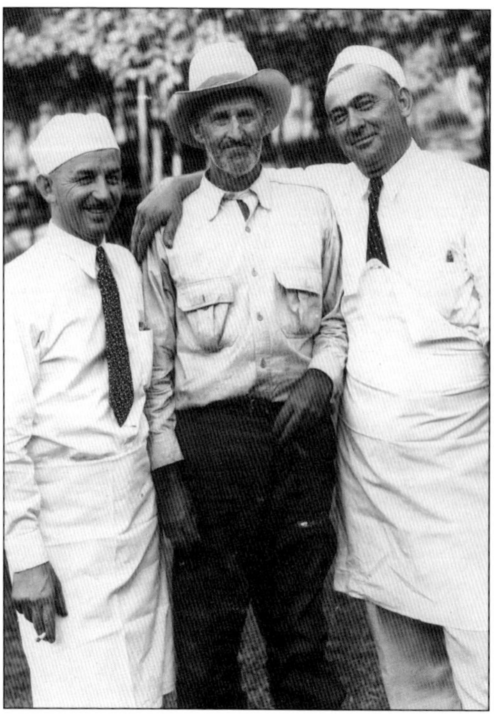

To put the outlaw in Cow Thieves and Outlaws, the infamous Oklahoma bank robber Henry Wells came to visit the party. As a part of the amnesty for the day, any individual that stepped onto Woolaroc property was immune from pursuit. For one day, the lawman and the outlaw could be friends. During his career in train and bank robbery, Wells pocketed over $100,000. Ironically, Grif Graham, former Washington County sheriff and Woolaroc ranch manager, had at times pursued Wells. Graham said the following about Wells upon his "retirement" from the "banking business" in 1945: "He was and is one of the greatest unschooled psychologists I ever knew, and the way he worked circles around peace officers and county attorneys in the early days in Oklahoma was a shame." Woolaroc legend tells of a kidnapping plot by Pretty Boy Floyd issued against the Phillips children. Supposedly, Wells alerted Frank Phillips, and from that time on, the two men were good friends.

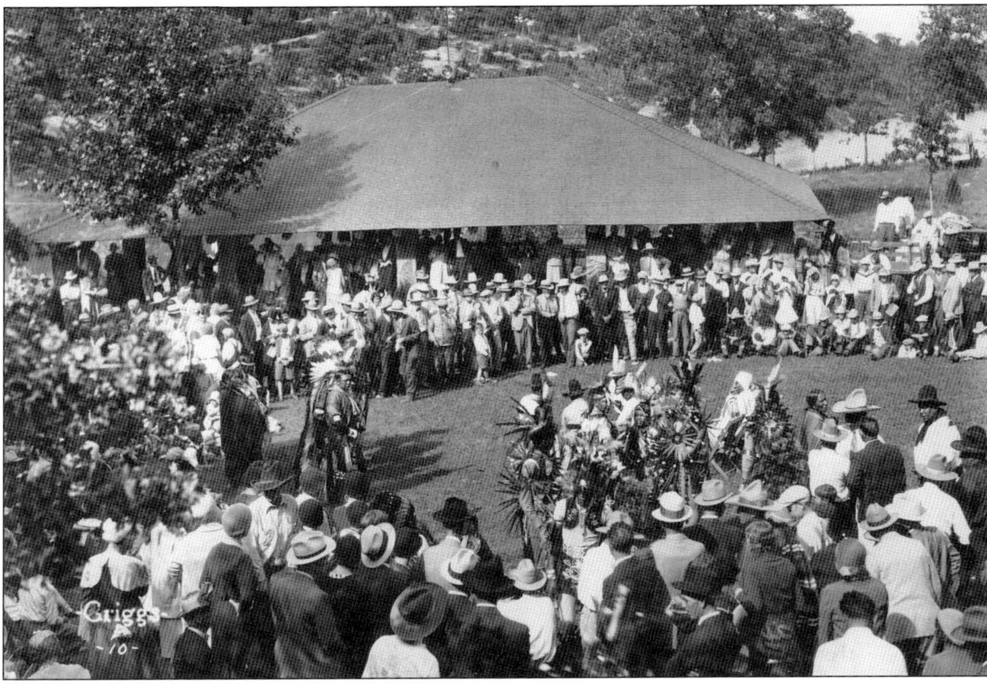

In this Cow Thieves and Outlaws Reunion scene, visitors gather along the banks of Clyde Lake near the pavilion to listen and watch American Indian drummers beat out their traditional songs. Dancers would spin and whirl, much to the delight of the crowds.

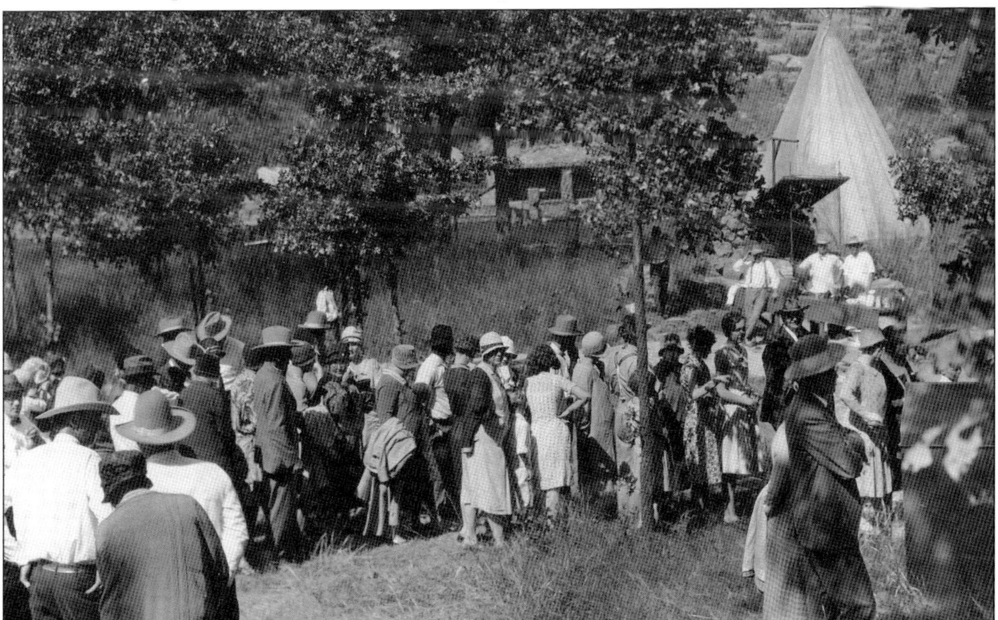

Next to the entertainment and good times, people attended Cow Thieves and Outlaws for some of the best barbecue cooking in the state of Oklahoma. With the cooks set up to the top right near the white tepee, the food line stretches back as hungry partygoers wait to eat. Along with the incredible food, beverages flowed plentifully. Despite Prohibition, beer was a party favorite.

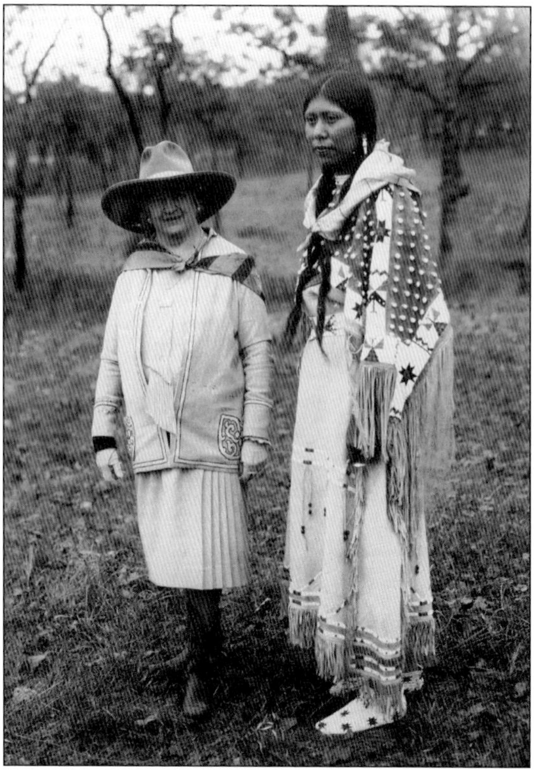

Jane Phillips loved Cow Thieves and Outlaws and embraced the spirit of the West as well. Photographed here with one of the many American Indian performers, Jane sports her cowgirl boots and hat with her very stylish attire that looks more appropriate for afternoon tea, not an afternoon in the Wild West.

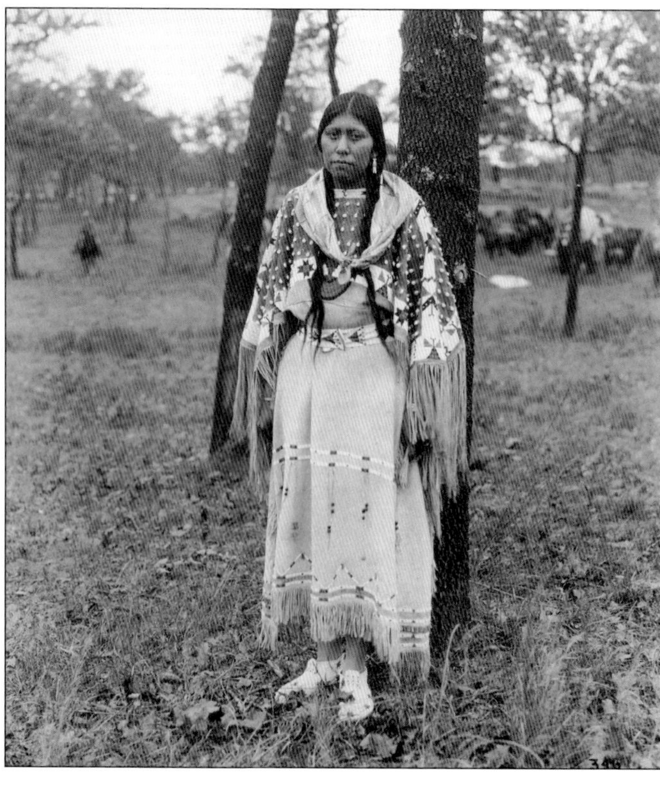

This American Indian woman, one of the numerous brought by Pawnee Bill or the Miller Brothers, is captured on film by Frank Griggs. Her intricate clothing, all hand made, adorned with elk teeth, and hand beadwork, is itself a work of art and testimony to the creative talents of her people.

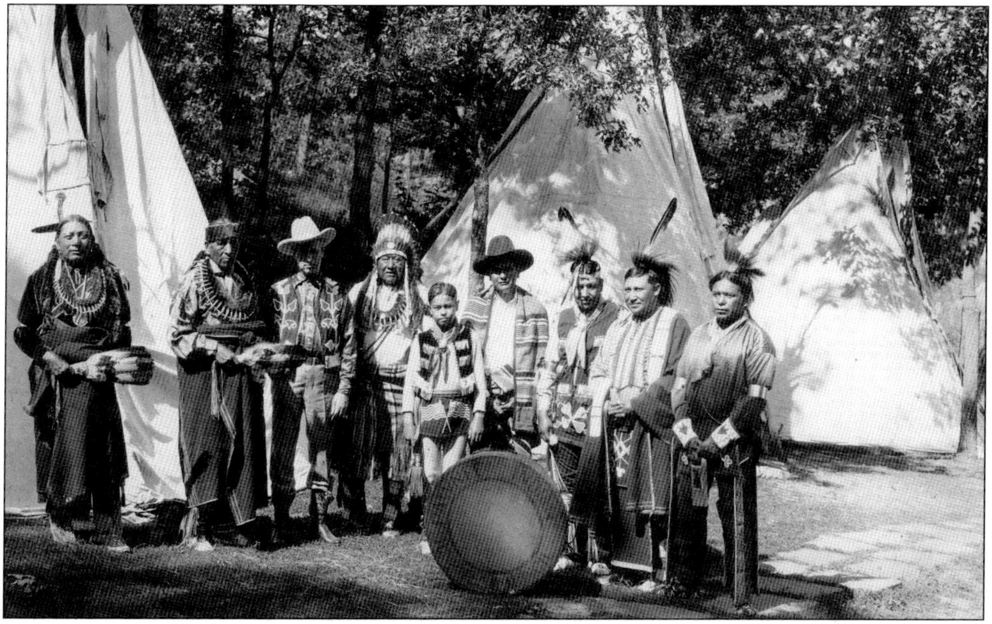

Gathered around a drum at the Cow Thieves and Outlaws Reunion, a group of American Indian men pose for Griggs's camera. Their traditional clothing is indicative of their tribal affiliations—Pawnee, Osage, and Sioux. Frank Phillips was fascinated by American Indian culture and enjoyed their presence at the Cow Thieves events immensely.

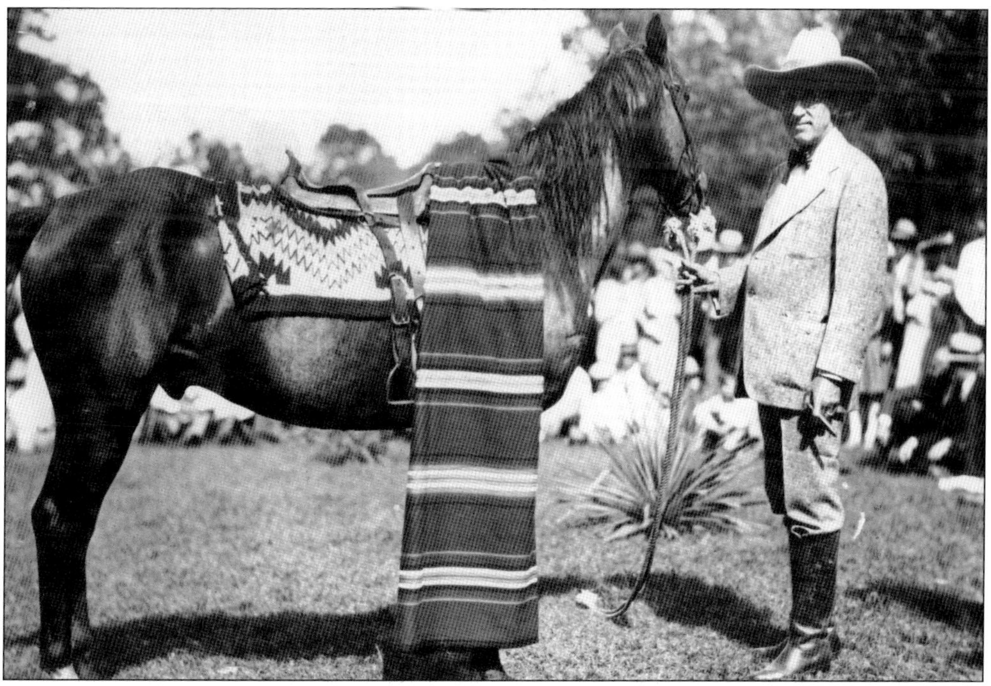

At the Cow Thieves and Outlaws reunion in 1930, Chief Fred Lookout of the Osage presented Frank Phillips with this handsome horse, saddle, and blanket. This would be the first step in his adoption into the Osage tribe as Eagle Chief. Those who knew Phillips well proclaimed this one of his proudest moments.

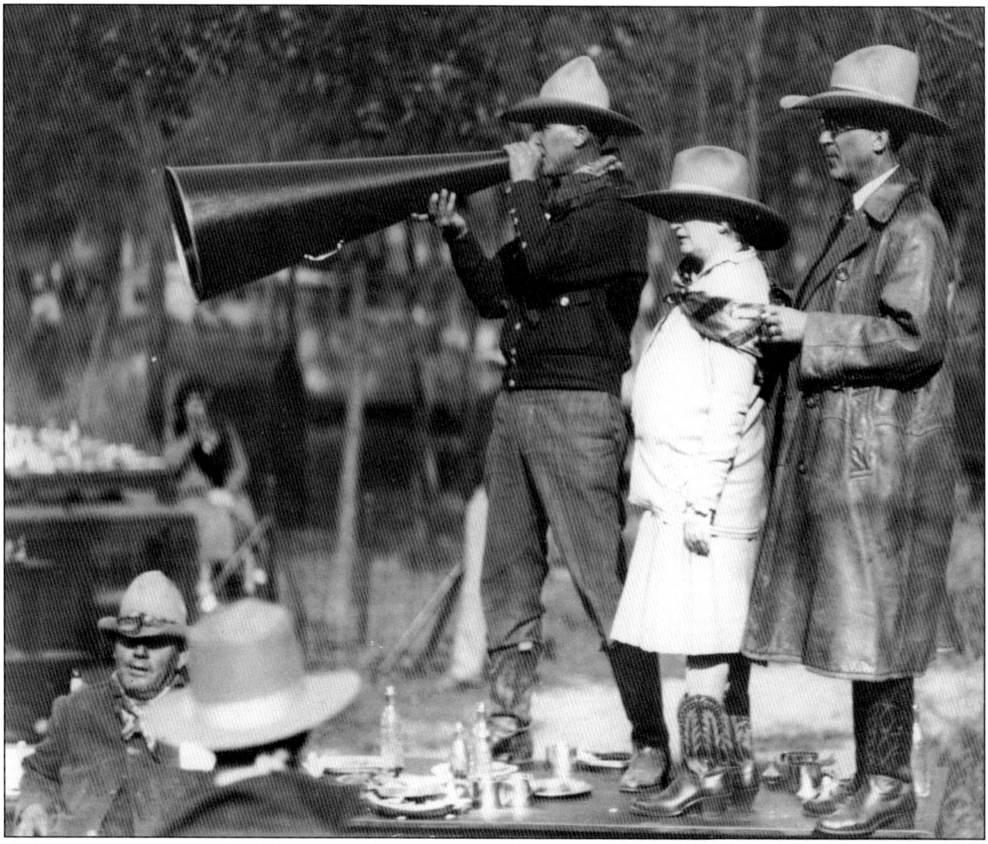

Addressing partygoers at the Cow Thieves and Outlaws Reunion, Grif Graham uses a megaphone to get the crowd's attention as Jane and Frank Phillips watch. The reunions were a favorite event that Frank and Jane enjoyed.

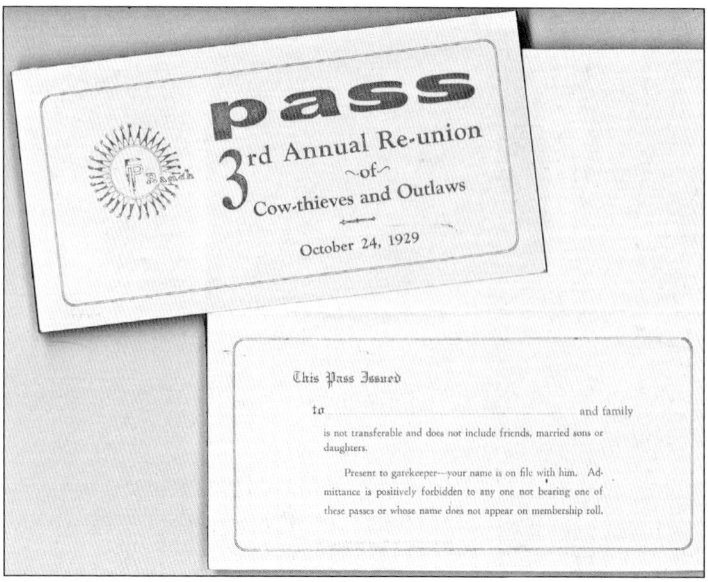

pass

3rd Annual Re-union

~of~

Cow-thieves and Outlaws

October 24, 1929

This Pass Issued

to .... and family

is not transferable and does not include friends, married sons or daughters.

Present to gatekeeper—your name is on file with him. Admittance is positively forbidden to any one not bearing one of these passes or whose name does not appear on membership roll.

As with any good social event, invitations were issued to the Cow Thieves and Outlaws Reunion at Woolaroc. These passes from October 24, 1929, still survive in the archival collection at the Woolaroc Museum. Admittance was strictly limited to those individuals named on the passes, and they were not transferable to anyone else. Gate crashing was a serious offense and not tolerated.

"Don't ware yer guns cause we ain't allowin' to have no shootin'," proclaimed the 1929 Cow Thieves and Outlaws Reunion invitation.

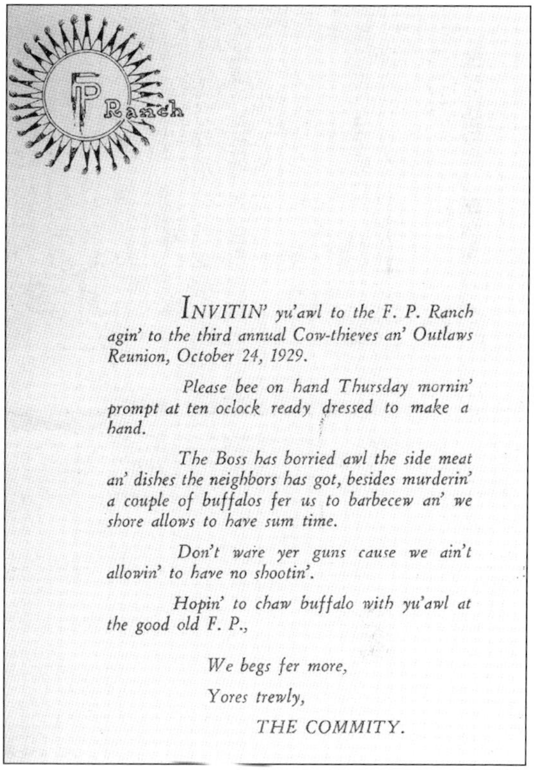

INVITIN' yu'awl to the F. P. Ranch agin' to the third annual Cow-thieves an' Outlaws Reunion, October 24, 1929.

Please bee on hand Thursday mornin' prompt at ten oclock ready dressed to make a hand.

The Boss has borried awl the side meat an' dishes the neighbors has got, besides murderin' a couple of buffalos fer us to barbecew an' we shore allows to have sum time.

Don't ware yer guns cause we ain't allowin' to have no shootin'.

Hopin' to chaw buffalo with yu'awl at the good old F. P.,

We begs fer more,

Yores trewly,

THE COMMITY.

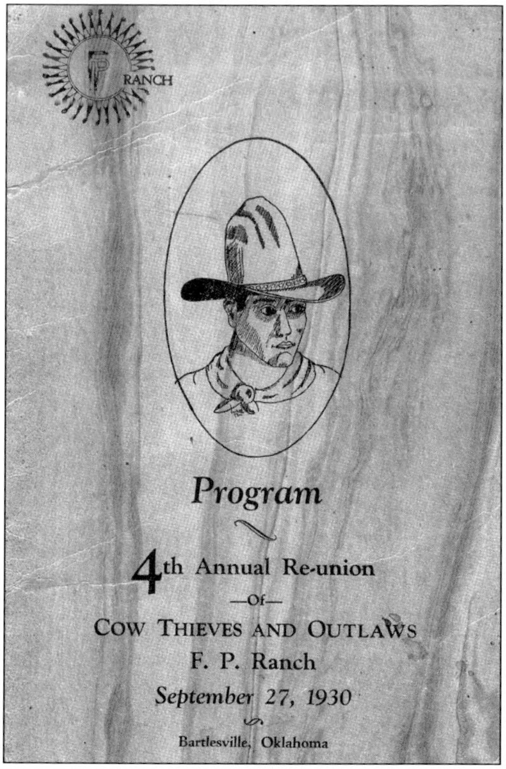

This program from the 1930 Cow Thieves and Outlaws Reunion is part of the archival collection at the Woolaroc Museum. Passes, programs, and invitations all proclaimed amnesty from the law for the day, good food, plenty of drink, and lots of tall tales around the campfire for all.

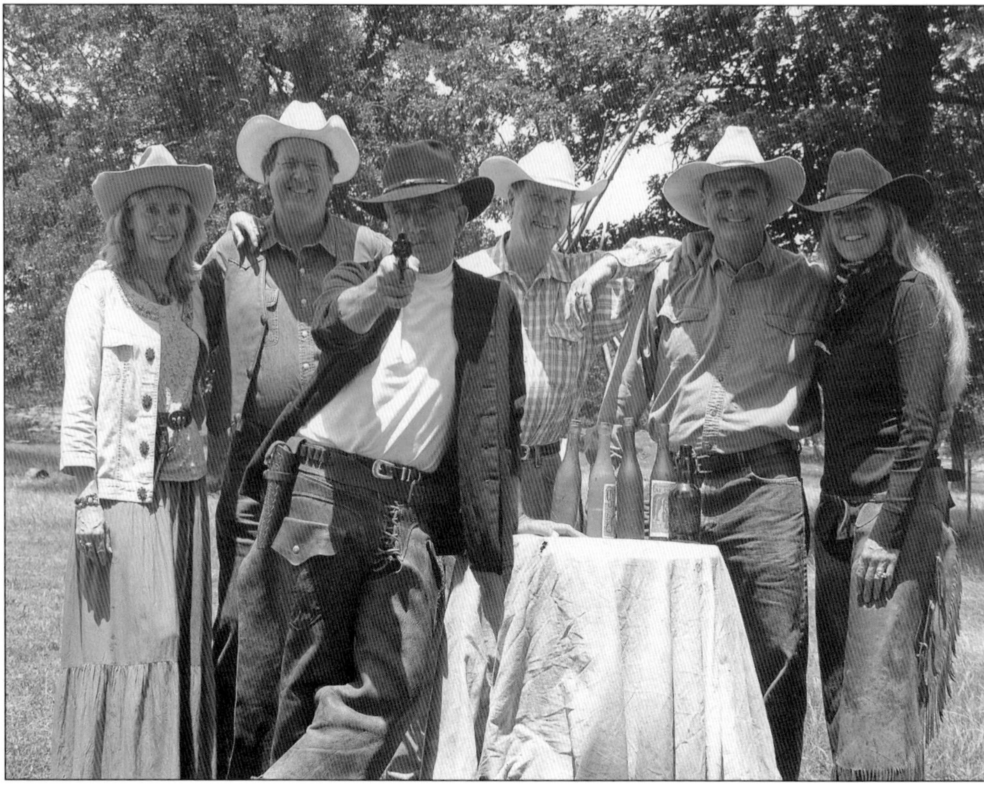

The Cow Thieves and Outlaws Reunion has been revived in the form of a fundraiser held each fall at Clyde Lake. The Cow Thieves Committee, pictured here, plan food and entertainment and throw the gates open just like Frank and Jane Phillips did so long ago. All funds raised at the event support the Frank Phillips Foundation, Inc., and further its charge to preserve, promote, and share Frank and Jane's amazing Osage Hills retreat, ranch, and museum with new generations. (Author's collection.)

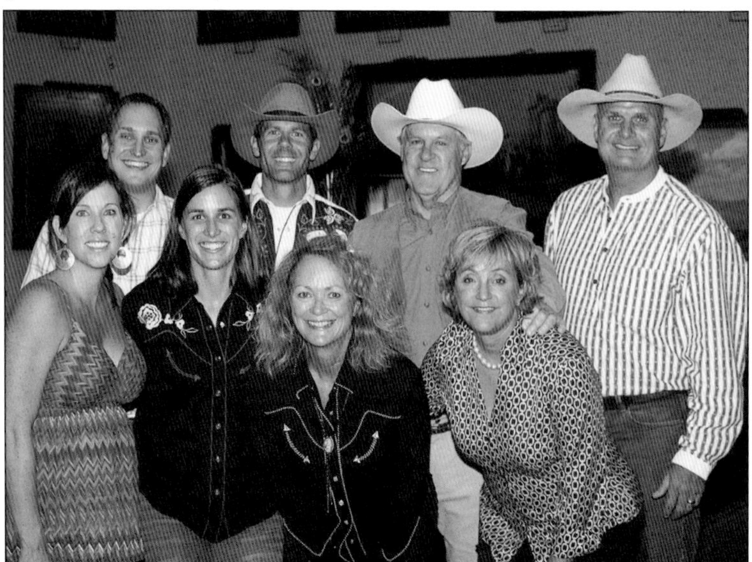

Each fall the Cow Thieves and Outlaws Reunion is the hottest ticket in Oklahoma and draws partygoers from across the state of Oklahoma and from neighboring states as well. Gathering in the spirit of Frank and Jane Phillips, attendees enjoy and evening of food and entertainment and recreate history. (Author's collection.)

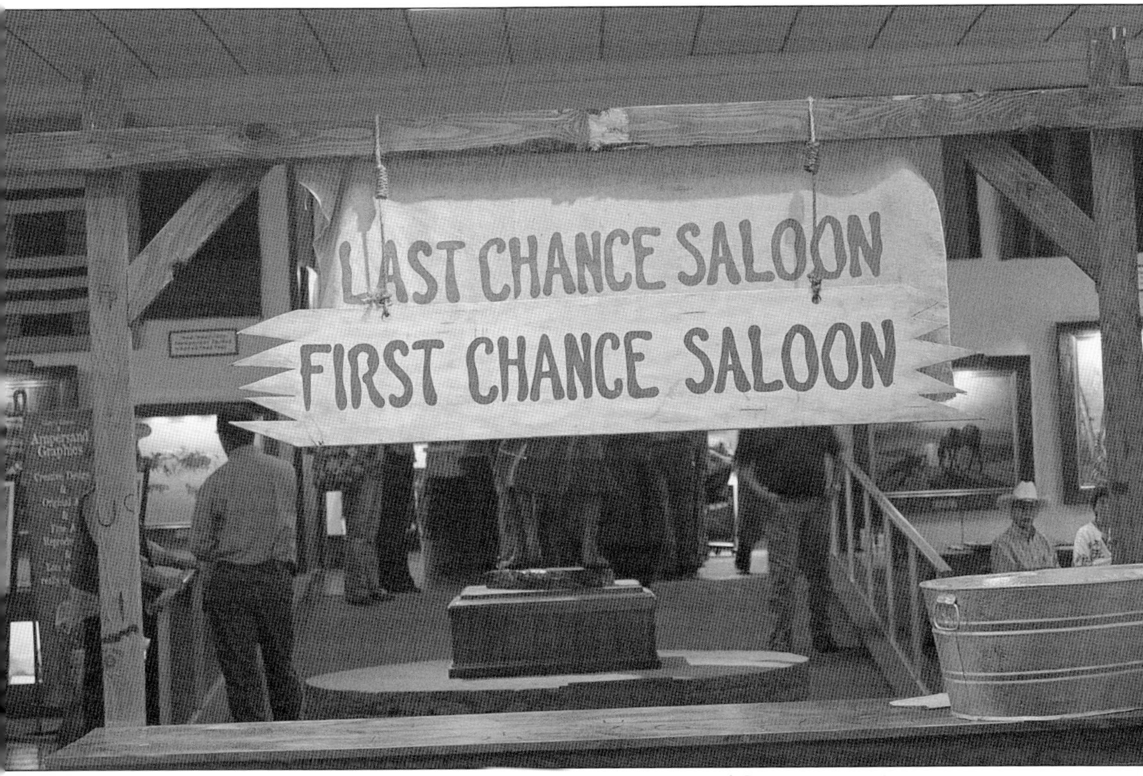

The Last Chance Saloon First Chance Saloon has been a part of Cow Thieves history since its birth in 1927. Visitors can belly up to the bar and enjoy cold frosty refreshment or their favorite beverages, just like Frank and Jane's guests did during Prohibition. (Author's collection.)

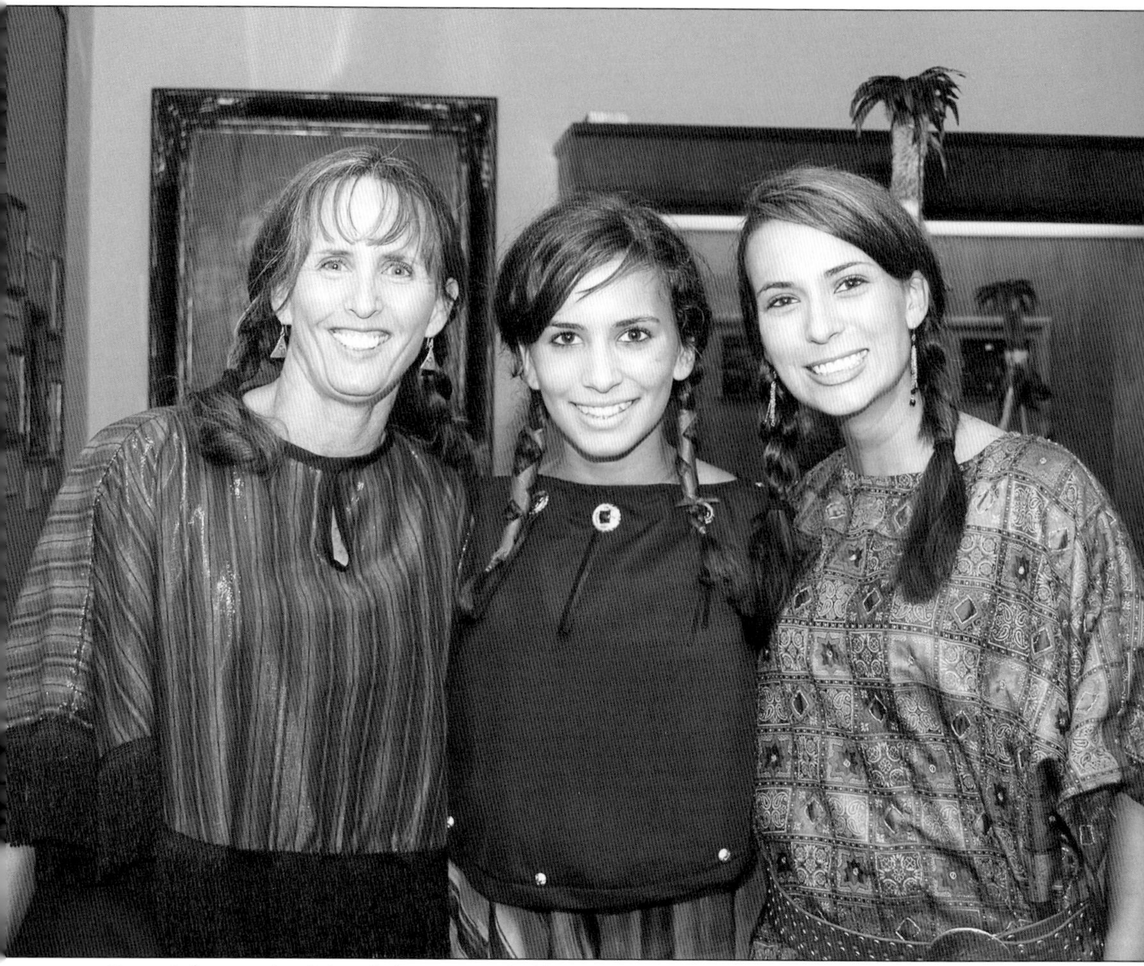

From left to right, Meredith Fraser, Shelby Fraser, and Jordan Fraser Ihrig get into the Cow Thieves spirit with their American Indian–inspired clothing at a Cow Thieves event. The Cow Thieves and Outlaws Reunion seeks to not only raise funds for the foundation but also to keep the spirit of the Old West that Frank Phillips loved so much alive and well in the 21st century. (Author's collection.)

About Woolaroc

Founded in 1937 by Frank and Jane Phillips, the Frank Phillips Foundation, Inc., ensures that the magic, majesty, and beauty of Woolaroc will be preserved and protected for future generations. In keeping with Frank's vision, Woolaroc's employees help preserve the history of the American West, educate future generations, and entertain them with Oklahoma hospitality in the spirit of Frank and Jane Phillips.

Each year, the staff of Woolaroc dedicate themselves to providing visitors with magical experiences that will last a lifetime. From the splendor of Wonderland of Lights to the joy of children playing on the Western Town playground, Woolaroc continues the legacy that Frank and Jane Phillips set out to accomplish so many years ago. With special events throughout the year, Woolaroc shares the history, art, culture, and spirit of the American West with visitors the world over.

For more information on how you can visit Woolaroc and support the efforts of the Frank Phillips Foundation, Inc., visit www.woolaroc.org. You can also follow them on Facebook and Twitter.